SCHOLASTIC

ENCYCLOPEDIA OF THE UNITED STATES

JUDY BOCK AND RACHEL KRANZ

Bascom Communications

SCHOLASTIC
REFERENCE

New York   Toronto   London   Auckland   Sydney
Mexico City   New Delhi   Hong Kong

A NOTE TO THE READER

Every best effort has been made to ensure the accuracy of this book and we have consulted the most authoritative sources during its writing.

Please be aware that you may find state areas in this book that differ from other books. The reason is that the people who measure the size of the states do so at different times of year. In the winter, surface water of a state may be frozen (and smaller in size) or liquid (and larger in size) in the spring or summer. Also, natural erosion and landfills affect measurements all the year round.

The people who measure also use different ways of totaling surface water such as lakes and rivers, and this also can lead to differences among books.

Also, the population statistics are **estimates** for the year 1996. These figures come from The Population Distribution Branch, U.S. Bureau of the Census, Consistent with Department of Commerce Press Release CB96-10.

The following have been most helpful in giving us correct information for this book: The Bureau of the Census: Geography Division • The Cartography Department of the National Geographic Society • The Department of Defense • The National Bureau of Statistics • The U.S. Geological Survey: Inquiry Group

ACKNOWLEDGMENTS

Many thanks to Betsy Ryan, president of Bascom Communications, who produced this book with intelligence and care. A great debt of gratitude is also owed to its editor at Scholastic, the peerless Carolyn Jackson. Dr. Alex Moore, Director of the Historic Society of Charleston, was gracious and generous with his time, as was Ann Grant of the Federal Museum in Arkansas.

Michael Schulman at Archive Photos is a true professional, gifted with patience and a rare sense of humor. Thanks also to the art directors: Kevin Callahan, Jonette Jakobson, Nancy Sabato, and the indefatigable David Saylor. Thanks also to Barbara Curry Walsh for her energetic assistance in photo research. And to Edward Morris, scholar and gentleman, gratitude for his constant assiduity. Thanks also to Doric Wilson.

Library of Congress Cataloging-in-Publication Data

ISBN 0-590-94747-8 (hc)
ISBN 0-439-14722-0 (pb)

10 9   04

Printed in the U.S.A.   09
First printing, August 1997
First paperback printing, October 1999

Table of Contents

Alabama

The Basics

POPULATION: 4,447,100
23rd most populous state
AREA: 52,423 square miles
30th largest state
STATE CAPITAL: Montgomery
STATE BIRD: Yellowhammer (also called yellow-shafted woodpecker, flicker)
STATE FLOWER: Camellia
STATE TREE: Southern pine (also known as the longleaf yellow pine)
NICKNAMES: Yellowhammer State, Camellia State, the Heart of Dixie
STATE MOTTO: *Audemus Jura Nostra Defendere* (Latin for "We dare defend our rights")
STATE FRESHWATER FISH: Largemouth bass
STATE SALTWATER FISH: Tarpon
STATE MINERAL: Hematite (red iron ore)
STATE ROCK: Marble
STATE FOSSIL: *Basilosaurus cetoides*
STATE NUT: Pecan
STATE DANCE: Square dance
STATE DRAMA: *The Miracle Worker* by William Gibson (story of Alabama native Helen Keller)
STATE SONG: "Alabama," words by Julia S. Tutwiler, music by Edna Glockel Gussen
STATE HISTORIC PARKS: Burritt Museum and Park, Huntsville; Museum Village at Constitution Hall Park, Huntsville; Old North Hull Street Historic District, Montgomery; Pike Pioneer Museum, Troy
STATE FESTIVALS: Joe Wheeler Civil War Reenactment, Decatur (September); National Peanut Festival, Dothan (October); National Shrimp Festival, Gulf Shores (October); Tale Telling Festival, Selma (October)

The Basics column gives you fast facts about each state: its size, population, capital, motto, flower, tree—and much more

The **locator map** shows where each state is.

2

Entrance to Bellingrath Park, Mobile   **22nd state to enter the Union, December 14, 1819**

This Deep South state is filled with beauty, from the red clay soil and forests of the northern part of the state to the pine forests and rolling grasslands farther south. The Mobile Delta, just above the Gulf of Mexico, is full of swamps and bayous, while the coastline and Dauphin Island have some of the nation's most beautiful beaches. Alabama, full of variety, even has an industrial region, around Birmingham.

ROCKETS AND PLANTATIONS Most of Alabama has a hot, wet climate, barely cooled by breezes from the Gulf of Mexico. In the northern part of the state, though, are the southernmost mountains of the great Appalachians, and the weather is somewhat cooler.

Alabama was once primarily rural, but now more than 60 percent of Alabamans live in such cities as Birmingham, Mobile, Montgomery, and Huntsville.

Yet when most people think of Alabama, they picture the antebellum (pre-Civil War) mansions built by the owners of the huge Southern plantations. You can still visit such mansions in and around Mobile, Montgomery, Selma, and Monroeville. But now Alabama also has a more modern image—the Alabama Space and Rocket Center at Huntsville, where NASA scientists developed the first rocket that put people on the moon. Visitors can take a bus tour of NASA labs and visit the space museum. Children go to Space Camp here, too.

Folk dancing at Landmark Park, Dothan

MANY PEOPLES Alabama's first inhabitants were Native Americans, mainly Chickasaw, Cherokee, Creek, and Choctaw. In 1540, the Spanish explorer Hernando de Soto led an expedition through the area and defeated a Choctaw army led by Chief Tuscaloosa. The first permanent European settlement was founded by the French, who settled Mobile in 1711.

The United States took control of the area in 1813—but conflict with Native Americans was not yet over. In the 1830s the Creek Indians were moved from their land to Oklahoma, despite U.S. treaties that had said they could stay. In 1836-37 the Cherokee were also forced off their land. This forced migration of Native Americans throughout the Southeastern United States was known as the Trail of Tears. The "removals" occurred in a series of waves between 1831 and 1835.

In the nineteenth century, Alabama's economy depended on huge cotton

The center part of each page tells you the history, geography, and industry of each state. You will also see photographs of famous people who were born or who lived in the state, or festivals or interesting places to visit.

plantations, which in turn relied on the labor of African-American slaves. When President Abraham Lincoln was elected in 1860, many in the South feared that he would put an end to slavery. So in 1861 Alabama and 10 other Southern states seceded from the Union to form the Confederate States of America. For a brief time, Montgomery was the capital of this new nation, and the Confederate flag was first designed and flown there. You can still visit the "First White House of the Confederacy" near today's state Capitol building.

The Great Secession led to the Civil War, which ended in the defeat of the South and the abolition (end) of slavery. After federal troops left, supporters of the old order passed laws to keep African Americans from voting and to promote segregation—keeping black and white people as separate as possible, using separate schools, hospitals, even water fountains.

Civil Rights Memorial, Montgomery

In the 1950s the civil rights movement gained power. Its goal was to win for African Americans the same rights that white people had always taken for granted. African Americans wanted to be integrated (allowed to use the same facilities as whites). In 1953 Autherine Lucy won the right to attend the previously all-white University of Alabama. Lucy was so badly harassed, however, that she decided not to continue.

In 1955, in Montgomery, Rosa Parks refused to sit in the separate section for African Americans in the back of the bus. Her action sparked a bus boycott that lasted more than a year, which finally led to integration on buses. One of the boycott leaders was the Reverend Martin Luther King, Jr., who went on to lead many other civil rights activities.

The civil rights movement succeeded in making vast changes in Alabama. By 1984, for example, Alabamans had elected 25 black mayors. As a reminder of those earlier times, architect Maya Lin designed the Civil Rights Memorial in Montgomery. She created a 40-foot black granite wall over which water flows into a pool. Engraved on the wall is a quote from the Bible that Martin Luther King, Jr., used in one of his famous speeches, and on a nearby tablet are engraved the names of those who died in the movement for civil rights.

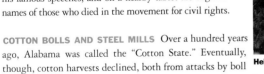

Helen Keller

COTTON BOLLS AND STEEL MILLS Over a hundred years ago, Alabama was called the "Cotton State." Eventually, though, cotton harvests declined, both from attacks by boll weevils (insects), and because the soil became worn out. George Washington Carver taught Alabama farmers how to rotate crops. By growing crops that added nitrogen back to the soil, farmers got better harvests and enriched the soil. They began to grow peanuts and soybeans alternately with cotton.

Alabama's many forests are used to produce timber, pulp, and paper. After the Civil War, the region of Birmingham was developed—the only big industrial city in the South. Iron and steel are still produced there. More recently, the space center in Huntsville has spurred the development of an electronics and space industry.

Fascinating Facts

FAMOUS PEOPLE BORN IN ALABAMA:
• Harper Lee, author of *To Kill a Mockingbird*, Monroeville (1926-)
• Country singer Hank Williams, Grace (1923-1951)
• Hugo L. Black, U.S. Supreme Court Justice, Harlan (1886-1971)

DID YOU KNOW THAT... William Gibson's play about Helen Keller, *The Miracle Worker*, is performed every year at "Ivy Green," Keller's home at Tuscumbia.

HOW ALABAMA GOT ITS NAME: The name was used as an Indian nation in the Creek confederacy. Then the Alabama River was named for the Indians, and the state was named for the river.

HOW ALABAMA GOT ITS STATE BIRD: The yellowhammer was chosen because its colors were the same as those worn by a company of Alabama Confederate soldiers.

ALABAMA SPORTS HALL OF FAME:
• Legendary University of Alabama football coach William "Bear" Bryant (1913-1983)
• Olympic Gold Medal track star Jesse Owens (1913-1980)
• Record-setting hitter New York/San Francisco Giants Willie Mays (1931-)
• Home run record-setter Atlanta Braves Hank Aaron (1934-)

ALABAMA HOT TIMES: Alabama is tied with Nevada for third-hottest recorded temperature in the U.S.: 122 degrees Fahrenheit in Centreville, Sept. 5, 1925.

ALABAMA IS TOPS IN...
• cast-iron and steel pipe products

ALABAMA HAD THE WORLD'S FIRST:
• electric trolley system—Montgomery—1886

DID YOU KNOW THAT... In the 1880s, Alabama scientist George Washington Carver discovered 300 new uses for the peanut and 175 for the sweet potato, which revitalized Alabama's farm economy.

3

The **Fascinating Facts** column tells you state firsts, mosts, bests, and lists famous people born in the state. This column changes a little from state to state, and you'll always find a fact that you never knew before. We promise.

Alabama

The Basics

POPULATION: 4,447,100
23rd most populous state
AREA: 52,423 square miles
30th largest state
STATE CAPITAL: Montgomery
STATE BIRD: Yellowhammer (also called yellow-shafted woodpecker, flicker)
STATE FLOWER: Camellia
STATE TREE: Southern pine (also known as the longleaf yellow pine)
NICKNAMES: Yellowhammer State, Camellia State, the Heart of Dixie
STATE MOTTO: *Audemus Jura Nostra Defendere* (Latin for "We dare defend our rights")
STATE FRESHWATER FISH: Largemouth bass
STATE SALTWATER FISH: Tarpon
STATE MINERAL: Hematite (red iron ore)
STATE ROCK: Marble
STATE FOSSIL: *Basilosaurus cetoides*
STATE NUT: Pecan
STATE DANCE: Square dance
STATE DRAMA: *The Miracle Worker* by William Gibson (story of Alabama native Helen Keller)
STATE SONG: "Alabama," words by Julia S. Tutwiler, music by Edna Glockel Gussen
STATE HISTORIC PARKS: Burritt Museum and Park, Huntsville; Museum Village at Constitution Hall Park, Huntsville; Old North Hull Street Historic District, Montgomery; Pike Pioneer Museum, Troy
STATE FESTIVALS: Joe Wheeler Civil War Reenactment, Decatur (September); National Peanut Festival, Dothan (October); National Shrimp Festival, Gulf Shores (October); Tale Telling Festival, Selma (October)

Entrance to Bellingrath Park, Mobile

22nd state to enter the Union, December 14, 1819

This Deep South state is filled with beauty, from the red clay soil and forests of the northern part of the state to the pine forests and rolling grasslands farther south. The Mobile Delta, just above the Gulf of Mexico, is full of swamps and bayous, while the coastline and Dauphin Island have some of the nation's most beautiful beaches. Alabama, full of variety, even has an industrial region, around Birmingham.

ROCKETS AND PLANTATIONS Most of Alabama has a hot, wet climate, barely cooled by breezes from the Gulf of Mexico. In the northern part of the state, though, are the southernmost mountains of the great Appalachians, and the weather is somewhat cooler.

Alabama was once primarily rural, but now more than 60 percent of Alabamans live in such cities as Birmingham, Mobile, Montgomery, and Huntsville.

Yet when most people think of Alabama, they picture the antebellum (pre-Civil War) mansions built by the owners of the huge Southern plantations. You can still visit such mansions in and around Mobile, Montgomery, Selma, and Monroeville. But now Alabama also has a more modern image—the Alabama Space and Rocket Center at Huntsville, where NASA scientists developed the first rocket that put people on the moon. Visitors can take a bus tour of

Folk dancing at Landmark Park, Dothan

NASA labs and visit the space museum. Children go to Space Camp here, too.

MANY PEOPLES Alabama's first inhabitants were Native Americans, mainly Chickasaw, Cherokee, Creek, and Choctaw. In 1540, the Spanish explorer Hernando de Soto led an expedition through the area and defeated a Choctaw army led by Chief Tuscaloosa. The first permanent European settlement was founded by the French, who settled Mobile in 1711.

The United States took control of the area in 1813—but conflict with Native Americans was not yet over. In the 1830s the Creek Indians were moved from their land to Oklahoma, despite U.S. treaties that had said they could stay. In 1836-37 the Cherokee were also forced off their land. This forced migration of Native Americans throughout the Southeastern United States was known as the Trail of Tears. The "removals" occurred in a series of waves between 1831 and 1835.

In the nineteenth century, Alabama's economy depended on huge cotton plantations, which in turn relied on the labor of African-American slaves. When President Abraham Lincoln was elected in 1860, many in the South feared that he would put an end to slavery. So in 1861 Alabama and 10 other Southern states seceded from the Union to form the Confederate States of America. For a brief time, Montgomery was the capital of this new nation, and the Confederate flag was first designed and flown there. You can still visit the "First White House of the Confederacy" near today's state Capitol building.

The Great Secession led to the Civil War, which ended in the defeat of the South and the abolition (end) of slavery. After federal troops left, supporters of the old order passed laws to keep African Americans from voting and to promote segregation—keeping black and white people as separate as possible, using separate schools, hospitals, even water fountains.

Civil Rights Memorial, Montgomery

In the 1950s the civil rights movement gained power. Its goal was to win for African Americans the same rights that white people had always taken for granted. African Americans wanted to be integrated (allowed to use the same facilities as whites). In 1953 Autherine Lucy won the right to attend the previously all-white University of Alabama. Lucy was so badly harassed, however, that she decided not to continue.

In 1955, in Montgomery, Rosa Parks refused to sit in the separate section for African Americans in the back of the bus. Her action sparked a bus boycott that lasted more than a year, which finally led to integration on buses. One of the boycott leaders was the Reverend Martin Luther King, Jr., who went on to lead many other civil rights activities.

The civil rights movement succeeded in making vast changes in Alabama. By 1984, for example, Alabamans had elected 25 black mayors. As a reminder of those earlier times, architect Maya Lin designed the Civil Rights Memorial in Montgomery. She created a 40-foot black granite wall over which water flows into a pool. Engraved on the wall is a quote from the Bible that Martin Luther King, Jr., used in one of his famous speeches, and on a nearby tablet are engraved the names of those who died in the movement for civil rights.

Helen Keller

COTTON BOLLS AND STEEL MILLS Over a hundred years ago, Alabama was called the "Cotton State." Eventually, though, cotton harvests declined, both from attacks by boll weevils (insects), and because the soil became worn out. George Washington Carver taught Alabama farmers how to rotate crops. By growing crops that added nitrogen back to the soil, farmers got better harvests and enriched the soil. They began to grow peanuts and soybeans alternately with cotton.

Alabama's many forests are used to produce timber, pulp, and paper. After the Civil War, the region of Birmingham was developed—the only big industrial city in the South. Iron and steel are still produced there. More recently, the space center in Huntsville has spurred the development of an electronics and space industry.

Alaska

The Basics

POPULATION: 607,007
48th most populous state
AREA: 656,424 square miles
largest state
STATE CAPITAL: Juneau
STATE BIRD: Willow ptarmigan
(pronounced *tar-mi-gan*)
STATE FLOWER: Wild forget-me-not
STATE TREE: Sitka spruce (also called
yellow, tideland, western, coast, or
Menzies' spruce)
NICKNAMES: The Land of the Midnight
Sun, America's Last Frontier
STATE MOTTO: North to the future
STATE SPORT: Dog mushing
STATE FISH: King salmon
STATE MARINE MAMMAL: Bowhead
whale
STATE MINERAL: Gold
STATE GEM: Jade
STATE SONG: "Alaska's Flag," words by
Marie Drake, music by Elinor Dusenbury
STATE LANDMARK: Aniakchak, Cape
Krusenstern
NATIONAL PARKS: Glacier Bay National
Park, near Juneau, where 11 glaciers meet
the water; Denali, near Healy; Gates of
the Arctic, near Big Lake; Katmai, near
King Salmer; Kenai Fjords, near Homer;
Kobus Valley, near Kotzebue; Lake Clark,
near Anchor Point; Wrangell-St. Elias,
near Cordova
HISTORICAL PARK: Sitka National
Historical Park, featuring authentic
totem poles
STATE FESTIVAL: Ice Climbing Festival,
Valdez (February)

Mt. McKinley National Park

Alaska seems to call for superlatives—most, highest, only. Alaska is the only state to include part of the Arctic. It has America's highest point—Denali, formerly Mt. McKinley; our westernmost—Cape Wrangell; and our northernmost—Point Barrow. Alaska is our largest state—twice as big as Texas—and our wildest. Thousands of acres have never been explored by Europeans. And Alaska is our coldest state: the U.S. record was set at Prospeck Creek near Barrow on January 23, 1971: 80 degrees Fahrenheit below zero.

LAND OF THE MIDNIGHT SUN Most Alaskans live along the southern coast, near the archipelago of islands that extend into the Gulf of Alaska and the Bering Sea, or on the fertile interior basin that nestles below the Alaskan Range. Farther north is the Yukon, a demanding region with winter temperatures as low as -50 degrees F, where in winter darkness or twilight lasts virtually around the clock. Farther north still is the North Slope in the Arctic Circle, a land of tundra and permafrost (permanently frozen ground). There, winter brings 67 straight days of darkness, while from mid-May through July the sun never sets.

A RUSH TO RICHES Alaska's dramatic landscape and abundant natural resources have helped to shape its history. From fur trappers to gold prospectors to wilderness buffs, thousands of people have come to Alaska seeking fortune, opportunity, and adventure.

The first Alaskans were the Inuit (Eskimo), Aleuts, Athabascans, Haida, Tlingit, and Tlairda, whose rich heritage survives today. The word Alaska comes from the Aleutian word Alaxsxaq—mainland.

Danish navigator Vitus Bering visited Alaska on behalf of the Russian czar in 1728 and took sea otter furs

Inuit children in traditional dress

back home. The Russians loved the furs, and the first Alaska rush was on. Hundreds of trappers quickly depleted the sea otter population, killing or enslaving Aleuts as well. The Russian government founded the Russian-American Company in 1799 to run the fur trade and establish peaceful relations with Aleuts.

U.S. Secretary of State William Seward arranged to buy Alaska for $7.2 million in 1867. Critics called it Seward's Folly and Seward's Icebox because they believed Alaska had no value for the U.S.

They were proved wrong when, in 1897, gold was discovered in the Klondike, just across the border, in Canada. The second rush to Alaska began. In 1899 gold was discovered in Nome, and soon 10,000 gold-seekers swarmed into that region. More gold was found in Fairbanks, and near the Yellow, Iditarod, and Yukon Rivers—and each discovery brought more prospectors. But miners' camps were dismal and dangerous, and more miners went away disappointed than rich. Still, by 1910 over $100 million worth of gold had been found by a lucky few.

Alaska grew again in 1957 when oil fields were discovered in the Kenai peninsula. More oil deposits were discovered on the Alaska North Slope in 1968. To transport the oil, the Alaska government built the 800-mile-long Trans-Alaska Pipeline. Alaska has made so much money from its oil fields that it doesn't have to charge any income tax. Instead, it pays money to each person who lives there every year!

Today, many people move to Alaska to enjoy its wide open spaces and outdoor activities. The most famous is the Iditarod, an 1100-mile dogsled race held each winter. Champion racer Susan Butcher holds the Iditarod record with four victories.

A carved raven's head tops this Tlingit totem pole.

BRINGING IN A NEW ERA The second-floor visitors' gallery at the State House of Representatives is named for Elizabeth W. Peratrovich, a Tlingit (pronounced klink-it) woman who came to live in Juneau in the 1940s. There she found such signs as "No dogs, no natives" and "No Indians allowed." In 1945, she spoke before the legislature in defense of a bill that would grant full equal rights to Native Americans. Thanks to her speech, the bill passed—and, in the words of Governor Ernest Gruening, "a new era in Alaska's racial relations had begun."

WEALTH FROM THE EARTH Most of Alaska's wealth comes from its natural resources: oil, natural gas, copper, coal, and gold. Fish are also a key source of wealth, especially salmon, king crab, shrimp, and halibut. Tourism is a fast-growing industry—so much so that Alaska has more tourists than residents! The government is also a major Alaska employer, hiring people to run military bases as well as national and state parks.

Preservation of the environment is a key issue in Alaska. In 1980, Congress passed the Alaska Lands Bill, setting aside more than 104 million acres as wilderness. In 1989 the oil tanker *Exxon Valdez* ran aground in Prince William Sound, causing one of the worst oil spills in history. Environmentalists are concerned about the effects of the spill—and about how to prevent future disasters. Environmentalists also clash with developers who want to cut more timber or drill for more oil.

Arizona

The Basics

POPULATION: 4,428,068
21st most populous state
AREA: 114,006 square miles
6th largest state
STATE CAPITAL: Phoenix
STATE BIRD: Cactus wren
STATE FLOWER: Saguaro flower
STATE TREE: Paloverde (Green-barked Acacia)
NICKNAMES: Grand Canyon State, Apache State, Copper State, Valentine State, the Italy of America, the State Where You Can Always Expect to Enjoy the Unexpected
STATE MOTTO: *Ditat Deus* (Latin for "God enriches")
SPORTS TEAMS: Arizona Cardinals (Phoenix), football; Phoenix Suns, basketball
STATE GEM: Turquoise
STATE NECKWEAR: Bola tie
STATE SONG: "Arizona March Song," words by Margaret Rowe Clifford and music by Maurice Blumenthal
STATE LANDMARKS: Grand Canyon; Painted Desert; Petrified Forest (an ancient forest that turned to brightly colored stone about 150 million years ago); Navajo National Monument; Hubbell Trading Post (Ganado)
ARIZONA FESTIVALS: Chili Cook-Off, Kingman (May); "Helldorado" Historic Reenactment, Tombstone (October); *La Vuelta de Bisbee* Bicycle Races, Bisbee (April); Sawdust Festival Loggers' Competition, Payson (July)

The Grand Canyon

48th state to enter the Union, February 14, 1912

Arizona is a state marked by overwhelming beauty: the Painted Desert, the Petrified Forest, mountains, plateaus, and the spectacular Grand Canyon, one of the seven natural wonders of the world. Southeast of Flagstaff, there's even a meteor crater—a hole 600 feet deep and a mile wide—left from when a giant meteor crashed into Arizona millions of years ago.

CACTUS AND CANYONS   The Colorado Plateau, a flat, dry area marked by canyons and mesas, occupies the northeastern two-thirds of Arizona. The rest of the state is an arid or semi-arid region that includes the Sonoran Desert in the state's southwestern corner. Despite the name, however, only one percent of Arizona is true desert although over forty percent is desert scrub. Southeastward, near Tucson, is the Saguaro National Park, featuring fifty-foot cacti whose "arms" extend in bizarre shapes.

Although you can see working cowboys in Arizona, some 84 percent of this state's residents live in cities and towns. Urban residents have accounted for most of Arizona's phenomenal population growth: the state has more than tripled in size since World War II, and just since 1980 its population has risen by almost 35 percent. The state's hot, dry climate has made it popular with senior citizens who come to retire in Phoenix, Tucson, Sun City, and other Arizona places in ever-increasing numbers.

Geronimo, the brave leader of the Apache, led many uprisings.

GERONIMO'S LAST STAND   Arizona's history begins almost two thousand years ago, with the ancient Hohokam, Mogollan, and Anasazi cultures. The best known of these is the Anasazi (a Navajo word meaning "the ancient ones"), who lived in pueblos (Spanish for village), a type of communal house that resembled modern apartment buildings, with many small rooms built into the sides of cliffs. You can still see Anasazi ruins at the Canyon de Chelly National Monument.

These ancient civilizations mysteriously disappeared around the beginning of the fifteenth century, to be replaced by other native peoples. Arizona is still home to more Native Americans, including Apache, Hualapai, Maricopa,

Papago, Pima, Southern Paiute, Yavapai, and most notably, Hopi and Navajo, than any other state.

The first Europeans came to Arizona in 1539, searching for the famous Seven Cities of Cibola, which, according to legend, were rich in gold, silver, and jewels. In 1539 the Franciscan friar Marcos de Niza arrived. He was followed in 1540 by Francisco Vasquez de Coronado. The explorers attacked and destroyed many villages—only to discover that there were no riches, after all. (If you drive on U.S. Route 66, you'll be taking Coronado's route.) In 1692, Spanish Jesuit missionaries came to convert Indians away from their own religions to Christianity.

In 1821 Arizona became part of Mexico which had recently won its own independence from Spain. Arizona was still primarily settled by Native Americans although some American trappers—Bill Williams, Pauline Weaver, and the legendary Kit Carson—established trails.

Some of the rock formations in Monument Valley rise as high as 1000 feet.

When the United States acquired Arizona in 1853, new waves of settlers moved in from Texas and the East but they were soon met with fierce resistance from the Apache, led by Mangas Coloradas, Cochise, and most famously, Geronimo. Indian resistance continued for decades. Then in 1876, the U.S. Army tried to move the Apache onto a reservation. Geronimo (1829-1909) fled with his followers and fought the U.S. Army so successfully that the federal government came to consider Geronimo its chief enemy and even offered a $25,000 reward for his capture. Much of the heaviest fighting was conducted by the Ninth and Tenth cavalries, the all-black Buffalo Soldier units stationed at Fort Bowie.

Geronimo resisted so successfully that many people came to believe that he had supernatural powers. After ten years, however, on September 4, 1886, Geronimo was captured and forced onto a reservation in Florida.

Today, Arizona's territory includes several Indian reservations operating under Indian sovereignty. Oraibi, on the Hopi Reservation, has been home to the Hopi for over 800 years—longer than any other Indian settlement in the United States.

ORANGES AND AIRPLANES Agriculture is one of Arizona's most important industries—85 percent of the state's water supply is used to irrigate crops. Arizona is among the country's leading producers of oranges and lemons, but the state's most important crop is cotton. At an average size of 4,557 acres, Arizona's farms are by far the largest in the United States. Mining has historically been a key Arizona industry as well, particularly copper mining.

One of the most important industries in Arizona is aircraft manufacturing. Electronics—stereos, telephones, and computer printers—has become an increasingly major part of the economy as well.

Fascinating Facts

ARIZONA HAD THE FIRST...
• competitive annual rodeo—begun on July 4, 1888, Prescott, Arizona

DID YOU KNOW THAT... Arizona was the last of the 48 *contiguous* (touching) states to be admitted to the Union.

HOW ARIZONA GOT ITS NAME:
Although no one knows for sure, the state's name may have come from the Spanish pronunciation of the Pima Indians' Papago dialect: *Aleh-zon* or *Arizonac*, meaning "little spring place," referring to a spring in the southern part of Arizona territory (now in Mexico). The name may also have come from an Aztec word, *Arizuma*, meaning "silver-bearing."

ARIZONA HOT SPOTS:
• The second-hottest temperature in the United States was recorded in Parker, Arizona, on July 7, 1905—127 degrees Fahrenheit.
• The sunniest city in the United States is Yuma, Arizona, which receives less than two inches of rain each year and is sunny 90 percent of the time.
• On average, the hottest U.S. city is Arizona's capital, Phoenix.

GRAND CANYON FACTS:
• 277 miles long
• 2 billion years old
• 17 miles across at its widest spot
• one mile deep—so deep that it has different climates at different levels!

FAMOUS ARIZONAN:
• Senator Barry Goldwater, born in Phoenix, 1909, Republican nominee for President in 1964

ARIZONA IS TOPS IN:
• copper production. Over fifty percent of U.S. copper comes from Arizona.

ARIZONA BRIDGES:
• London Bridge really was falling down— so it was transported from England to Arizona, where tourists can visit it.
• Arizona has the only bridge in the world built just for sheep, on the Salt River, northeast of Mesa. This unique bridge is just one sheep wide!

Arkansas

The Basics

POPULATION: 2,673,400
33rd most populous state
AREA: 53,182 square miles
29th largest state
STATE CAPITAL: Little Rock
STATE BIRD: Mockingbird
STATE FLOWER: Apple blossom
STATE TREE: Pine
NICKNAMES: Land of Opportunity, Razorback State, the Natural State, the Bowie State, the Toothpick State, the Hot Water State
STATE MOTTO: *Regnat Populus* (Latin for "The people rule")
STATE INSECT: Honeybee
STATE MINERAL: Quartz crystal
STATE ROCK: Bauxite
STATE GEM: Diamond
STATE DRINK: Milk
STATE MUSICAL INSTRUMENT: Fiddle
STATE SONG: "Arkansas," words and music by Eva Ware Barnett
NATIONAL PARKS: Hot Springs, near Mountain Pine; Ouachita National Forest, near Hot Springs; Ozark National Forest, near Russellville; Buffalo National River, near Harrison; Felsenthal National Wildlife Refuge, near Crossett
STATE PARKS: Bull Shoals; Crater of Diamonds, Murfreesboro; DeGray Lake Resort, Bismarck; Petit Jean, Morrilton; Toltec Mounds Archaeological State Park, Scott
HISTORIC SITES: Arkansas Territorial Restoration, Little Rock; Mountain Village 1890, Bull Shoals; Old Washington Historic State Park, Hope; Ozark Folk Center State Park, Mountain View; Pioneer Village, Rison; Robinson Farm Museum and Heritage Centers, Valley Springs

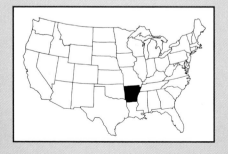

The landscape of this rural, southern state may remind you of its neighbors. To the east are cotton plantations like the ones in Alabama and Mississippi. To the southwest are Texas-style cattle ranches and grazing ranges. To the southeast are bayous, swamps, and moss-hung oak trees that look very like the Louisiana lowlands. To the north, however, Arkansas is truly unique among its neighbors for there are the Boston Mountains, part of the Ozarks, whose hills and ridges are home to Arkansas's mountain people.

DIAMONDS AND QUILTS The Ozark Folk Center in northwest Arkansas is dedicated to preserving traditional mountain culture. Visitors can explore a Victorian-era village or look at local crafts: hand-carved fiddles, straw baskets, and intricately patterned quilts. In the summer, you can see people building a pioneer settlement out of logs.

William Jefferson Clinton, our 42nd president, was born in the town of Hope.

Nearby is Blanchard Springs Caverns, one of the largest caves in the world. The surrounding area offers forested mountains and blue lakes.

In western Arkansas are the Ouachita (wah-chee-tah) Mountains, whose Hot Springs have been famous for two centuries. The earth heats spring waters from 95 to 147 degrees Fahrenheit, and many people believe the waters have healing power. The region also features an alligator farm, a working riverboat, and the Crater of Diamonds, where tourists can keep any jewels they might dig up.

A BARGAIN AT ANY PRICE When Spanish explorer Hernando de Soto visited Arkansas in 1541, he found a confederacy of native peoples: the Osage, Caddo, and Quapaw. In 1682 French explorer La Salle mapped the area and claimed it for France. (The state's name comes from the French pronunciation of the Algonquin name for the Quapaw—the Kansas, or "downstream people.")

When Thomas Jefferson was elected president in 1800, relations between the United States and France were not good. Jefferson became afraid that France would prevent American traders from shipping their goods along the Mississippi River. So in 1803, Jefferson asked to buy a small parcel of land around the river's mouth. To his surprise, the French offered instead to sell almost 800,000 square miles of territory for only $15 million. The sale, known as the Louisiana Purchase, included all of present-day Arkansas, Missouri, Iowa, North Dakota, South Dakota, Nebraska, Oklahoma, and Kansas, as well as parts of Louisiana, Wyoming, and Colorado.

FROM CIVIL WAR TO CIVIL RIGHTS When the Civil War began in 1861, Arkansas sent 60,000 soldiers to fight for the South. But 9,000 white Arkansans and 5,000 African Americans fought for the Union instead. In 1864, some Arkansas leaders even held a Unionist convention that attempted to abolish slavery in the state.

After the war, the federal government sent troops to the South to protect African Americans from those white people who thought they should not have equal rights. During this period, called Reconstruction, ex-Confederate soldiers were not allowed to vote. That made it possible for African Americans and sympathetic white people to work for equality. Many African Americans fought in the state militia against the Ku Klux Klan, an outlaw group that terrorized black people who tried to assert their rights. In 1874, however, former Confederate officers and soldiers were allowed to vote again. Soon, the Arkansas legislature was passing laws to keep black people from voting and to segregate them (keep them separate) in schools and other public places.

In 1954 the Supreme Court ruled that black and white children must be allowed to attend the same schools. On September 4, 1957, nine brave African-American students enrolled in Little Rock's all-white Central High School. Hundreds of angry white people gathered outside the school, trying to keep black students out. Arkansas's Governor Orval Faubus sent national guard troops to keep the "Little Rock Nine" from entering the building. Finally, on September 20, President Dwight Eisenhower sent federal soldiers to integrate Central High. The rest of the nation was so shocked at the image of national guardsmen aiming guns at high school students that school desegregation went more smoothly else-where. Today, almost half the students at Central High are black.

Little Rock's Old Statehouse was used for official business from 1836 to 1910.

FROM COTTON TO COAL In the state's early days, agriculture was the mainstay of the economy, especially cotton farming. Then three important discoveries changed the state's economy. Bauxite—aluminum ore—was discovered in 1887, diamonds in 1906, and oil in 1921. Now Arkansas produces these products plus coal and natural gas. Arkansas is still one of the nation's three leading cotton states, as well as a producer of cattle, corn, soybeans, and rice. One-half of the state is covered in forests, so timber is also a key Arkansas product. Nevertheless, in the 1960s, Arkansas went from being a farm state to one that relies on manufacturing.

PRESIDENT BORN IN ARKANSAS:
• Bill Clinton (1946-), 42nd President

OTHER FAMOUS PEOPLE BORN IN ARKANSAS:
• Actress Mary Steenburgen, Newport, (1953-)
• General Douglas MacArthur, Little Rock (1880-1964)
• Baseball great Dizzy Dean, Lucas (1911-1974)

ARKANSAS IS TOPS IN:
• aluminum ore production—95 percent of U.S. ore comes from Bauxite (the name of a town, also the name of the ore itself)
• diamond mines—the Murfreesboro field is the only one in North America
• mineral springs
• mineral variety—in Magnet Cove, there are over 60 different minerals, more than in any other single region of the world
• archery bow production—Pine Bluff
• earthquakes—the 1811 quake has been called the strongest on the continent

ARKANSAS HAD THE FIRST:
• aluminum ore mine—at Bauxite—1887
• national park—Hot Springs—1932
• national river—Buffalo—1972
• woman senator—Hattie Caraway—1931

ARKANSAS IS THE ONLY STATE TO... pass a resolution on how to pronounce its name, with the last *s* silent. The state legislature decreed this in 1881.

DAVY CROCKETT SAID: "If I could rest anywhere it would be Arkansas, where the men are of the real half-horse, half-alligator breed such as grows nowhere else on the face of the universal earth."

THINGS THAT USED TO BE ILLEGAL IN ARKANSAS:
• to blindfold cows on public highways
• to file down a mule's teeth
• to set up a lunch counter on Memorial Day within a half-mile of a Confederate cemetery
• to drive an automobile without a man walking in front carrying a red flag

California

The Basics

POPULATION: 33,871,648
most populous state

AREA: 163,707 square miles
3rd largest state

STATE CAPITAL: Sacramento

STATE BIRD: California Valley quail

STATE FLOWER: Golden poppy

STATE TREE: California Redwood

NICKNAMES: The Golden State, Empire State of the West

STATE MOTTO: *Eureka!* (Greek for "I have found it!")

SPORTS TEAMS: California Angels, Los Angeles Dodgers, Oakland Athletics, San Diego Padres, San Francisco Giants, baseball; Golden State Warriors, Los Angeles Clippers, Los Angeles Lakers, Sacramento Kings, basketball; Los Angeles Rams, Los Angeles Raiders, San Francisco 49ers, San Diego Chargers, football ; Los Angeles Kings, San Jose Sharks, hockey;

STATE ANIMAL: Grizzly bear

STATE FISH: Golden trout

STATE INSECT: Dog-Face butterfly

STATE MARINE MAMMAL: Gray whale

STATE REPTILE: Desert tortoise

STATE MINERAL: Native gold

STATE ROCK: Serpentine

STATE FOSSIL: Saber-Toothed cat

STATE SONG: "I Love You, California," words by F.B. Silverwood, music by A.F. Frankenstein

STATE LANDMARK: Disneyland, Anaheim; La Brea Tar Pits, Los Angeles—bones of Ice Age animals stuck in oil

STATE NATIONAL PARKS: Yosemite; Sequoia; Kings Canyon; Inyo National Forest

From the days of the gold rush, California has had a magical allure for people in the rest of the United States. Whether people were rushing here to prospect gold, make a movie, or just enjoy the year-round sunshine, they saw California as the land of their dreams.

FROM THE SIERRA NEVADA TO DEATH VALLEY California occupies most of the West Coast. The state is shaped by two great mountain ranges—the Coastal and the Sierra Nevada. Between them lies the fertile Central Valley. At the southern end of the Sierra Nevada is the barren Death Valley, and below that is the Mojave Desert. Along the coast, southern California is blessed with a mild, sunny climate, and beautiful beaches. Northern California has a cooler climate, stunning mountain scenery, and a dramatic rocky coastline.

Yosemite Falls are the highest waterfalls in North America.

From San Diego to Sonoma, a chain of Spanish missions stretches up the California coast. These were built in the late 1700s by people hoping to convert the Indians to Catholicism. One of the most famous missions is San Juan Capistrano, known for the swallows that travel back every spring to nest there.

A GOLDEN DESTINY Throughout its history, California has been a place to start life anew. The first Europeans to visit the area were the Spanish. They had read stories about a rich land called "California." Explorer Juan Rodriguez Cabrillo "discovered" the real California in 1542. He found none of its fabled riches, though—only the Paiute, Shoshone, Maidu, Mohave, Yuma, and some 500 other native peoples who had been living there for many years. In the late 1700s, Spanish missionaries arrived, intending to convert the Indians to Christianity. Settlers from Mexico soon followed. California became part of newly independent Mexico in 1821 and was acquired by the U.S. in 1848 after the Mexican War.

That year, gold was discovered at Sutter's Mill, and by 1849, 40,000 "forty-niners" had swarmed into the state. In one year, they found over $30 million in gold. Moses Rodgers, an African American, gained fame as one of the best mining engineers around. He used his vast earnings to free other African Americans being held as slaves in the South.

A cross-country railroad was completed in 1869, allowing farmers to come more easily to California's rich farmland, and land values rose sharply. Just in

1885, the price of an acre jumped from $350 to $10,000. In the early 1900s, moviemakers set up shop in a small town called Hollywood. Soon the very name stood for movie magic.

In 1929 America was struck by an enormous depression that put almost one-third of the country out of work. A drought hit Texas and Oklahoma, and farmers had to leave their land. Many of these displaced farmers came to California to look for work. Often they ended up living in dismal migrant labor camps. They were known, insultingly, as "Okies."

Over the years, many Japanese had become successful small farmers in California. When America went to war with Japan in 1941, some people thought these Japanese Americans would be loyal to the enemy. In 1942, the U.S. forced them into internment camps in Montana, Idaho, and other states that had no access to the ocean, so that they could not communicate with Japan. (America was also at war with Germany, but German Americans were never put in camps.) When the war was over, Japanese Americans were released—but by then, many had lost their homes, businesses, and savings. Years later, some received payment from the U. S. Congress for some of what they had lost.

California-born author, Amy Tan

After the war many Californians found jobs in the state's new aircraft factories—including the "Okies," once so scorned. The 1970s brought new glory to California as a vibrant computer industry blossomed in San Jose's Silicon Valley. Every year, its high-tech companies invent new computer products used around the world.

Also after the war, California became a land of theme parks. Knotts Berry Farm, Marineland, Sea World, and, of course, Disneyland offered tourists a new kind of day out. Disneyland, which first opened in 1955, is still the nation's most famous theme park. Its attractions include Fantasyland, full of fairy castles and storybook rides; Frontierland, which recreates the Wild West; Tomorrowland, "world of the future"; and Adventureland, where you explore jungles and haunted houses.

Redwood trees often grow 300 feet high.

SO MUCH TO DO! If California were an independent country, its economy would be the sixth largest in the world! Although only about one percent of the state's people work on farms, California leads the country in agricultural production. Airplanes and cars dominate California manufacturing, as well as high-tech industries, which employ one in every five California workers. Mining gold, silver, copper, mercury, zinc, and tungsten is also big business. With 47,000 oil wells, California ranks fourth in U.S. oil production. Of course, tourism, television, movies, and other glamour industries are key to the Golden State's economy.

Cesar Chavez, labor leader

Colorado

The Basics

POPULATION: 3,822,676
25th most populous state

AREA: 104,100 square miles
8th largest state

STATE CAPITAL: Denver

STATE BIRD: Lark bunting

STATE FLOWER: Rocky Mountain columbine

STATE TREE: Colorado blue spruce (also called Blue spruce, Colorado spruce, Balsam, and the Prickly, White, Silver, or Parry's spruce)

NICKNAMES: The Centennial State, the Highest State, the Switzerland of America

STATE MOTTO: *Nil sine numine* (Latin for "Nothing without Providence")

STATE SPORTS TEAMS: Colorado Rockies, baseball; Denver Broncos, football; Denver Nuggets, basketball; Colorado Avalanche, hockey

STATE ANIMAL: Rocky Mountain Bighorn sheep

STATE GEM: Aquamarine

STATE COLORS: Blue and white

STATE SONG: "Where the Columbines Grow," words and music by A.J. Flynn

STATE NATIONAL PARKS: Mesa Verde; Rocky Mountain; Great Sand Dunes National Monument—mountains of sand almost 700 feet high

STATE FESTIVALS: Renaissance Festival, Larkspur (June-August); Boom Days and Burro Race, Leadville (August); *Flauschink* Ski Events, Crested Butte (April); Kinetic Conveyance Challenge, Boulder (May); National Footbag Championship, Golden (July); World's Championship Pack Burro Race, Fairplay (July)

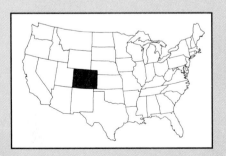

The Continental Divide   **38th state to enter the Union, August 1, 1876**

Tall, snowy mountains under a bright blue sky and sparkling sunshine… 54 of the nation's highest peaks, including Mt. Elbert, the second highest mountain in the United States—no wonder some people call Colorado the "American Switzerland!"

COWBOYS AND PIONEER WOMEN Colorado can be divided into three sections. To the east are dry, windy high plains. The central area is Colorado's Piedmont, a heartland containing 80 percent of the state's population. To the west are the Rocky Mountains, high and rugged. Through Colorado runs the Continental Divide, dividing rivers into those that run east and those that run west.

The capital and largest city is Denver, whose winter weather reports often begin with a rundown of skiing conditions. If you see a "D" under the date of any coin, it was made in the Denver mint.

Garden of the Gods—an 8000-year-old rock formation in Colorado Springs

Denver is a modern city, the commercial center of the Southwest. But you can find traces of its pioneer heritage throughout. The state Capitol building, for example, has a memorial window celebrating Aunt Clara Brown, a slave who bought her freedom in 1856 and worked her way west as a cook on a wagon train. At well over 50 years old, Brown began a new life, starting Denver's first laundry. In Denver's Black American West Museum and Heritage Center, you can learn about African-American cowboys such as Nat Love, who also started life as a slave but ended as a gunslinger on the frontier. South of Denver, black explorer Jim Beckwourth founded the frontier town of Pueblo. Beckwourth was an explorer, a fur trapper, an honorary war chief with the Crow Indians, and the man who discovered California's Beckwourth Pass.

Colorado's second city is Boulder, home of the University of Colorado. There you can take a tour of the Celestial Seasonings tea company. Colorado Springs is the home of the U.S. Olympic Center, where athletes train for the worldwide contest. It's also the site of the United States Air Force Academy and the North American Air Defense Command (NORAD).

In northwest Colorado, skiers head for Vail and Aspen. Southwest Colorado is famous for Mesa Verde, the U.S.'s largest cliff dwelling. The Anasazi, ancestors of today's Pueblo Indians, built multistoried buildings and created black-on-white pottery there between 550 and 1300.

PIKES PEAK OR BUST About four hundred years ago, Colorado was occupied by Cheyenne, Arapaho, and Ute, who chased the buffalo on Colorado's plains and lived in tipis—cone-shaped tents made of buffalo skin. The United States

Mesa Verde National Park, site of ancient Indian cliff dwellings

had acquired the territory by 1848, however, and first settled it in 1851. Between 1858 and 1891, gold and silver were discovered in Colorado, first near Denver, then at Central City, then at Leadville, and finally at Cripple Creek. Thousands of prospectors and settlers rushed into the state between the first discovery in 1858 and the last one in 1891. Pikes Peak or Bust! was their slogan, as they tried to reach Colorado's famous mountain.

Slowly and reluctantly, in response to U.S. troops, the native peoples began to give up their homeland. In 1861 for example, the Cheyenne ceded a great portion of their territory to the United States. In 1864, angered by the U.S. massacre of 150 Indians at Sand Creek, the Cheyenne and the Arapaho began to fight again. But by 1867, they were defeated and forced to go to Indian Territory in Oklahoma. Likewise, in 1879, the Ute fought against U.S. encroachment, but by 1880 they had been relegated to a small reservation.

MASSACRE AT LUDLOW In 1914, another kind of massacre took place in Colorado. For many years, workers in the gold, silver, and copper mines had tried to win better wages and working conditions through their union, the Western Federation of Miners. But employers fought bitterly against these efforts, even calling in the State and National Guards to break strikes in 1903 and 1904. Ten years later, striking miners at the Colorado Fuel and Iron Corporation were horrified when the National Guard set fire to a tent colony for miners and their families at Ludlow, killing 20 people including 12 children.

Coyotes roam over the western United States.

Over 1,000 miners took up arms in a 10-day uprising against the company, which was owned in part by John D. Rockefeller. The company called in federal troops to stop the uprising—and break the strike. Later, the miners erected a monument to those who had died.

AIRPLANES, AEROSPACE, AND ELECTRONICS Once agriculture was the mainstay of Colorado's economy. Even today, two-fifths of the state's land is used to graze cattle. Next, mining was king in Colorado—and uranium, gold, silver, copper, and oil are still big business. But Colorado's future lies in the aerospace, electronics, and research and development industries in and around Denver and Colorado Springs, inspired in part by the U.S. government's support for military research and nuclear power.

Fascinating Facts

COLORADO HALLS OF FAME:
• Figure Skating Hall of Fame, Colorado Springs
• Pro Rodeo Hall of Champions, Colorado Springs

DID YOU KNOW THAT... Boulder is the only city in the world that owns a glacier—Arapahoe Glacier. As the glacier melts, the city uses its water.

FAMOUS PERSON BORN IN COLORADO:
• Writer Ken Kesey, La Junta (1935-)

DID YOU KNOW THAT... Explorer Zebulon Pike was *not* the first person or the first European American to see Pikes Peak. Native Americans had known of the mountain for thousands of years; U.S. trapper James Purcell saw it in 1804.

IT USED TO BE ILLEGAL IN COLORADO:
• to watch a dogfight
• to hunt ducks from an airplane
• to throw shoes at a bridal couple

HOW COLORADO GOT ITS NAME: Colorado is Spanish for "red." The state was named for the Colorado River, which flows through canyons of red stone.

DID YOU KNOW THAT... When World War II began, Nazi dictator Adolf Hitler owned 8,960 acres of prime Colorado land.

COLORADO HAS THE NATION'S HIGHEST:
• state capital, Denver—one mile above sea level
• settlement—Climax—11,560 feet above sea level
• mean (average) altitude for a state
• automobile road—up to the top of Mount Evans, west of Denver—14,264 feet

DID YOU KNOW THAT... The song "America the Beautiful" was written by Katherine Lee Bates in 1893 after she rode up Pikes Peak in a horse-drawn wagon and got a good look at the view.

Connecticut

The Basics

POPULATION: 3,274,238
28th most populous state
AREA: 5,544 square miles
48th largest state
STATE CAPITAL: Hartford
STATE BIRD: Robin (American robin)
STATE FLOWER: Mountain laurel
STATE TREE: White oak
NICKNAMES: The Constitution State, the Nutmeg State
STATE MOTTO: *Qui Transtulit Sustinet* (Latin for "He Who Transplanted Still Sustains")
SPORTS TEAMS: Hartford Whalers, hockey
STATE ANIMAL: Sperm whale
STATE INSECT: Praying mantis
STATE MINERAL: Garnet
STATE SHIP: *U.S.S. Nautilus*
STATE SONG: "Yankee Doodle Dandy," folk song
STATE LANDMARKS: State Capitol, Hartford; Mystic Seaport and Mystic Marinelife Aquarium, Mystic; Charter Oak Monument
NATIONAL PARKS: Weir Farm National Historic Site, Wilton, former home of artist J. Alden Weir; Salt Meadow Wildlife Refuge, Stewart B. McKinney Wildlife Refuge; Appalachian National Scenic Trail
STATE FESTIVALS: Balloons Over Bristol, Bristol (Memorial Day Weekend); Barnum Festival, Bridgeport (June-July); Powder House Day, New Haven (Spring); Shad Derby Festival, Windsor (May); Taste of Hartford, Hartford (May)

Connecticut

From the very beginnings of the United States, Connecticut has been a leader—in politics, in education, and in manufacturing. Today, the state has preserved its Colonial heritage—and gone on to be a leader in twentieth-century industry and finance.

VALLEYS AND SUBURBS You can divide Connecticut into four parts. To the northwest are the Western Uplands at the eastern end of the Berkshire Mountains. Below the mountains is the Connecticut Valley through which flows the Connecticut River. Farther east are the Eastern Uplands, hilly country occupied by dairy farms. And at the southern border of the state is the Long Island Sound with its inviting beaches and rocky coves.

Connecticut is an urban and suburban state, although you can also find plenty of rolling countryside dotted with small farms and scenic villages. The population is organized around two major urban areas. In the south are suburbs of New York City. Farther north, residents work at jobs in and around Hartford, the state capital.

Other major Connecticut cities include Bridgeport, the former home of circus showman P.T. Barnum (you can visit the Barnum Museum there), and New Haven, site of Yale University. Historic sites abound in this state. In Hartford, you can visit Mark Twain's home, right next door to the house of Harriet Beecher Stowe, author of *Uncle Tom's Cabin*. Nearby is the birthplace of Noah Webster, who published the first American dictionary. Revolutionary War spy Nathan Hale once taught school in East Haddam. And at Groton is a submarine base, from which the first atomic-powered submarine, the *U.S.S. Nautilus*, was launched in 1954.

Harriet Beecher Stowe (1811-1896) was born in Litchfield.

FUNDAMENTAL ORDERS Almost 150 years before the United States Constitution was signed, Connecticut residents met in Hartford to create the first constitution of a representative government. Known as the Fundamental Orders, the document declared that "the foundation of authority is in the first consent of the people." In other words, the people must agree to give authority to a government.

Connecticut residents had long prized independence. In 1636 Thomas Hooker led over a hundred settlers from Massachusetts to Connecticut to escape the harsh rule of the Puritans. The Fundamental Orders followed in 1639. In

1662 John Winthrop petitioned England's King Charles II for a charter that would make the colony almost independent of the British governor, Sir Edmund Andros. Charles agreed to Winthrop's request—but in 1687, the charter was revoked. Andros wanted to destroy the document, but the colonists were too fond of their liberty. According to legend, they hid the charter in a tree, the "Charter Oak," to guard their rights.

Yale University, New Haven, CT. One of America's oldest institutions.

Later, in 1770 Old Lyme residents had a "tea party" years before the one in Boston. They seized and burned a peddler's tea to protest the high British taxes on that product. In Lebanon, a group of citizens drafted a declaration of rights and liberties. When the Revolutionary War finally came, Connecticut furnished the United States with more soldiers and money than any other colony except Massachusetts. This state's food, clothing, and supplies were so important that George Washington called Connecticut "the Provisions State."

Square rigger at Mystic seaport

THE INSURANCE CAPITAL OF THE WORLD Early Connecticut was full of ports: New Haven, New London, and Bridgeport. Whalers sailed out of Mystic and Stonington, while Hartford linked the ocean and the Connecticut River.

Today, the sea is less important to this industrial state although the Coast Guard Academy is in Connecticut, as well as a naval submarine base. More important, however, is the massive finance industry in and around Hartford, the "Insurance Capital of the World."

Connecticut has also led in the development of modern industry. In 1798 Eli Whitney figured out that guns could be made more quickly and cheaply if some of the parts were machine-made to the same size every time. This made the parts interchangeable so that they always fit together. No longer did one worker make each gun separately. This idea was central to the system of mass production that we have today. Today, Connecticut leads the nation in production of small firearms, computers, helicopters, jet aircraft engines, submarines, ball and roller bearings, pins and needles, silverware, and thread.

Deer become a nuisance when people encroach on their land.

There is some farming in Connecticut, notably of apples, beef, eggs, milk, shrubs, flowers, and vegetables. Connecticut farmers also grow a special kind of tobacco used as the outside leaves on cigars.

Delaware

The Basics

POPULATION: 783,600
45th most populous state

AREA: 2,489 square miles
49th largest state

STATE CAPITAL: Dover

STATE BIRD: Blue hen chicken

STATE FLOWER: Peach blossom

STATE TREE: American holly (also known as holly, white holly, evergreen holly, and Boxwood)

NICKNAMES: The First State, the Diamond State, the Blue Hen State, the Peach State

STATE MOTTO: Liberty and Independence

STATE FISH: Weakfish

STATE BUG: Ladybug

STATE MINERAL: Sillimanite

STATE COLORS: Colonial blue and buff

STATE DRINK: Milk

STATE SONG: "Our Delaware," words by George B. Hynson, music by Will M. S. Brown

STATE LANDMARKS: Fort Delaware, Pea Patch Island; Odessa, featuring 200-year-old houses; Swedish log house, Wilmington, a 1638 log cabin; Winterthur Museum, Garden, and Library, outside Wilmington, a nine-story, 196-room mansion displaying two centuries of American furniture, china, and silver collected by Henry Francis du Pont; Nemours Mansion and Gardens, Wilmington, displaying luxury automobiles, antiques, and French gardens; Brandywine Zoo, Wilmington; Cypress Swamp, the U.S.'s northernmost natural stand of cypress trees

NATIONAL PARKS: Bombay Hook National Wildlife Refuge, near Smyrna; Prime Hook National Wildlife Refuge, near Milton

Delaware

16

Bombay Hook Wildlife Refuge

1st state to enter the Union, December 7, 1787

Delaware is the only colony to have been claimed by Sweden, Holland, and England. Delaware is notable for another reason: More than half of the nation's biggest companies are incorporated in Wilmington. Truly, the most important business in Delaware is business itself.

SHIPPING STATE ON THE SEABOARD Most of Delaware is a low, flat plain—farming country—although there are some rolling hills and valleys to the north. This mid-Atlantic state is strategically located along the Eastern seaboard, making it a key shipping center between New York and Washington, D.C. Its only major city, Wilmington, is conveniently situated within 10 miles of New Jersey, Pennsylvania, and Maryland.

LAND OF THE LOG CABIN Henry Hudson was probably the first European to visit Delaware when he sailed his famous ship, *Half Moon*, into Delaware Bay in 1609. He was followed in 1610 by Captain Samuel Argall of Virginia Colony. The first settlers, though,

Henry Hudson

were the Dutch who in 1631 founded the town of Swaanendael near today's town of Lewes.

After the Indians drove out the Dutch, the Swedes arrived in 1638 to found Fort Christina (now part of Wilmington), named for their famous queen. The Dutchman Peter Minuit was hired by the Swedes to lead their expedition. The Swedes built the first American log cabins.

The Dutch still considered that they owned Delaware, however, and in 1656 Peter Stuyvesant brought a large fleet to enforce that claim. Then, in 1664, the English took over, making Delaware part of New York Colony. In 1673 the Dutch took the state again but returned it peacefully to the English in 1674.

Delaware's owners continued to change. In 1682 the state was given to William Penn as part of his new state, Pennsylvania. In fact, Penn's first landing in the United States was at Battery Park, New Castle, five miles south of Wilmington. Finally, in 1701 Penn gave Delaware its own separate legislature.

The people of Delaware had learned to prize their independence. Although he was dying of cancer, Delawarean Caesar Rodney made a famous ride from Dover to the Continental Congress in Philadelphia to cast the deciding vote in favor of independence. On December 7, 1787, Delaware became the first state to sign the Constitution. And during the Civil War, Delaware was one of four slave states to stick with the Union.

AMERICA'S FIRST BLACK CHURCH   In the eighteenth century, there were slaves throughout the United States, north and south. And free African Americans were segregated everywhere. Even in churches, they were often required to sit in separate sections or not allowed to attend at all.

Richard Allen decided to change all that. In 1794 he founded the African Methodist Episcopal (AME) Church, the oldest and largest institution of African Americans. Allen grew up in Dover as a slave on the Stockley family plantation. There he had a religious awakening, converted his owner, and managed to buy his freedom. You can visit a marker commemorating this important man just north of the State Capitol.

BUSINESS HEADQUARTERS TO A NATION   Delaware was once the center of the flour industry. Indeed, the price of wheat was set in Wilmington. In 1802, however, the Du Pont family built a gunpowder mill on the Brandywine River. This event marked the beginning of the Du Ponts' influence—and the start of Delaware's history as a manufacturing state. (At the Hagley Museum in Wilmington, you can still see the gunpowder mills, an old machine shop, and the Du Pont family mansion.)

The Delaware River was a key artery for shipping goods along the east coast, which helped bring more factories to Wilmington. In the nineteenth century, they made engines and railroad equipment. In the twentieth century, they produced machinery, ammunition, and aircraft.

Wilmington also became a major chemical center. Paints, dyes, and synthetic fabrics such as nylon and orlon are made there. These factories have brought prosperity to the state, but they may have also exposed many of Delaware's workers to toxic products, possibly leading to an unusually high rate of cancer in the state.

Delaware's orchards produce apples and peaches, while its poultry farms produce eggs and chickens. Delaware Bay yields a rich harvest of oysters, crabs, clams, and sea trout. And truck farms on Delaware's fertile plains produce soybeans, potatoes, corn, and vegetables.

But Delaware's economy relies most of all on the corporate headquarters that are based here. The state charges

The state Hall of Records in Dover

no income tax or corporate tax, making it a favorable location for over 200,000 corporations. Even companies who actually do business elsewhere may officially incorporate in Delaware to take advantage of its tax laws. Banks from all over the nation have established their credit-card companies here.

Fascinating Facts

HOW DELAWARE GOT ITS NAME: Sir Thomas West, Lord de la Warr, was the first governor of the Virginia Colony. The Delaware River was named for him, and the state was named for the river. The British also used the name for the Delaware Indians, who in their own language were called the Lenni-Lenape.

DELAWARE HAD THE FIRST:
• steam railroad—out of New Castle—1831

DID YOU KNOW THAT...
• Johan Prinz, the governor of New Sweden from 1643 to 1653, weighed 400 pounds and was called the "Big Tub."
• When a ship carrying peas foundered on a sandbar, the peas grew and collected sand—forming Pea Patch Island.

FAMOUS PERSON BORN IN DELAWARE:
• Astronomer Annie Jump Cannon, Dover (1863-1941)

HOW DELAWARE GOT ITS NICKNAMES: Delaware was the "First State" to ratify the Constitution. Later, President Thomas Jefferson said Delaware was like a diamond, small but of great value—hence, "the Diamond State."

A CITY NICKNAME: Wilmington, Delaware, makes so many chemicals— the Du Pont Company is headquartered here—that it is called the Chemical Capital of the World.

DELAWARE INVENTIONS:
• nylon—This useful synthetic fabric was invented here and has become a mainstay of Delaware's textile industry.
• milling grain into flour—A Delaware mill was the first to put together all the steps in this process.

DID YOU KNOW THAT... since Delaware was the first state to ratify the Constitution, it gets to lead the parade of states every four years when the President is inaugurated.

DELAWARE IS TOPS IN:
• broiler chickens

District of Columbia

The Basics

POPULATION: 572,059
AREA: 68.25 square miles
OFFICIAL BIRD: Wood thrush
OFFICIAL FLOWER: American Beauty rose
OFFICIAL TREE: Scarlet oak
NICKNAMES: The Nation's Capital, America's First City
OFFICIAL MOTTO: *Justitia Omnibus* (Latin for "Justice for all")
SPORTS TEAMS: Washington Redskins, football
STATE FLAG: based on George Washington's coat of arms
LANDMARKS: Capitol, White House, Washington Monument, Jefferson Memorial, Lincoln Memorial, Vietnam Veterans Memorial, Smithsonian Institution, National Gallery of Art, Library of Congress, U.S. Supreme Court Building, Kennedy Center, the Pentagon (home of the Department of Defense), United States Holocaust Memorial Museum, National Museum of Women in the Arts, The Shakespeare Theater.
HISTORIC SITES: Frederick Douglass National Historic Site—the abolitionist's home; Chesapeake & Ohio Canal, 19th-century waterway that carried lumber, coal, iron, and flour into Maryland; Washington Navy Yard
PARKS AND GARDENS: National Arboretum; Rock Creek Park; U.S. Botanic Garden
KEY RIVER: Potomac
D.C. FESTIVAL: Easter Egg Roll on the White House Lawn
ARTS GROUPS: National Symphony; Shakespeare Theater; Ford's Theater; Washington Opera society

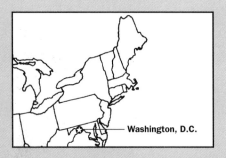
Washington, D.C.

18

The White House was designed by James Hoban   **Established December 1, 1800**

Visitors to Washington, D.C., have the chance to see United States history come to life. The historic buildings represent our nation's government, while the tradition of protest marches represents our democratic ideals.

MONUMENTS AND MUSEUMS   The city of Washington and the District of Columbia are one and the same. That's why the city is often called just "D.C." or "The District." This city, which belongs to no state, is the capital of the whole United States. Here are our government buildings, along with monuments and museums that preserve our history and art. If you go to the National Archives, for example, you can see the original Declaration of Independence and Constitution.

The Jefferson Memorial commemorates our third President, Thomas Jefferson, who wrote the Declaration. In the spring, some 3,000 Japanese cherry blossom trees bloom along the Tidal Basin at the foot of the Jefferson Memorial.

U.S. Marine Monument depicting the flag raising on Iwo Jima during WWII. This is north of Arlington Cemetery, across the Potomac.

The Lincoln Memorial honors President Abraham Lincoln, who saw the nation through the Civil War. This memorial features a huge statue of Lincoln staring thoughtfully at the reflecting pool below.

Washington memorials do not only honor single individuals. Some, like the Vietnam Veterans Memorial, honor groups, such as the 58,000 Americans who were killed in Vietnam. This monument was designed by architect Maya Lin, who also designed the Civil Rights Memorial in Alabama. It consists of two black granite walls etched with the names of the dead. Nearby, the Vietnam Women's Memorial honors the women who served as nurses and soldiers.

Another highlight of Washington is the Smithsonian Institution, a huge complex of museums, including the National Air and Space Museum, the National Gallery of Art, the National Museum of Natural History, and the National Museum of American History. In these buildings, you can find everything from dinosaur bones to the evening gowns worn by first ladies at their husbands' inaugurations.

The city of Washington is laid out like a big wheel. Huge, tree-lined avenues are the spokes of the wheel, and the Capitol—where Congress meets—is the hub. That way, visitors will always remember that the main business of Washington, D.C., is to govern our country.

BUILDING THE NATION'S CAPITAL The idea of a District of Columbia began in 1783 when the Continental Congress decided that our nation needed a capital. It seemed unfair for any one state to have that honor. So Maryland and Virginia offered some of their land to create a new entity, the District of Columbia, named for Christopher Columbus.

The name Washington, of course, came from our nation's first President. In 1791 he was allowed to choose the exact site of the new capital. He also appointed French architect Pierre Charles L'Enfant to design the city and its buildings. In 1793 George Washington, a former surveyor, laid the cornerstone of the new Capitol himself.

In June 1800 the government moved from Philadelphia to Washington, even though the Capitol building wasn't yet finished. Ironically, Washington was the only President who never lived in Washington. The second President, John Adams, was the first to live in the White House.

"MARCH ON WASHINGTON" America has a long tradition of protest, and often that protest has centered on Washington. In 1894, for example, Jacob Coxey and his 500 followers, known as Coxey's Army, marched into the nation's capital to protest unemployment and demand government action to create jobs. Coxey was arrested for walking on the grass, and the protest fell apart. But in 1931 and 1932 the Great Depression brought the hardest time the United States had ever known. Hunger marchers converged on Washington, D.C., demanding social programs to help cope with their new poverty. In 1932 veterans who were not receiving their promised government bonuses actually rioted in Washington, until the U.S. Army was called in.

Civil rights and African-American equality was the theme of the famous 1963 "March on Washington." Half a million people gathered in front of the Lincoln Memorial to hear Dr. Martin Luther King, Jr., give his now-famous speech, "I Have A Dream."

In 1969 marchers came to Washington to protest the war in Vietnam. Since then, people have marched for equal rights, freedom of choice, and

U.S. Supreme Court Building

Right to Life. Labor unions have marched for better treatment of working people, and gay and lesbian people have marched for their own civil rights. Other marchers have both supported and opposed equal rights for women and for gays. Still others have demonstrated for better treatment of workers and of children. In 1995 black men participated in the Million Man march to encourage increased family responsibility. Marching on Washington to make your voice heard is clearly an American tradition.

Fascinating Facts

DID YOU KNOW THAT... The United States had 36 Presidents before the people of Washington, D.C., were allowed to vote for their first President. Washington residents could not vote for President until 1964, and they couldn't elect their own Mayor until 1975. They still have no voting representative in Congress. This issue is known as *Home Rule*, and is still quite controversial in Washington.

FAMOUS PEOPLE BORN IN THE DISTRICT OF COLUMBIA:
• Actress Helen Hayes (1900-1993)
• Actress Goldie Hawn (1945-)
• Actor William Hurt (1950-)

CAPITOL FACT:
• One early plan for the Capitol called for the statue of a large rooster on top.

WASHINGTON TRAGEDIES:
• On April 14, 1865, President Abraham Lincoln was shot while attending a play at Ford's Theater.
• On September 19, 1881, President James Garfield died from an assassination attempt made at a Washington rail station.

DID YOU KNOW THAT...
• Roosevelt Island in the Potomac River at Theodore Roosevelt Memorial Bridge "grows" about 20 acres every hundred years. That's because new land forms around the brush that floats down the river and catches on the island.

WASHINGTON MONUMENT FACTS:
• 555 feet tall, obelisk-shaped
• Construction, begun in 1848, was interrupted by the Civil War—hence the color change one-third of the way up. It was completed in 1884.
• When temperature inside the monument goes up quickly, moisture condenses—and produces an indoor "rain."

IT USED TO BE ILLEGAL IN THE DISTRICT OF COLUMBIA:
• to drive a taxicab without a broom and shovel in the car
• to punch a bull in the nose

Florida

The Basics

POPULATION: 14,399,985
4th most populous state
AREA: 65,758 square miles
22nd largest state
STATE CAPITAL: Tallahassee
STATE BIRD: Mockingbird
STATE FLOWER: Orange blossom
STATE TREE: Palmetto palm
NICKNAMES: The Sunshine State, the
Alligator State, the Everglades State, the
Orange State
STATE MOTTO: "In God We Trust"
STATE ANIMAL: Florida panther
STATE FRESHWATER FISH: Largemouth
bass
STATE SALTWATER FISH: Atlantic
sailfish
STATE MARINE MAMMAL: Manatee
STATE SALTWATER MAMMAL: Porpoise
STATE STONE: Agatized coral
STATE SHELL: Horse conch
STATE GEM: Moonstone
STATE DRINK: Orange juice
STATE AIR FAIR: Central Florida Air Fair
STATE FESTIVAL: Calle Ocho-Open
House 8, Miami
STATE PAGEANT: "Indian River"
STATE PLAY: "Cross and Sword"
STATE LITTER CONTROL SYMBOL:
"Glenn Glitter"
STATE SONG: "Old Folks at Home" (also
known as "Swanee River"), words and
music by Stephen Foster
STATE LANDMARKS: John F. Kennedy
Space Center at Cape Canaveral; Thomas
A. Edison Home and Museum, Ft. Myers
NATIONAL PARKS: Everglades National
Park; Biscayne National Park; Big
Cypress National Preserve

The Everglades

27th state to enter the Union, March 3, 1845

Most of Florida is a peninsula—a long piece of land extending into the Atlantic Ocean and the Gulf of Mexico, connected to the mainland by only a tiny piece of land. Florida has the second-longest coastline in the United States (after Alaska)—4,000 miles—known for its white, sandy beaches and sparkling sapphire waters. No wonder the "Sunshine State" is such a popular spot for both tourists and retirees.

PANTHERS, CROCODILES, AND MICKEY MOUSE Florida is the southernmost state on the U.S. mainland. Over 30,000 lakes dot this humid, low-lying land. The largest lake, Okeechobee, covers 700 square miles. Florida's northern panhandle is rural, hilly country with a temperate climate, but the southern peninsula has tropical weather with very high temperatures and a long rainy season. Florida's most famous natural feature is the Everglades, one of the world's largest swamps, full of alligators, crocodiles, panthers, bobcats, and sea turtles.

Pastel-colored Victorian houses are seen all over Key West.

Off the state's southern tip, are the Florida Keys, a 31-island chain curving out into the Gulf of Mexico. The most famous islands are Key West and Key Largo whose landscape and climate resemble those of other Caribbean islands.

Florida's largest city is Miami. More than half the people in Miami are of Latino heritage, many of them from families that emigrated from Cuba during the twentieth century. Other Cuban emigrés went to Ybor City, near Tampa, creating the famous cigar-making industry there.

The city of Orlando is famous for its many theme parks: Sea World, Cypress Gardens, Disney World, and Splendid China, which re-creates many of China's most beautiful monuments and palaces. Tampa has many theme parks as well, including Busch Gardens and a Seminole Indian village where you can see people wrestling with alligators. Farther south, in Sarasota, circuses come to spend the winter, as you can learn at the Ringling Museum.

An important Florida historical site is Bethune-Cookman College in Daytona Beach. There, in 1904, Mary McLeod Bethune opened the Daytona

Playful dolphins are crowd favorites at Sea World.

Educational and Industrial Training School for Negro Girls. Although it had little money, the school's enrollment grew to 250 within its first two years, and in 1923 it merged with Cookman College, the first state school to offer higher education to African-American males. Bethune was active in civil rights and in education until she died in 1955.

African-American writer, Zora Neale Hurston was born in Eatonville, just north of Orlando. At that time—1901—Eatonville was the only incorporated black town in the nation. Hurston went on to write novels and to collect African-American folklore.

FROM ST. AUGUSTINE TO CAPE CANAVERAL The first permanent European settlement in North America was St. Augustine, founded by Spanish explorers in 1565. For the next two hundred years, the English and the Spanish fought over Florida as pirates and buccaneers raided the coast. In 1750, Creek Indians from Georgia also came into the area, where they were joined by runaway slaves and became known as the Seminoles.

When the Revolutionary War was fought in 1777, Florida was in British hands. In 1783 Florida passed back into Spanish hands. But by 1821 the United States had acquired Florida from Spain.

In 1835 the United States began a seven-year war with the Seminoles, but this was the only Indian war the United States did not win.

Over a century later, Florida won world fame for its role in the space program. In 1961 Commander Alan Shepard was launched from Cape Canaveral to become the first American in space, and the next year Colonel John

Seminole clothes hang from the walls of this museum.

Glenn became the first American to orbit the earth. In 1969 Neil Armstrong left Florida to become the first person to walk on the moon. Today you can visit Spaceport USA at the John F. Kennedy Space Center in Cape Canaveral.

TOURISTS IN THE SUNSHINE STATE Tourism is probably Florida's most important industry, as more than 25 million people visit the state each year. Farming in Florida is dominated by citrus—oranges, grapefruit, and lemons. The state also produces corn, peanuts, soybeans, pecans, avocados, and flowers. Florida industry makes pulp and paper from the state's trees, and processes food, especially frozen orange juice. Electronic products are manufactured from industries clustered around Cape Canaveral.

Fascinating Facts

FLORIDA ANIMALS:
• On Lake George, near Seville, hogs swim out into the shallow waters to catch fish for dinner.
• At Hialeah Park, you can see pink flamingos eat only with their heads upside down.

FLORIDA HAS THE LONGEST...
highway built over ocean waters—the Overseas Highway, running from Miami to Key West over the Florida Keys.

FLORIDA IS TOPS IN:
• cypress; turpentine; cigars; grapefruit (70% of world's crop)

FLORIDA HAD THE NATION'S FIRST:
• permanent European settlement— St. Augustine, founded by the Spanish in 1565

FLORIDA HAS THE NATION'S LARGEST:
• peninsula—over 400 miles of land between the Atlantic and the Gulf of Mexico
• cruise-ship port—Miami

DID YOU KNOW THAT... Florida's population was the nation's fastest-growing between 1980 and 1990.

HOW FLORIDA GOT ITS NAME: Spanish explorer Ponce de León landed on the Florida coast on Easter Sunday. He named the land *La Florida*, to honor the Easter feast of flowers, *Pascua Florida*.

DID YOU KNOW THAT... During the hurricane of 1926, the Miami barometer reached a record low—and hundreds of people fainted for lack of oxygen.

FLORIDA HALLS OF FAME:
• International Swimming Hall of Fame, Fort Lauderdale
• Professional Golf Association Hall of Fame, Palm Beach Gardens

IT USED IT BE ILLEGAL IN FLORIDA:
• to lure a neighbor's cook away and then hire that cook
• to stay in an election booth more than five minutes

Georgia

4th state to enter the Union, January 2, 1788

The Basics

POPULATION: 7,353,225
10th most populous state
AREA 59,441 square miles
24th largest state
STATE CAPITAL: Atlanta
STATE BIRD: Brown thrasher
STATE FLOWER: Cherokee rose
STATE TREE: Live oak
NICKNAMES: The Empire State of the South, the Peach State, the Goober State, Yankee-Land of the South, the Buzzard State
STATE MOTTOES: *Agriculture and Commerce,* and *Wisdom, Justice, Moderation*
SPORTS TEAMS: Atlanta Braves, baseball; Atlanta Falcons, football; Atlanta Hawks, basketball
STATE FISH: Largemouth bass
STATE INSECT: Honeybee
STATE MARINE MAMMAL: Right whale
STATE MINERAL: Staurolite
STATE FOSSIL: Shark tooth
STATE GEM: Quartz
STATE ATLAS: *The Atlas of Georgia*
STATE SONG: "Georgia on My Mind," words by Stuart Gorrell, music by Hoagy Carmichael; originally "Georgia," words by Lottie Bell Wylie, music by Robert Loveman (changed in 1979)
STATE WALTZ: "Our Georgia," words and music by James B. Burch
STATE LANDMARK: Ocmulgee National Monument, near Macon—preserving Indian ways of life from 8000 B.C. to 1717 A.D.
STATE FESTIVALS: Appalachian Wagon Train, Chatsworth (July); Bite of the 'Boro, Statesboro (May); Okefenokee Spring Fling, Waycross (March); Tybee Jubilee, Tybee Island (September)

22

Georgia is an intriguing mix of old and new. In the old town of Savannah, you can still see gracious pre-Civil War mansions with their white pillars and manicured lawns. But you can also see the glass-and-steel skyscrapers of Atlanta, the new commercial center of the South.

MANY LANDSCAPES Georgia is the largest state east of the Mississippi, with a wide variety of landscapes. To the northeast are the Blue Ridge Mountains, while to the northwest are the Appalachians. Moving south, you find the fertile Appalachian Valley and below that, the Piedmont Plateau. Offshore are Jekyll, Sea and St. Simons Islands—once home to some of the richest families in the nation. And in the southeastern corner of the state is the Okefenokee Swamp, over 700 square miles of tropical wilds with 54 species of reptile (including alligators!), 49 different types of mammals, and 234 different kinds of birds.

Georgia's capital and largest city is Atlanta, a town that sprang to new life after it was burned by troops under Union General William Sherman. Today it's headquarters to the Coca-Cola corporation and to Ted Turner's communications empire, including CNN. The 1996 Summer Olympics were held in Atlanta. And Atlanta is the site of Ebenezer Baptist Church, where Martin Luther King Jr. first preached.

Savannah is Georgia's oldest city. General Sherman occupied it for more than a year at the end of his march, but it was never burned. Today it's the place to see historic homes from the 1700s, including the home of Girl

An alligator basking in the sun

Scout founder Juliette Low. Also noteworthy are Athens, home of the University of Georgia, and Augusta, site of the Master's Golf Tournament.

AMERICA'S FIRST HAVEN In 1733 British General James Oglethorpe arrived in Georgia with 120 people, intending to found a colony as a haven for England's poor and oppressed. He made two rules: no drinking of alcohol, and no slaves. Georgia was the last colony created by the British in America.

Less than fifty years later, Georgia fought with its fellow colonies against the British. It soon allowed both drinking and slavery. And in 1793 Georgia resident Eli Whitney invented a machine that would make slavery even more profitable. Until then, cotton seeds had to be separated from cotton fibers by hand, a slow and expensive process. But Whitney's cotton gin could separate

500 pounds of cotton in a single day. Suddenly, cotton plantations could make huge fortunes. Plantation owners were more eager than ever to save money by using slaves to grow, tend, and pick their cotton.

When the election of President Lincoln seemed to threaten slavery, Georgia, like its Southern neighbors, seceded from the Union. The Civil War was extremely hard on many Georgians. Some 90 percent of Atlanta's buildings were destroyed in the 117-day siege of that city.

Juliette Gordon Low (1860-1927)

CARPETBAGGERS AND THE KU KLUX KLAN

After the war, Georgia still refused to recognize African-American rights. It wouldn't ratify the 14th amendment, which guaranteed equal protection under the law regardless of race, color, or creed. Nor would it ratify the 15th amendment, guaranteeing voting rights. A white terrorist group, the Ku Klux Klan, was formed to harass and kill African Americans who exercised their rights. After supporters of the Confederacy were barred from holding office, "carpetbaggers"—northerners who had come South—dominated Georgia's government. In 1870, a legislature that included African Americans and their supporters accepted the 15th Amendment, and Georgia rejoined the Union.

The Klan continued to operate. And when Georgia's old leaders got back into power, they continued to oppose African-Americans' rights into the twentieth century. In 1948 Governor Herman Talmadge said he'd support segregation at all costs. These racists had opposition from Ralph McGill, the editor of the Atlanta Constitution, and Mayor Ivan Allen, which is why Georgia was considered more progressive than its

Nobel prize winner
Dr. Martin Luther King, Jr.

neighbors. And in 1966, Lester Maddox, who had closed his Atlanta restaurant rather than integrate it, was elected governor. In 1961 black students Charlayne Hunter and Hamilton Holmes had to get a court order to attend the all-white University of Georgia. Even in 1987 the Ku Klux Klan was active in the town of Cumming. But some 10,000 civil rights supporters marched to protest the Klan. Times had finally changed.

A WEALTHY LAND   Georgia has one of the most prosperous economies in the South, with factories to process the food and timber that it grows in its farms and forests. Agricultural products include peanuts, corn, tobacco, sugar, pecans, and the famous Georgia peaches. Industries make peanut butter and peanut oil, and make paper from the state's forests. Atlanta is also a hub of commercial and financial activity.

Fascinating Facts

GEORGIA HAD THE FIRST:
• U.S. gold rush—-at Dahlonega—1829
• cotton gin—invented by Eli Whitney—1793
• steamship to cross the Atlantic—the *Savannah*—sailed from Atlanta, 1819
• Coca-Cola served—in an Atlanta drugstore—1887

PRESIDENT BORN IN GEORGIA:
• Jimmy Carter (1934-), 39th President

OTHER FAMOUS PEOPLE BORN IN GEORGIA:
• *Uncle Remus* author Joel Chandler Harris, Eatonton (1848-1908)
• Baseball player "Ty" Cobb, Narrows (1886-1961)
• Blues singer Gertrude "Ma" Rainey, Columbus (1886-1939)
• Writer Carson McCullers, Columbus (1917-1967)
• Baseball pioneer "Jackie" Robinson, Cairo (1919-1972)
• Civil Rights Leader Martin Luther King, Jr., Atlanta (1929-1968)
• Writer Alice Walker, Eatonton (1944-)

GEORGIA HAS THE NATION'S LARGEST:
• freshwater swamp—the Okefenokee
• urban landmark—Savannah's historic district
• isolated granite boulder—Stone Mountain, Atlanta—825 feet high, 7 billion cubic feet

HOW GEORGIA GOT ITS NAME: James Oglethorpe honored the English King George II who had given him the charter for the land.

DID YOU KNOW THAT... Although Georgia was the fourth state to ratify the Constitution, it didn't ratify the Bill of Rights until 1939.

GEORGIA IS TOPS IN:
• turpentines and resins
• peanuts and pecans
• lima beans and pimiento peppers

DID YOU KNOW THAT... In the 1740s, Mary Jones was the captain of Fort Wimberley during a Spanish attack. She and her British forces were victorious.

Hawaii

The Basics

POPULATION: 1,211,537
42nd most populous state
AREA: 10,932 square miles
43rd largest state
STATE CAPITAL: Honolulu
STATE BIRD: Nene (Hawaiian goose)
STATE FLOWER: Yellow hibiscus
STATE TREE: Kukui (Candlenut)
NICKNAMES: The Aloha State, the Pineapple State, the Paradise of the Pacific, the Youngest State
STATE MOTTO: *Ua Mau ke Ea o ka Aina i ka Pono* (Hawaiian for "The life of the land is perpetuated in righteousness")
STATE COLORS: Each inhabited island has its own color: Hawaii, Red; Maui, Pink; Molokai, Green; Kahoolawe, Gray; Lanai, Yellow; Oahu, Yellow; Kauai, Purple; Nihau, White
STATE SONG: "Hawaii Ponoi," folk song
OFFICIAL LANGUAGES: English and Hawaiian
NATIONAL PARK: Hawaii Volcanoes; Haleakala
STATE FESTIVAL: Hula Festival, Honolulu (August)

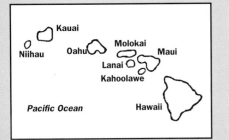

Hawaii is beloved by natives and tourists for its lush tropical growth, beautiful beaches and perfect climate. The weather is so good here that the Hawaiian language has no word for "weather"!

VOLCANO ISLANDS The word "Hawaii" refers both to a single island and to a chain of 132 islands stretching over 1,500 miles across the Pacific Ocean. These islands were formed by undersea volcanoes thrusting up 15,000 feet from the ocean floor. Only the eight largest islands are inhabited.

Statue of the Hawaiian war god Kamehameha

Most people live on Oahu, the home of Hawaii's capital and largest city, Honolulu. Here you can visit the only royal palace in America, the Iolani Palace, built in 1882. Nearby is the Kawaiahao Church, built in 1842 of solid blocks of coral and used by Hawaiian royalty for coronations, weddings, and funerals. Just outside Honolulu is Waikiki Beach, as well as Diamond Head, an extinct volcano. On Diamond Head Road is a bronze tablet honoring Amelia Earhart—who in 1935 became the first pilot ever to make the 18-hour solo flight from Hawaii to North America.

The largest Hawaiian island is Hawaii itself. Here you can see cowboys herding cattle, dense rain forests, snow-covered mountains, black sand beaches, ancient temples, and the largest active volcano in the world, Mauna Loa. Here, too, is Akaka Falls, 442 feet high.

Kauai, the "Garden Island," has huge sugar plantations. It's also home to Waimea Canyon—3,600 feet deep, 2 miles wide, and 10 miles long.

PEARL HARBOR: A DAY OF INFAMY AND COURAGE At Oahu is Pearl Harbor, where a United States naval base was attacked by the Japanese on December 7, 1941, prompting the United States to enter World War II. This surprise attack revealed the heroism of Dorrie Miller, an African-American mess attendant on the battleship *Arizona.* At that time, the navy was segregated: black sailors were not even trained for combat. But when the bombing began, Miller ran up on deck and pulled an injured officer to safety. Then he took an anti-aircraft gun, which he had never been trained to use, and shot down four Japanese planes. Finally, he was ordered to abandon the ship, which sank soon after. Five months later, he was awarded the Navy Cross for "extraordinary courage." In 1988 he was awarded the Congressional Medal of Honor to commemorate his bravery.

Queen Liliuokalani, Hawaii's last monarch (1838-1917)

ONE LAND, MANY PEOPLES Hawaii today has the most diverse racial and cultural mix in the world, with some 60 different combinations of ancestry and no racial majority. About 20 percent of the population is native Hawaiian (Polynesian), 23.2 percent is Japanese, 11.3 percent is Filipino, and less than one-fourth is of European ancestry. The history of Hawaii explains how this unique cultural mix came to be.

The first settlers of the Hawaiian islands were probably the Polynesians, who between A.D. 300 and 750 arrived in their huge, double-hulled canoes. As many as 100 people rowed a single boat as these Indo-Malaysians sailed thousands of miles across the Pacific Ocean.

In 1778 Captain James Cook and his followers landed at Kauai. Cook called the land the Sandwich Islands, after his patron, the Earl of Sandwich. Because of his many injustices to the islanders, he was killed in a quarrel in 1779. Soon, though, missionaries, traders, and whalers came to Hawaii, transforming the land as their influence was felt. In the 1820s, for example, traders depleted the island's sandalwood. Hawaii's population dropped rapidly as they were exposed to unfamiliar diseases. Meanwhile, in 1810 King Kamehameha united the islands into one kingdom, recognized by the United States in 1843.

Throughout the late 1800s the United States expanded its influence in Hawaii. The first major step towards statehood came in 1875 when the U.S. won exclusive rights to Pearl Harbor. In 1893 Queen Liliuokalani was overthrown in a bloodless revolution. A republic was established in 1894 with an American, S. B. Dole, as its president. In 1898 Hawaii was annexed by the United States and in 1900 became a territory with Dole as its first governor. It did not become a state, however, until 1959.

In 1903 pineapples introduced from South America became a key crop for Hawaii. Filipino and Japanese workers were brought into the area to harvest and pack this valuable fruit. Thus Hawaii created its unique mixture of European, Asian, and South Pacific ancestry.

PINEAPPLES AND SUGAR Tourism is the biggest industry in Hawaii. Next in importance are sugar and pineapple. Recently, macadamia nuts and coffee have become significant crops as well. In the late 1980s Japanese and U.S. investors increased their investment in real estate, hoping to benefit both from tourism and from the U.S. citizens retiring here.

Costumed children perform a traditional dance.

Fascinating Facts

HAWAII IS THE ONLY STATE:
• not in North America
• made up of islands
• with two official languages, English and Hawaiian
• with a tropical climate
• ever governed by monarchs who were recognized by international law

THE EIGHT LARGEST HAWAIIAN ISLANDS: From northwest to southeast: Niihau, Kauai, Oahu, Molokai, Lanai, Maui, Kahoolawe, Hawaii

HAWAIIAN SUPERLATIVES:
• southernmost state
• wettest place on earth—Mt. Waialeale, on Kauai—460-inch average annual rainfall
• world's largest inactive volcano crater—on Maui
• world's longest island chain

HAWAII IS TOPS IN:
• canned pineapple products

THE ALOHA STATE: "Aloha" has many different meanings: *welcome, goodbye, love,* and *friendship.*

DID YOU KNOW THAT... Surfing was invented in Hawaii by kings and chieftains. Today it's a popular sport among many adults and children.

HOW HAWAII GOT ITS NAME: The islands were named by King Kamehameha I in 1819, possibly from Hawaii Loa, who according to native folklore first discovered the islands. The name may also have come from two Hawaiian words, *Hawa,* meaning "homeland," and *ii,* meaning "small."

DID YOU KNOW THAT... The Hawaiian language has only 12 letters: H, K, L, M, N, P, W, and the five vowels. Every consonant must be followed by a vowel, and each word ends with a vowel.

BIG AND SMALL: One large Hawaiian fish is called *O.* Another much smaller fish is called *Humuhumunukunukuapua'a.*

IT USED TO BE ILLEGAL IN HAWAII:
• to put pennies in your ears
• for a barber to lather a customer with a shaving brush

Idaho

The Basics

POPULATION: 1,293,953
39th most populous state
AREA: 83,574 square miles
14th largest state
STATE CAPITAL: Boise
STATE BIRD: Mountain bluebird
STATE FLOWER: Idaho syringa
STATE TREE: Western White Pine (also
known as the White pine, the Idaho
white pine, the Finger Cone pine, the
Mountain pine, the Little Sugar pine, and
the Mountain Weymouth pine)
NICKNAMES: The Gem State, the Gem
of the Mountains, the Potato State
STATE MOTTO: *Esto perpetua* (Latin for "It
is forever")
STATE HORSE: Appaloosa
STATE GEM: Star Garnet
STATE SONG: "Here We Have Idaho,"
lyrics by McKinley Helm and Albert J.
Tompkins, music by Sallie Hume Douglas
STATE LANDMARKS: Thousand Springs
(in which each spring sprouts from the
side of a single cliff); Birds of Prey World
Center, Boise (with the world's largest
collection of living raptors); Hell's
Canyon (5,500 feet deep—deeper than
the Grand Canyon); Sacagawea's
birthplace; Nez Percé National Historic
Park, Spalding
NATIONAL PARKS: Challis National
Forest; Sawtooth National Forest; Silent
City of the Rocks National Reserve
STATE PARKS: Harriman State Park,
including the world-famous fly-fishing
stream, Henry's Fork of the Snake River;
Ponderosa State Park

idaho is a Rocky Mountain state, and no matter where you go, you're rarely out of sight of a mountain. Some people say that if you flattened all the mountains in Idaho, the state would be bigger than Texas!

WATERFALLS, TROUT STREAMS, AND THE CRATERS OF THE MOON
Northern Idaho is famous for its forests—home to deer, elk, and other game. It has the greatest concentration of lakes anywhere in the country, as well as many streams that are rich in trout and salmon.

Central Idaho features one of Idaho's most famous landmarks, the Craters of the Moon. These brightly colored lava fields and craters of extinct volcanoes bear an eerie resemblance to the barren, windswept landscape of the moon, and NASA astronauts used to train here. Nearby Sun Valley is the site of America's first ski resort founded in 1935, the first place where ski chairlifts were used.

Southern Idaho is flatter and more diverse, featuring desert, farms, and ranchland. You can still see cowboys

Silver City, Idaho. When the gold ran out this mining town became a ghost town.

herding cattle near such towns as Bungalow Cow Camp and Coffee Can Saddle. Snake River in southern Idaho is home to the giant white sturgeon, the biggest freshwater fish in North America. Some weigh more than 1,000 pounds, and fishermen have to use a two-horse wagon to pull them out of the water. In southwest Idaho, near the town of Twin Falls, the Snake River drops 212 feet over the Shoshone Falls, which are higher than New York's Niagara. Most people in Idaho live on or near the banks of the Snake, which provides most of the state's electrical power.

ON THE TRAIL OF LEWIS AND CLARK For thousands of years, Idaho has been home to such Indian peoples as the Kootenai, Nez Percé, Coeur d'Alene, Shoshone, and Paiute. Sometime around 1786, near the present town of Salmon, Sacagawea, a Shoshone, was born. Sacagawea eventually served as a translator for Meriwether Lewis and William Clark as they explored the Northwest Territory for the United States. Lewis and Clark passed through the northern part of the Idaho "panhandle" in 1805, much aided by the Nez Percé Indians.

The first European outpost in Idaho was the trading post established in 1809 by David Thompson of the North West Company on the eastern shore of Lake

A baby timber wolf and its mother

Pend Oreille (the lake's name comes from the French word for "earring"). In 1834 the Army constructed Fort Hall and Fort Boise (later Idaho's capital, from the French word bois, meaning "forest"). Forts and trading posts formed the basis of the Oregon Trail, which by 1845 was a well-traveled road. Travelers tended to pass through Idaho on their way to the more hospitable lands of the West Coast, however, and the first permanent settlement in Idaho was not established until June 15, 1860, when a group of Utah Mormons settled at Franklin. Idahoans now celebrate this day as Pioneer Day. As in most Western states, Indians were gradually resettled onto smaller reservations as settlers arrived.

GOLD, SILVER, AND LEAD Gold was first mined in Idaho in the 1860s. The mines relied heavily on Chinese workers. In 1870 some one-third of Idaho's 15,000 residents were Chinese, despite the anti-Chinese violence of 1866-1867 that had left almost one hundred people dead.

The discovery of silver in the 1880s brought in new mine workers, who responded to harsh working conditions by forming unions, such as the Western Federation of Miners. In 1892, federal troops were called in and martial law declared to break the strikes that had spread through northern Idaho. More than 600 union supporters were arrested. Martial law was established again in 1899, when hundreds more miners were imprisoned for six months.

Union Station in Boise, Idaho

The often bloody battles between workers and owners continued into the twentieth century. In 1906, for example, labor leader "Big Bill" Haywood was arrested for "conspiracy" after former governor Frank Steunenberg was assassinated. Famed defense lawyer Clarence Darrow successfully defended Haywood and other accused union leaders. Also active in Idaho were the "Wobblies," members of the so-called Industrial Workers of the World (IWW), of which Haywood was also a leader. The IWW organized miners, lumberjacks, and migrant farmworkers.

Today many of Idaho's mines have closed. The IWW has long since disappeared, and the unions there now are both weaker and more accepted by employers. Idaho no longer produces gold, but it still produces almost half of the nation's silver and all of the nation's antimony, which is used in making alloys (combinations of metals), storage batteries, cable sheathing, and paint pigments. It ranks second among states in the production of lead and vanadium, used in alloys. Other important Idaho products include potatoes and sugar beets. Tourism is also becoming a major industry.

Fascinating Facts

IDAHO IS TOPS IN...
- silver production (Sunshine mine, in Shoshone County, is the nation's largest)
- potatoes
- barley
- trout
- antimony

IDAHO POTATO FACTS:
- One fourth of the U.S. potato crop comes from Idaho.
- Two thirds of all U.S. *processed* potatoes come from Idaho.
- Each year, Idaho grows 27 billion potatoes—enough for every person in the United States to have 120 potatoes each.

AN IDAHO FOOTBALL CHEER: "Dice 'em, hash 'em, boil 'em, mash'em! Idaho! Idaho! Idaho!"

DID YOU KNOW THAT...
- Idaho's Malad River is the shortest river in the world.
- Idaho had one of the U.S.'s first "crime centers"—the Old West boom town of Idaho City in the 1860s. Of the 200 people buried in the pioneer cemetery there, only 28 died of natural causes.

HOW IDAHO GOT ITS NAME: Idaho is an artifical Indian word invented by George M. Willing. It's apparently based on the word *Idahi*, which the Kiowa-Apache people called the Comanches—but no one knows exactly what the word means; perhaps "fish eaters" or "mountain gem." The Shoshone phrase *Ee-dah-how*—"Sunup!" or "Behold the sun coming down the mountain"—may have been the basis for Willing's invention.

IDAHO'S POET LAUREATE... Irene Welch Grissom lived on a farm on the Snake River, near Idaho Falls. "A Pioneer Woman," one of her poems, declared
Go tell the world that women give
In an equal share with man!

IT USED TO BE ILLEGAL IN IDAHO:
- fishing for trout from a giraffe's back
- buying a chicken after dark without the permission of the sheriff
- for a man to give his sweetheart a box of candy that weighed less than 50 pounds

Illinois

The Basics

POPULATION: 11,846,544
6th most populous state
AREA: 57,918 square miles
25th largest state
STATE CAPITAL: Springfield
STATE BIRD: Cardinal (also called
Red bird, Kentucky cardinal)
STATE FLOWER: Violet
STATE TREE: White oak
NICKNAMES: Land of Lincoln, the
Prairie State, the Corn State, the Sucker
State
SPORTS TEAMS: Chicago Cubs, Chicago
White Sox, baseball; Chicago Bears,
football; Chicago Bulls, basketball;
Chicago Blackhawks, hockey
STATE MOTTO: "State Sovereignty—
National Union"
STATE ANIMAL: White-tailed deer
STATE INSECT: Monarch butterfly
STATE MINERAL: Fluorite
STATE SONG: "Illinois," words by C. H.
Chamberlain, music by Archibald
Johnston
STATE LANDMARKS: Chicago Museum
of Science and Industry; Field Museum
of Natural History, Chicago; Lincoln
Park Zoo and Brookfield Zoo, Chicago;
Shedd Aquarium, Chicago; Lincoln's
home and tomb, Springfield; Ulysses S.
Grant's home, Galena
NATIONAL PARK: Shawnee National
Forest
STATE PARK: Starved Rock State Park

"Hog Butcher for the World, Tool Maker, Stacker of Wheat," wrote poet Carl Sandburg about Illinois's largest city, Chicago, in 1914. And indeed, livestock, farm machinery, and wheat are still major products of Illinois, still processed, manufactured, and shipped through Chicago and its industrial neighbors Rockford, Peoria, East St. Louis, and Elgin. Does that make Illinois an urban or a rural state? Surprisingly, the answer is both: some 80 percent of Illinois's population lives in urban areas, while over 80 percent of the state's land is farmed.

Ulysses S. Grant lived in Galena for many years.

FROM THE GLACIERS TO SECOND CITY Most of Illinois is prairie, covered with a thick, dark blanket of fertile soil. That's the legacy of the glaciers that rolled across the state millions of years ago, leaving it flat as a pancake. There are only a few small variations. Northwest are some uplands that the glaciers missed. In the south are the rocky wooded hills of the Ozarks. And in the southernmost tip of the state, the land is part of the Gulf Coast plain.

Illinois is crisscrossed with over 500 rivers. The largest of these, the Mississippi, makes up most of the state's western border. However, in 1881 the mighty river flooded its banks and broke through a narrow peninsula that separated it from the mouth of the Kaskaskia River. As a result, the little town of Kaskaskia found itself on the west side of the river, instead of the east side.

Chicago used to be known as the Second City, because for many years it was second only to New York in population. Now Los Angeles holds that rank, but many Chicago names still include the term Second City, including a famous comedy club, where such entertainment greats as movie director Mike Nichols, screenwriter Elaine May, and much of the original cast of *Saturday Night Live* (Gilda Radner, Bill Murray, and others) got their start.

Chicago itself was founded by African-American explorer Jean Baptiste Pointe du Sable, who in the 1770s built himself a cabin and later a trading post on the marshy banks of the Checagou River. Today, Chicago is home to a rich mix of ethnicities and cultures. You'll find Eastern Europeans, Greeks, Germans, and Irish, who came here for factory and stockyard jobs in the nineteenth century. African Americans steadily emigrated from the South after slavery ended. And Asians and Latin Americans came later in the twentieth century, seeking industrial jobs like the immigrants who had come before them.

The first European settlers who came to Illinois, however, were from the American Southeast, such as the Lincoln family from Kentucky. Abraham Lincoln grew up in Illinois, worked as postmaster in New Salem, and practiced law in Springfield until he became President in 1861.

Home of Abraham Lincoln in Springfield

THE SLAVERY DEBATES Illinois first became part of the United States in 1787, as part of the Northwest Territory. By the time it became a state in 1818, slavery was a hot issue. There were already several thousand slaves within state borders, the property of settlers who had come from Kentucky and the Carolinas. In 1837 abolitionist Elijah Lovejoy actually died protecting his anti-slavery newspapers from an angry mob. Illinois didn't abolish slavery until 1848 but that didn't end the controversy. In 1853 the legislature passed a law forbidding free African Americans from entering the state. In 1858 Stephen Douglas and Abraham Lincoln had a series of seven famous debates in their race for the U.S. Senate. The pro-slavery Douglas won that election. Two years later, though, Lincoln became the president who eventually emancipated all Southern slaves. And in 1865, Illinois became the first state to ratify the 13th Amendment that finally abolished slavery throughout the United States.

AN INDUSTRIAL PIONEER Illinois has always been a pioneer in America's industrial development. In 1837 John Deere of Grand Detour invented a steel plow that could break the prairie sod. His plant at Moline still makes farm equipment. In 1847 Cyrus McCormick built a factory to make his mechanical reaper. And in 1874 Joseph Glidden opened the nation's first barbed-wire factory at De Kalb.

Today Chicago is the number one livestock marketing and meatpacking center in the nation. It is a major center for steel, printing, and manufacturing, along with its industrial neighbors. Some three-fifths of Illinois's factories are in the Chicago area.

Illinois also has some of the nation's largest coal reserves. Although burning soft or bituminous coal creates more pollution than hard coal, advances in technology may solve those problems soon.

Of course, farming remains an important part of Illinois's economy. Corn, wheat, soybeans, dairy farming, hogs, and cattle all create wealth for this midwestern state.

Wrigley Field, home of the Chicago Cubs and one of the oldest baseball parks in America

Indiana
INDIANAPOLIS MOTOR SPEEDWAY

19th state to enter the Union, December 11, 1816

The Basics

POPULATION: 6,080,485
14th most populous state
AREA: 36,420 square miles
38th largest state
STATE CAPITAL: Indianapolis
STATE BIRD: Cardinal (Red bird,
Kentucky Cardinal)
STATE FLOWER: Peony
STATE TREE: Tulip poplar (Tulip tree,
Yellow poplar, Blue poplar, Hickory
poplar, Basswood, Cucumber tree,
Tulipwood, White poplar, Poplar,
Old-Wive's-Shirt tree)
NICKNAME: The Hoosier State
STATE MOTTO: The Crossroads of
America
SPORTS TEAMS: Indianapolis Colts,
football; Indiana Pacers, basketball
STATE STONE: Limestone
STATE POEM: "Indiana" by Arthur
Franklyn Mapes
STATE SONG: "On the Banks of the
Wabash, Far Away," words and music by
Paul Dresser
STATE LANDMARKS: Lincoln Boyhood
National Memorial, Lincoln City—the
farm where President Lincoln lived for 14
years as a boy; Benjamin Harrison
National Historic Landmark, Indian-
apolis—home of the 23rd President
NATIONAL PARKS: George Rogers Clark
National Historical Park, Vincennes;
Indiana Dunes National Lakeshore,
Porter; Hoosier National Forest,
STATE PARKS: Falls of the Ohio, New
Albany, with 220 acres of fossil beds;
Lincoln State Park, Lincoln City; Spring
Mill, Mitchell, with a restored 1800s
pioneer village; Turkey Run, Marshall;
Pokagon State Park, Angola

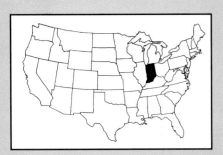

HOOSIER HYSTERIA! That's the slogan for the basketball madness that grips Indiana every season—from the professional team of the Pacers down through the national college champs at Indiana University and Purdue, all the way to the high school teams who compete for the state championship on national television. Fans also flock to see football played by the professional Colts in Indianapolis and Notre Dame's Fighting Irish in South Bend. And of course, racing cars compete in the Indianapolis 500 every Memorial Day. This midwestern state has rich farm country and prosperous industry, but when most people think Indiana, they think sports.

GLACIER FOOTPRINTS The level, fertile farmland of Indiana makes this a typical midwestern state. The flat northern land was formed by glaciers in the last Ice Age—glaciers that also left behind a great deal of gravel and sand and formed many small lakes. Farther south along the Ohio River, you find rolling hills, mineral springs, and huge limestone caves such as the one at Wyandotte—the second largest in the United States.

If you'd like to see what life was like a hundred years ago, you might visit the Amish and Mennonite communities in Berne, Goshen, and other northern Indiana towns. Both groups emigrated from Europe in the nineteenth century to preserve their religious ways of life. They avoid such modern inventions as

The Raggedy Ann doll was created by Marcella Gruelle in Indianapolis in 1914.

tractors and telephones, using their ancestors' methods to work the land and liv-ing as simply as possible.

Although 80 percent of the state is farmland, Indiana is a major manufactur-ing state. Principal industrial cities include Indianapolis, Gary, Fort Wayne, Evansville, and South Bend. Yet, each urban center is only minutes away from a rural way of life. West of Indianapolis, for example, is the area known as the "covered bridge capital of the world," featuring more than 30 bridges. And each winter, Parke County is dotted with "sugar shacks" as local maple trees are tapped for syrup.

TIPPECANOE AND TECUMSEH For centuries Indiana was inhabited by many native peoples, including the Illinois, Miami, and Shawnee. The area became first French, then British, then American. The British captured it for a time during the Revolutionary War but the Americans took it back in 1779.

Indians continued to oppose the Americans and in 1790-1791 the Miami chief Little Turtle defeated federal troops two times. However, in 1794 American troops under General "Mad" Anthony Wayne won a key battle at Fallen Timbers. In 1811 Tecumseh and his Shawnee were defeated by the troops of U.S. General William Henry Harrison in the Battle of Tippecanoe.

Finally, in 1812, the Miami were defeated near the town of Peru. That was the end of Indian activity in Indiana, "land of the Indians." (Later, in 1840, Harrison ran successfully for president with a running mate named John Tyler, using the slogan, "Tippecanoe and Tyler, Too!" Harrison became the only president to die after one month in office.)

A STOP ON THE UNDERGROUND RAILROAD "They must have an underground railroad running hereabouts, and Levi Coffin must be the president of it," said one disgruntled slave-hunter looking for runaways. Historians believe that's how the famous phrase was born.

From 1827 to 1847 Levi and Catharine Coffin hid slaves in the attic of their Fountain City house by day and helped them find the best route north by night. They helped some 2,000 runaway slaves escape from the South to Canada, including "Eliza," model for the character of the same name in Harriet Beecher Stowe's novel, *Uncle Tom's Cabin*. The Coffins were the models for Simeon and Rachel Halliday in the same book.

AUTOMOBILES AND VIOLINS Indiana has been a leader in U.S. manufacturing for most of this century. Before World War I, Indiana—especially South Bend—was the U.S. center for making automobiles. Gary became a steeltown in 1905 when U.S. Steel opened its largest plant there. Fort Wayne is known for machinery, Evansville for refrigeration equipment, Indianapolis for making books and chemicals, and Elkhart for producing musical instruments. Moreover, the Bedford quarries produce limestone. Mines in southwest Indiana bring forth bituminous coal, and the Indianapolis area is the longtime home of a major oil refinery.

Indiana is well placed. Shipping vessels can sail from Lake Michigan to the Atlantic or go inland on the Ohio River. Indiana is also a big farm state, leading the nation in corn, soybeans, and tomatoes; producing grain, spearmint, and peppermint; and raising hogs and cattle.

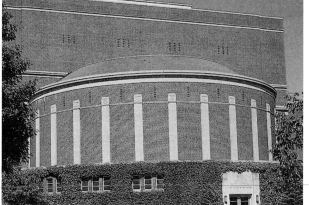

With 6,027 seats, the Elliot Hall of Music Building at Purdue University contains the largest theater in America.

Iowa

The Basics

POPULATION: 2,926,324
30th most populous state
AREA: 56,276 square miles
26th largest state
STATE CAPITAL: Des Moines
STATE BIRD: Eastern goldfinch
STATE FLOWER: Wild rose
STATE TREE: Oak (all varieties)
NICKNAMES: The Hawkeye State, the
Land Where the Tall Corn Grows, the
Nation's Breadbasket, the Corn State
STATE MOTTO: Our Liberties We Prize,
and Our Rights We Will Maintain
STATE ROCK: Geode
STATE SONG: "The Song of Iowa," words
by S.H.M. Byers set to the music of the
old Christmas carol "O Tannenbaum"
UNOFFICIAL STATE SONG: "Iowa Corn
Song," words and music by George
Hamilton
STATE LANDMARKS: Fort Atkinson
State Preserve; Herbert Hoover National
Historic Site, West Branch; Homestead,
Amana Colonies; South Amana, Amana
Colonies
HISTORICAL PARKS: Kaslow Prairie,
near Fort Dodge—preserving the
unplowed, virgin prairie; Living History
Farms, near Des Moines—three working
farms, from the 1840s, 1900s, and the
future; Heritage Village, Des Moines;
Bentonsport-National Historic District,
Fairfield; Kalona Historical Village,
Kalona; Nelson Pioneer Farm and Craft
Museum, Oskaloosa; Pella Historical
Village Museum, Pella

Iowa is one of America's leading farm states   **29th state to enter the Union, December 28, 1846**

When you think Iowa, think farmland. Some 97 percent of this state's land is cultivated. Only Texas and California produce more foodstuffs—yet California is three times Iowa's size, and Texas is five times bigger. This rural, farm state has another statistic to be proud of: over 99 percent of its people can read and write, a higher literacy rate than anywhere in the United States.

THE LAND WHERE THE TALL CORN GROWS Iowa's eastern border is the Mississippi River. The river lowlands are marked by bluffs and forested hills. You can see this beautiful country by driving along the Great River Road, which hugs the Mississippi all the way up the state.

Iowa's land gradually rises into flat prairie until it meets its western border, the Missouri River. In the northwest corner of the state is Iowa's resort area, the six "Iowa Great Lakes," including Spirit Lake and West and East Okoboji.

Iowa's largest city and capital is Des Moines, known as the home of the Iowa caucuses, which begin the Presidential campaign every four years.

Iowa has many covered bridges.

Another principal city is Cedar Rapids, in east central Iowa. This region was home to many Czech immigrants who came in the nineteenth century to farm. To find out more about how they lived, you can visit Czech Village. Cedar Rapids also has a museum dedicated to the art of Grant Wood, who painted *American Gothic,* a famous painting that shows a stern farmer and his wife.

In the nineteenth century the Swiss philosopher Christian Metz founded a cluster of utopian colonies (colonies to serve as a model for the ideal society). People in his Amana colonies were supposed to share everything and live peacefully together. They tried to be self-supporting by making and selling furniture, woolen goods, baked goods, and wine. Although in 1932 the colonists voted to give up their communal way of life, they have become famous as the makers of home appliances, such as dishwashers and washing machines.

Another kind of communal life was practiced by the Native Americans who lived in Iowa for hundreds of thousands of years before the Europeans came. Effigy Mounds National Monument features prehistoric Native American burial mounds in animal shapes, created over 2500 years ago.

IOWA SUFFRAGISTS   Two famous activists for women's rights lived in Iowa. Carrie Chapman Catt grew up in Charles City. In 1872, at age 13, she was heard to wonder aloud why women couldn't vote. When she grew up, she went on to head the National American Woman Suffrage Association. After women finally won the vote in 1920, Catt founded the League of Women Voters. She had an unusual arrangement with her second husband, George W. Catt. In a premarriage contract, they agreed that she would get two months off in the fall and two months in the spring to work for suffrage.

Amelia Bloomer spent the last forty years of her life in Council Bluffs, from 1855 to 1894. Girls and women who wear pants have Amelia Bloomer to thank. In the 1840s she invented a kind of long, loose pants for women—the first ever. At the time, they were considered scandalous.

FARMERS WORK TOGETHER   Iowa farmers have often had hard times. In the 1870s they had to pay the high prices demanded by the railroads to ship their goods to market. Corn and wheat farmers had to store their goods in local grain elevators, which also charged high prices. So Iowa, Minnesota, and Illinois farmers formed the Granger Movement. ("Grange" comes from an old English word meaning "farm.") "Grangers" started low-priced cooperative grain elevators and worked together in other ways.

Still, many farmers had to borrow from banks to buy the things they needed. Then, in the 1930s, many farmers couldn't pay back their loans. So the banks took away their farms and then held auctions to sell the farms and all their equipment. Sometimes farmers turned these auctions into "penny sales." No one would bid more than a few pennies, no matter what was being sold. Neighbors would buy a family's property for a few dollars—and then give it all back. If someone tried to bid more, to keep the property for himself, neighbors would threaten to beat him up.

The Capitol building in Des Moines

After the Depression, Iowa became one of the wealthiest farm states. In times of plenty, many farmers took out government-supported loans to expand their farms or buy new equipment. Then, in the 1980s, the government's rules about the loans changed, and farmers had to pay them back more quickly. Many farmers could not afford to do this. Once again, farmers lost their land, even though they were still growing large crops or raising huge herds of hogs and cattle.

Still, Iowa continues to be first or second in producing corn for the nation, and is a leader in hogs, cattle, hay, and soybeans as well. Its industry also relates to agriculture—food processing, farm machinery, tools, and fertilizer. Des Moines is also a major insurance center, with over 50 insurance companies headquartered there.

Kansas

The Basics

POPULATION: 2,688,418
32nd most populous state
AREA: 82,282 square miles
15th largest state
STATE CAPITAL: Topeka
STATE BIRD: Western meadowlark
STATE FLOWER: Sunflower (Helianthus)
STATE TREE: Cottonwood
NICKNAMES: The Sunflower State,
the Cyclone State, the Squatter State,
the Jayhawk State
STATE MOTTO: *Ad astra per aspera* (Latin
for "To the stars through difficulties")
STATE ANIMAL: American buffalo
STATE REPTILE: Ornate box turtle
STATE INSECT: Honeybee
STATE SONG: "Home on the Range,"
words by Dr. Brewster Higley, music by
Dan Kelly
STATE MARCH: "The Kansas March" by
Duff E. Middleton
STATE LANDMARK: Eisenhower Library
and Museum, Abilene
HISTORICAL SITES: Fort Larned
National Historical Site; Hollenberg Pony
Express Station, Hanover; Barton County
Historical Village, Great Bend; Fort
Markley and Indian Village, Seneca; Fort
Scott National Historic Site; Historic
Front Street, Dodge City; "Old Abilene
Town"; Old Fort Bissell, Phillipsburg;
Old Shawnee Town, Kansas City
STATE FESTIVALS: Buffalo Bill Cody
Days, Leavenworth (September); Good Ol'
Days Celebration, Fort Scott (June);
International Pancake Race, Liberal
(Shrove Tuesday); John Brown Jamboree,
Osawatomie (June)

Kansas is famous for its cowboy history. Dodge City, for instance, was once known as "the wickedest little city in America." Rowdy cowboys and buffalo hunters drank and gambled there, kept in line by such legendary sheriffs as Bat Masterson and Wyatt Earp. You can still see cowboys herding cattle in Dodge City, but now they ride on motorcycles!

AMBER WAVES OF GRAINS Those famous words might have been written to describe the golden wheatfields of Kansas, stretching for miles across this flat, rural, Great Plains state. The eastern part of Kansas, the Osage Plains, features gently rolling hills. Then, central Kansas levels off into a region of high plains and harsh weather. Western Kansas will remind you of old cowboy movies—a remote, windy, treeless land, marked by blowing tumbleweed.

A little-known part of Kansas history can be seen at Nicodemus. After the end of Reconstruction (the period of readjustment in the South after the Civil War), many African Americans seeking better conditions left the South and went to Kansas. Between 1875 and 1881, some 60,000 black people—the "Exodusters"—came to this state. (They were named after the biblical exodus, or journey, that Moses had led out of Egypt.) Benjamin "Pap" Singleton organized new farming colonies for the Exodusters, but most ended up in Kansas City and Topeka. But if you visit Kansas today, you can still see his surviving colony of Nicodemus.

Amelia Earhart was the first person to fly from Hawaii to California.

BLEEDING KANSAS Kansas was once home to the Kansa, Osage, Wichita, Comanche, Cheyenne, Pawnee, and many other native peoples. The name Kansas comes from the French spelling of KanNze, a native word meaning "people of the south wind." These were the people discovered by Spanish explorer Coronado, who came looking for gold in 1541, and found instead a network of Indian trails. These became the Chisholm, Santa Fe, and Oregon Trails, used by thousands of pioneers crossing from East to West.

The United States bought Kansas as part of the Louisiana Purchase in 1803. Fifty years later, this western state was drawn into a huge battle begun in the East. Slave and free states were battling over what type of nation the United States should be. Should new territories joining the Union allow slavery? Formerly, the Missouri Compromise had said that for every free state let into the Union, one slave state had to be admitted, and vice versa. But when this compromise was repealed, the Kansas-Nebraska Act of 1854 let citizens of the new territory decide for themselves.

Immediately, both abolitionists and proslavery people swarmed into Kansas to help decide the issue. In 1855 the proslavery territorial legislature passed the infamous Black Laws. They gave the death penalty to anyone who helped a runaway slave and made it illegal to spread antislavery opinion. But later that year a convention in Topeka wrote an antislavery constitution. Then in 1856 the antislavery town of Lawrence was attacked. Noted abolitionist John Brown had settled in Osawatomie to defend the idea of liberty for all. He responded to the Lawrence raid with a raid of

This museum in Topeka presents artifacts from prehistoric times.

his own, executing five proslavery men near Potawatomi Creek. Open war broke out in Bleeding Kansas. One of Brown's sons was killed later that year and part of Osawatomie was burned by raiders from Kansas City. In 1859 Kansas finally approved an antislavery constitution and joined the Union as a free state in 1861.

BUFFALO BILL AND THE WILD WEST The first railroad arrived in Kansas in 1860 bringing new settlers and new activity. Texas cattle could now be driven to cow towns on the railroad line—Abilene, Dodge City, and Wichita—and shipped on to the East. But the railroad owners believed that this development could not take place if Indians still lived on the land as they had for thousands of years. To push away the Indians, they decided to destroy the huge buffalo herds on which the Indians depended. Sometimes men shot the

William F. Cody (1846-1917) worked in Kansas for the railroad.

buffalo just for fun from train windows. But the railroads also hired men like William "Buffalo Bill" Cody to kill buffalo. Buffalo Bill became famous for shooting 4,280 buffalo in 18 months. Later, he went on to start America's first Wild West show: cowboys and Indians performing daredevil stunts with horses and bulls.

WHEAT MILLS AND STOCKYARDS Today, Kansas City leads the nation in sorghum and wheat and is one of our major producers of beef cattle. It's also an important state for corn, soybeans, barley, alfalfa, and hogs. Its industry is centered on processing food—milling grain and packing meat. And Kansas is one of only two sources of helium in the U.S. Wichita is a major center for the construction of private aircraft.

Kentucky

The Basics

POPULATION: 4,041,769
25th most populous state
AREA: 40,411 square miles
37th largest state
STATE CAPITAL: Frankfort
STATE BIRD: Cardinal (also called Red bird, Kentucky cardinal)
STATE FLOWER: Goldenrod
STATE TREE: Coffee tree
NICKNAMES: The Bluegrass State, the Hemp State, the Tobacco State, the Dark and Bloody Ground
STATE MOTTO: United We Stand, Divided We Fall
STATE WILD ANIMAL GAME SPECIES: Gray squirrel
STATE FISH: Bass
STATE FOSSIL: Brachiopod
STATE SHAKESPEARE FESTIVAL: Shakespeare in Central Park, Louisville
STATE TUG-OF-WAR CHAMPIONSHIP: Nelson County Fair Tug-of-War Championship Contest
STATE SONG: "My Old Kentucky Home," words and music by Stephen Foster
STATE LANDMARK: Abraham Lincoln Birthplace National Historic Site, near Bardstown
NATIONAL PARKS: Mammoth Cave, near Bowling Green; Daniel Boone National Forest; Land between the Lakes, near Golden Pond
STATE PARKS: Cumberland Falls State Park—68-foot waterfall; Old Fort Harrod State Park, Harrodsburg—from the first permanent European settlement of 1774; Fort Boonesborough State Park—reconstruction of an early Daniel Boone Fort

Kentucky was the first U.S. state west of the Appalachian Mountains. The home of the famous pioneer Daniel Boone, it's also famous for its thoroughbred race horses, a key tobacco state, and birthplace of the Louisville Slugger baseball bat.

LANDSCAPE OF THE BLUEGRASS STATE Kentucky is bordered on three sides by rivers: the Mississippi to the west, the Ohio to the north, and the Cumberland to the east. Eastern Kentucky is a maze of steep mountains, narrow ridges, and coal valleys. Central Kentucky is bluegrass country—grass covered with small blue flowers. It's a land of blue-green meadows and manicured lawns, where the rich and famous come to buy and breed horses. Western Kentucky is coal country.

Daniel Boone (1734-1820)

In the center of the state is the famous Mammoth Cave, one of the seven natural wonders of the world. This underground wonderland was first explored by an African-American slave, Stephen Bishop, who later became a guide for tourists. You can still find Bishop's name smoked into the walls of some of the caverns, deep underground.

Mammoth Cave features over 150 miles of caverns below the earth, some high enough for a twelve-story building. You can find underground lakes, rivers, a subterranean sea, even waterfalls that rush below the earth. Thousands of years ago native peoples used the entrance to the cave for shelter. The remains of a young girl buried in a grass-lined grave were found near the mouth of the cave and estimated to be 3,000 years old. In 1935 two guides found one of the most famous mummies, "Lost John," a 45-year-old man who died two miles inside the cave when a six-and-a-half-ton rock fell on him.

Birthplace of Abraham Lincoln, Hardin County

RACE COURSES AND JOCKEYS The city of Lexington is the world capital of racehorse breeding. There you can find the Kentucky Horse Park, a shrine to the Kentucky thoroughbred. Outside the shrine is a memorial honoring the state's greatest jockey, Isaac Burns Murphy (1856-1896). This African-American horseman won an amazing 44 percent of his rides and was a three-time winner of the Kentucky Derby. Although many jockeys took bribes from bettors, Murphy had a reputation for complete honesty.

Murphy's career may be less unusual than it seems, for 13 of the 14 jockeys in the first Kentucky Derby in 1875 were African Americans. Black people frequently worked as trainers and riders in Kentucky before the Civil War. With their knowledge and experience, they remained expert horsemen throughout the nineteenth century.

In Louisville you can visit Churchill Downs where the Kentucky Derby is run on the first Saturday in May. On other Saturdays you might attend "Dawn at the Downs," the daybreak training session for horses. Other Louisville attractions include an authentic steamship ride on the 1914 vessel *Belle of Louisville,* and rides in old-fashioned horse-drawn carriages. Fans of new plays will enjoy a trip to the Actors Theatre of Louisville where many new American works are developed. Or you could visit the home of Mildred and Patty Hill, the Louisville sisters who in 1893 wrote the world's most oft-sung song— "Happy Birthday To You."

DARK AND BLOODY GROUND

Kentucky was once home to Chero-kee, Delaware, Iroquois, Shawnee, and other Indian nations. But when the first European settlers entered the region in the late 1770s, they and the Indians fought so bitterly that Kentucky was given its first famous nickname. One of the most famous early settlers was Daniel Boone, who in 1775 led pioneers across an old Indian trail through

Colt and his mother

the Cumberland Gap. Early Kentucky settlers built log cabins. Later settlers started horse farms.

This southern state had mixed feelings about slavery. In 1833, the state outlawed the importation of slaves—but this law was repealed in 1850, and Kentucky soon became an important slave center. Yet unlike its neighbors, Kentucky never seceded from the U.S. When the Civil War ended, some 45,000 Kentucky men had fought for the Confederacy—but 90,000 had fought for the Union.

TOBACCO AND COAL   Tobacco used to be Kentucky's only important crop. Indeed, merchants once accepted tobacco instead of money! Now, however, soybeans, corn, and wheat are also important crops, as well as vegetables, peaches, apples, and grass seed. Horse farms too are a key part of the state's economy.

Local manufacturing derives from agriculture: meatpacking, leather tanning, farm equipment. Kentucky is a major coal mining state, and also is rich in oil, gas, clay, limestone, and cement.

Louisiana

Traditional wrought-iron balcony, New Orleans   **18th state to enter the Union, April 30, 1812**

The Basics

POPULATION: 4,468,976
22nd most populous state
AREA: 51,843 square miles
31st largest state
STATE CAPITAL: Baton Rouge
STATE BIRD: Brown pelican (or Eastern brown pelican)
STATE FLOWER: Magnolia
STATE TREE: Bald cypress (also called cypress, cypress tree, Southern cypress, Red cypress, Yellow cypress, Black cypress, White cypress, Gulf cypress, Swamp cypress, Deciduous cypress, Tidewater Red cypress)
NICKNAMES: Bayou State, Fisherman's Paradise, Child of the Mississippi, Sugar State, Pelican State, Creole State
STATE MOTTO: *Union, Justice, and Confidence*
SPORTS TEAM: New Orleans Saints, football
STATE DOG: Louisiana Catahoula leopard dog
STATE INSECT: Honeybee
STATE CRUSTACEAN: Crawfish
STATE REPTILE: Alligator
STATE FOSSIL: Petrified palmwood
STATE GEM: Agate
STATE FRUIT: Changes annually
STATE SONGS: "Give Me Louisiana," words and music by Doralice Fontane; "You Are My Sunshine," words and music by Jimmy H. Davis and Charles Mitchell
LOUISIANA'S STATE PLEDGE OF ALLEGIANCE: "I pledge allegiance to the flag of the state of Louisiana and to the motto for which it stands: A state, under God, united in purpose and ideals, confident that justice shall prevail for all of those abiding here."

The rowdy crowds of Mardi Gras… alligators sunning themselves in the bayous… and the busy oil wells of Baton Rouge and Shreveport. These contrasting sights are all part of Louisiana.

FROM THE BAYOU TO BOURBON STREET

For over a thousand years, rivers carried bits of soil into Louisiana, creating the rich farmland of the Mississippi Delta in the lower third of the state. Just north and west of the Delta is bayou country—a land of swamps and marshes, home to pelicans and alligators. Still farther northwest is a drier, hillier region. The entire state, however, has a subtropical climate—hot and humid, subject to tropical storms and a six-month hurricane season.

Shadows-on-the-Teche, built in 1834, is in New Iberia.

Louisiana's economy has always depended on the Mississippi River, and the state's three largest cities—New Orleans, Baton Rouge, and Shreveport—all began as shipping centers along the famous river. Levees, like little dams, keep the Mississippi from flooding, for it can rise up to five feet higher than its banks.

Louisiana's largest city, New Orleans, has many claims to fame. It's known as the birthplace of jazz. It's also known for its French quarter, or Vieux Carré (vee-YUH kah-RAY), and for Bourbon Street, renowned for its jazz and nightlife. The New Orleans Mardi Gras ("Fat Tuesday," a celebration of the Catholic holyday of Shrove Tuesday) features a huge parade with marchers dressed in colorful and outrageous costumes.

THE STATE NAMED FOR A KING

For thousands of years Louisiana was home to many native peoples, including the Biloxi, Choctaw, Creek, Natchez, Opelousa, and Yazoo. Today, at Poverty Point in northwest Louisiana, you can see the embankments left by a complex civilization that flourished from about 1500 B.C. to 700 B.C.

The Spanish and French explored Louisiana in the sixteenth and seventeenth centuries. Some of their descendants married native peoples and African Americans. Now they're known as Creoles. Another people, the Cajuns, came to Louisiana from 1760 to 1790, from Acadia, a French colony in Nova Scotia, Canada, that was being taken over by the British. Their story is told in Henry

Wadsworth Longfellow's poem *Evangeline*.

For many years France, Spain, and the United States all took turns owning different parts of the Bayou State. For a short time there was even an independent Republic of Louisiana when colonists rebelled against Spain in 1768, the first North American revolution. Finally, in 1803 President Thomas Jefferson bought the western part of the state in the Louisiana Purchase and in 1810 the U.S. took the eastern part of the state from Spain. In 1812 the state of Louisiana joined the Union.

AN UNNECESSARY BATTLE On January 8, 1815 General "Stonewall" Jackson defeated the British at New Orleans in the last battle of the War of 1812. Unfortunately, neither Jackson nor the British knew that the United States and Britain had signed a treaty two weeks before! Communications were so slow that the armies hadn't heard about the peace.

PLANTATIONS AND POPULISM Like its Southern neighbors, Louisiana used enslaved African Americans to work its huge plantations. Even free black people had a hard time during slavery. Norbert Rillieux, an African-American engineer who had

Mardi Gras float—The first parade was held in 1827.

been educated in France, invented a ground-breaking method for processing sugar. Thousands of plantation owners benefitted from Rillieux's invention. But Rillieux left the state when an 1854 law required all black people, slaves or free, to carry passes.

Louisiana joined the Confederacy in 1861, then rejoined the Union after the Civil War. To oppose black people's rights, many people joined the White League, a violent group that in 1874 actually fought the New Orleans city police. In 1898 the state's new rules for voting effectively kept most black people from casting a ballot.

Louisiana continued to be a poor state. From 1928 to 1932, Governor Huey Long, nicknamed Kingfish, led a movement called Populism, designed to help poor people. There have been many kinds of populist movements in the United States. Long's version was especially controversial. He did help poor and working people. For example, he provided free textbooks to public schools, which no one had ever done before. But his dictatorial methods alienated many people. In 1935, when Long was a candidate for the Democratic presidential nomination, he was assassinated. Today people still argue about the value of his work.

THE RICHES OF THE DELTA Louisiana's economy relies primarily on the oil that was discovered there in 1901. The state is also second in the production of natural gas and sulfur. Louisiana's rich delta land produces sugar, cotton, and rice, while fishing the Mississippi yields fish, oysters, and shrimp.

Its rich and colorful history, great music and food ensure the strength of Louisiana's tourism industry year after year.

Fascinating Facts

DID YOU KNOW THAT... Seven different nations have claimed Louisiana: France, Spain, Britain, the Republic of West Florida, the Republic of Louisiana, the Confederacy, the United States

LOUISIANA NAMES:
• French explorer La Salle called the state *La Louisianne*, after Louis XIV.
• Baton Rouge ("red stick" in French) was named for a red-painted tree that marked the boundary between two Indian nations.

LOUISIANA HAD THE FIRST:
• movie theater, Vitascope Hall, which opened on June 26, 1896, in New Orleans
• tabasco sauce, created in the 19th century by McIlhenny's Tabasco Company
• advice column, begun in 1894 in the *New Orleans Picayune*, by "Dorothy Dix"

FAMOUS PEOPLE BORN IN LOUISIANA:
• Folksinger Huddie "Leadbelly" Ledbetter, near Shreveport (1888-1949)
• Jazz musician (Daniel) Louis "Satchmo" Armstrong, New Orleans (1901-1971)
• Playwright Lillian Hellman, New Orleans (1905-1984)
• Gospel singer Mahalia Jackson, New Orleans (1911-1972)
• Novelist Truman Capote, New Orleans (1924-1984)

LOUISIANA IS TOPS IN...
• salt production
• wild animal skins (nutria, muskrat)
• sweet potatoes
• frogs—the town of Rayne supplies most of the country's frogs for eating and for scientific experiments

DID YOU KNOW THAT... The world's longest bridge is near New Orleans: Lake Pontchartrain Causeway, which spans 24 miles of open water.

IT USED TO BE ILLEGAL IN LOUISIANA:
• for a beauty operator to put cold cream or powder on a customer's feet
• whistling on Sunday

Maine

The Basics

POPULATION: 1,274,923
40th most populous state
AREA: 35,387 square miles
39th largest state
STATE CAPITAL: Augusta
STATE BIRD: Chickadee (Black-capped chickadee)
STATE FLOWER: White pine cone and tassel
STATE TREE: White pine
NICKNAMES: The Pine Tree State, the Lumber State, the Border State, the Old Dirigo State
STATE MOTTO: *Dirigo* (Latin for "I direct")
STATE ANIMAL: Moose
STATE CAT: Maine coon cat
STATE FISH: Landlocked salmon
STATE INSECT: Honeybee
STATE MINERAL: Tourmaline
STATE FOSSIL: *Pertica quadrifaria*
STATE SONG: "State of Maine Song," words and music by Roger Vinton Snow
STATE LANDMARKS: Burnham Tavern, where Americans plotted the first naval battle of the Revolutionary War; Portland Head Light, built under orders of President George Washington
HISTORIC PARKS: Norlands Living History Center, Auburn; York Village, York
NATIONAL PARKS: Moosehorn; Rachel Carson National Wildlife Refuge; Acadia National Park, Mount Desert Island, Bar Harbor
STATE FESTIVALS: Maine Seafoods Festival, Rockland; Houlton Potato Feast, Houlton (August); Kenduskeag Steam Canoe Race, Bangor (April); Whatever Week, Augusta (July)

A lighthouse on Maine's picturesque coast   23rd state to enter the Union, March 15, 1820

If you had a dinner of lobster, boiled potatoes, and blueberry pie, you'd be eating foods that are all specialties of the state of Maine. And if you wanted to be the first person in the United States to see the sun rise one morning, all you'd have to do was go to the top of Mount Katahdin in eastern Maine, at the northern end of the Appalachian trail.

ROCKBOUND COAST AND SNOWBOUND FORESTS Maine is the largest New England state—and the wildest. It has two main regions. Along the rockbound coast are lowlands, marked by sandy beaches, tree-lined bays, lonely lighthouses. Inland, you find the heavily forested northern end of the Appalachian mountains, featuring lakes and rivers stocked with trout and perch. In northwest Maine, the winters often bring nine feet of snow—or more. And some parts of Maine are so wild that there aren't even any roads—you have to go there by canoe or seaplane.

In northern Maine is Acadia National Park, where the mountains come right down to the sea. Nearby Bar Harbor is a famous vacation spot.

Buoys and lobster traps for sale in Boothbay Harbor

Farther south near Maine's largest city of Portland, shines the Cape Elizabeth lighthouse. It gives off 500,000 candlepower worth of light—equal to half a million candles. In Portland itself, you can visit the home of Maine native, the poet Henry Wadsworth Longfellow.

Maine was the home of many other famous writers. Sarah Orne Jewett, for example, known for her stories about Maine, was born in South Berwick. There you can see both the house she grew up in and Hamilton House, the setting for her 1901 novel, *The Tory Lover*.

Environmental writer Rachel Carson gathered material for her book, *The Edge of the Sea*, in New Harbor, at what is now the Rachel Carson Salt Pond Preserve. If you visit, you can find the creatures she wrote about: blue mussels, hermit and green crabs, periwinkles, rock algae, starfish, and sea urchins. In Wells, you can go to the Rachel Carson National Wildlife Refuge, the wetlands and woodlands that she studied so often.

Maine was also the home of Dorothea Dix, who became one of the nation's first nurses during the Civil War and who went on to crusade for better treatment of the mentally ill. If you go to Hampden you can see the Dorothea Dix Memorial Park, commemorating her birthplace.

KING PHILIP'S WAR Although Leif Eriksson and his Vikings may have visited Maine in A.D. 1000, the first European explorers who left records were the French and the English, who arrived in the 1500s and 1600s. The first permanent European settlement was founded in 1623 near Saco. At that time, over 25,000 Algonquin lived on the Maine coast.

For a time, the Europeans and the Indians lived peacefully together. After all, in Massachusetts, Chief Massasoit of the Wampanoag had helped save the Pilgrims' colony with food for the first Thanksgiving and many other types of aid. But when Massasoit died, the English settlers saw it as a chance to take all of "New England" for themselves. They attacked the Wampanoag in 1675 setting off the conflict known as King Philip's War.

Massasoit's son, Metacom, led the Wampanoag against the English in a conflict that was even bloodier than the Revolutionary War. Metacom had been given a European name, "King Philip," by the English. He had acquired guns and armor from them as well, in the days when the two nations traded peacefully together. As a result, his people were able to fight long and hard. Finally, however, the English setttlers won. Metacom was killed, and his wife and son—grandson of the chief who had saved the Pilgrims—were sold into slavery in the West Indies.

Salisbury Cove, Mt. Desert Island

REVOLUTIONARY DAYS—AND BENEDICT ARNOLD In 1629 all Maine belonged to a single English family headed by Ferdinando Gorges. In 1677 Massachusetts bought the area for $6,000, so during the Revolutionary War, Maine was part of Massachusetts. When the British tried to take Maine's tall trees for their masts, coastal people fought back fiercely. And in 1775 U.S. Colonel Benedict Arnold led his troops up through Maine to attack the British in Canada. Their route was named the Arnold Trail in his honor. (Later, he betrayed the United States so that Benedict Arnold became another word for traitor.) Maine itself finally won independence from Massachusetts in 1819. It joined the Union the year after.

There are many sea otters who swim off the coast of Maine.

CHRISTMAS TREES AND ICEBOXES Nearly 90 percent of Maine's land is forest, so lumber, paper, and pulp are Maine's chief industries. Every year nearly a million Maine firs are cut for Christmas trees. Although Maine's soil is rocky and poor, it leads the nation in potatoes and also produces sweet corn, hay, apples, and blueberries. Fishing, especially lobstering, has long been a big Maine business. One abandoned Maine business is the export of ice. Before the days of refrigerators, over three million tons of ice a year were cut from Maine's ponds and sent to other states, as well as to Europe, India, and Africa.

Fascinating Facts

DID YOU KNOW THAT... The easternmost point in the United States is West Quoddy Head.

MAINE HAD THE FIRST:
- ship built in the western hemisphere—the *Virginia*—1607
- atomic submarine, the *Swordfish*
- sawmill in the United States
- woman Republican senator, Margaret Chase Smith, elected in 1948

DID YOU KNOW THAT... The first Maine settlers brought their own lumber for house-building—and were amazed to discover Maine's rich forests.

MAINE IS TOPS IN:
- canoes
- lobsters
- potatoes
- high tides—the world's highest tides are at Passamaquoddy Bay

MAINE FOLKLORE: Barney Beal of Beal's Island was so strong, he could knock out a horse with one blow. He once beat 15 men in a tavern fight.

DID YOU KNOW THAT... The Old Gaol (Jail) in York once served the entire state—even though it had only one cell! (However, the building was enlarged in 1720.)

HOW MAINE GOT ITS NAME: No one knows for sure. Two theories:
- French explorers named it after the ancient French province of Mayne.
- The English named it, referring to the term for a *main*land as opposed to an island.

DID YOU KNOW THAT... Maine is the only state to have a state cat—the Maine coon cat.

FAMOUS PEOPLE BORN IN MAINE:
- Author Stephen King, Portland (1947-)
- U.S. Senator Margaret Chase Smith, Skowhegan (1897-1995)

IT USED TO BE ILLEGAL IN MAINE:
- to lead a bear around on a rope
- to walk the streets with untied shoelaces
- to set fire to a mule

Maryland

The Basics

POPULATION: 5,296,486
19th most populous state
AREA: 12,407 square miles
42nd largest state
STATE CAPITAL: Annapolis
STATE BIRD: Northern oriole (formerly called the Baltimore oriole)
STATE FLOWER: Black-eyed Susan
STATE TREE: White oak (also known as Wye Oake, Wyle Mills)
NICKNAMES: The Old Line State, the Free State, the Pine Tree State, the Lumber State
STATE MOTTOES: *Fatti Maschii, Parole Femine* (Latin for "Manly Deeds, Womanly Words"); *Scuto Bonae Voluntatis Tuae Coronasti Nos* ("With Favor Wilt Thou Compass Us As With a Shield")
SPORTS TEAM: Baltimore Orioles, baseball
STATE SPORT: Jousting
STATE DOG: Chesapeake Bay retriever
STATE FISH: Rockfish and striped bass
STATE INSECT: Baltimore Checkerspot Butterfly
STATE SHIP: Skipjack
STATE THEATER: Center State, Baltimore
STATE SUMMER THEATER: Olney Theatre, Montgomery County
STATE SONG: "Maryland! My Maryland!", words by James Ruder Randall, set to the old tune "*Lauriger Horatius*"
STATE LANDMARKS: Fort McHenry National Monument, Baltimore; Star-Spangled Banner House (where the flag that inspired the national anthem was woven), Baltimore; U.S. Frigate *Constellation*, (oldest ship still afloat), Baltimore

Maryland

If you visit Baltimore, taste the city's famous crab cakes. If you take a trip to Maryland's eastern shore, you're sure to find clams on the menu. And if you drive through Maryland's farm country, you'll see roadside stands selling corn, strawberries, and tomatoes. As you can see, the state of Maryland draws riches from both land and sea.

AN OPEN DOOR TO THE SEA This South Atlantic state includes the Allegheny Mountains to the west, the Blue Ridge Mountains and Piedmont Plateau in central Maryland, and the lowlands of the Eastern Shore around Chesapeake Bay. Yet most of the state's people live in the Baltimore-Washington, D.C. metropolitan area.

Much of Maryland straddles the nation's largest bay, the Chesapeake. This bay is so deep that ocean-going vessels can sail right up to Annapolis and Baltimore. The Susquehanna River flows into the Chesapeake, linking ocean and inland.

Baltimore Oriole Cal Ripken, Jr., (1960-)

Baltimore, Maryland's major city, was once home to the writer Edgar Allan Poe. Poe fans can visit the house where he wrote his first horror story or take a trip to Westminster Church to see his grave.

Annapolis, Maryland's capital, was once the capital of the United States. From 1783 to 1784 Congress met in the State House there. Later, in 1791 Maryland gave the United States land on which to establish the District of Columbia. The Annapolis State House, built in 1772, is still Maryland's Capitol—the oldest capitol building still in continuous use.

Annapolis is also the home of the U.S. Naval Academy, where America's first great naval hero, John Paul Jones, is buried. During the Revolutionary War, when Jones encountered the British, he uttered the famous words "I have not yet begun to fight!"

BROUGHT BY THE *ARK* AND THE *DOVE* Originally Maryland was inhabited by the Nanticoke, Piscataway, and the Powhatan Confederacy. The first European settlement arrived in 1634 on two ships named for the biblical story of Noah, the *Ark* and the *Dove.* The expedition was led by Governor Leonard Calvert whose brother, Lord Baltimore, had been granted the land by the British crown in 1632.

In 1649, Maryland became the first place to be completely tolerant of all religions with the "Act Concerning Religion." During the Revolutionary War, Maryland soldiers fought bravely in the Battle of Long Island, holding the line against the British while General Washington and the rest of the troops escaped.

For many years Baltimore was one of the centers of the U.S. slave trade. But there was also a great deal of anti-slavery activity in Maryland, especially western Maryland. The great abolitionist and social reformer Frederick Douglass was born a slave in Maryland, from which he later escaped. Likewise, Harriet

Frederick Douglass (1817-1895)

Tubman grew up as a slave on a plantation in Cambridge. Tubman escaped slavery in 1849, but she returned to the South 19 times, rescuing over 300 slaves, including most of her family. She was never caught and she never lost anyone she tried to bring to freedom. During the Civil War Maryland was a "border state," one of the four Southern states that nevertheless fought with the Union.

FROM MARYLAND TO THE NORTH POLE
The first man to reach the North Pole was a Maryland native. Matthew Henson was born on a Maryland farm in 1866, a time when there were few opportunities for African Americans. Yet Henson was determined to "go places." He ran off to sea at the age of 13 and eventually met Admiral Robert E. Peary, a Naval officer who took Henson with him on his 1909 expedition to the North Pole. On the last two days of the trip, Peary's toes were frozen, so he couldn't walk and had to be pulled in a sled by four Eskimo natives. Henson walked ahead, blazing a trail across the ice. He was the one to actually plant an American flag on the Pole itself. For years, Peary got all the credit for the expedition, but, in 1945, after Peary had died, Congress gave Henson a medal in recognition of his achievement.

CRAB CAKES AND TOBACCO Maryland draws riches out of the Chesapeake Bay: fish, oysters, and soft-shell crabs. Truck farms on the Eastern Shore grow corn, wheat, strawberries, and tomatoes.

Tobacco is also a key industry, and Maryland's loose-leaf tobacco auctions are the largest in the world.

Baltimore has been a shipping center since colonial times, linking Atlantic Ocean trade with western destinations along the Susquehanna. Baltimore ships transport coal from Virginia and other coal states. Ships and transportation machinery are also made in Baltimore.

Today, most of Maryland's income comes from electric and electronic products, chemicals, and steel. Government employees, living in Maryland but working in Washington, D.C., also bring income into the state. A major part of Maryland's economy is the medical research center the National Institutes of Health, located in the Washington suburb of Bethesda.

Massachusetts

Fanueil Hall in Boston

6th state to enter the Union, February 6, 1788

The Basics

POPULATION: 6,349,097
13th most populous state
AREA: 10,555 square miles
44th largest state
STATE CAPITAL: Boston
STATE BIRD: Chickadee
STATE FLOWER: Mayflower
STATE TREE: American elm
NICKNAMES: The Bay State, the Old
Bay State, the Old Colony State, the
Pilgrim State, the Puritan State, the
Baked Bean State
STATE MOTTO: *Ense Petit Placidam Sub
Libertate Quietem* ("By the sword we seek
peace, but peace only under liberty")
SPORTS TEAMS: Boston Red Sox,
baseball; New England Patriots, football;
Boston Celtics, basketball; Boston
Bruins, hockey
STATE DOG: Boston terrier
STATE FISH: Cod
STATE INSECT: Ladybug
STATE MARINE MAMMAL: Right whale
STATE MINERAL: Babingtonite
STATE ROCK: Roxbury pudding stone
STATE FOSSIL: Dinosaur track
STATE GEM: Rhodonite
STATE DRINK: Cranberry juice
STATE HEROINE: Deborah Sampson
STATE SONG: "All Hail to Massachusetts,"
words and music by Arthur J. Marsh
STATE FOLK SONG: "Massachusetts,"
words and music by Arlo Guthrie
STATE LANDMARKS: Paul Revere's
House, Boston; the Witch House, Salem;
Museum of Afro American History,
Boston; the Whaling Museum, New
Bedford; the Basketball Hall of Fame,
Springfield; the Volleyball Hall of Fame,
Holyoke

Massachusetts has always been a national leader. In the seventeenth century it was one of the first American colonies. In the eighteenth century it saw the first events leading to the Revolutionary War. Before the Civil War it was a leader in the Abolitionist movement, the effort to abolish (get rid of) slavery. And in the nineteenth and twentieth centuries Massachusetts was the home of many of the nation's first factories... including its first woolen mills, iron works, and shoe factories. Today Massachusetts is a first with tourists, who enjoy its beaches, its cities... and its history!

This statue of Paul Revere commemorates his "midnight ride" of April 18, 1775.

FROM THE OCEANS TO THE MOUNTAINS Massachusetts has three main geographical areas. To the east is flat coastal land, home to fishing villages and vacation resorts. Boston and its surroundings make up one of the three major metropolitan centers of the East Coast. And to the west are the Berkshire Mountains and green, hilly country dotted with small cities and college towns.

PILGRIMS AND REVOLUTIONARIES The very first residents of Massachusetts were Native Americans. In fact, the state's name actually comes from the Massachusetts Indians. The word "Massachusetts" means "near the great hill" or "the place of the great hill." In 1614 English explorer Captain John Smith identified this place as the Great Blue Hill, just south of the present-day town of Milton. Other Native American nations located within the borders of present-day Massachusetts included the Massasoit, the Samoset, and many others.

In 1620 the Pilgrims—a group of English colonists, landed at Plymouth Rock. In 1621 the Pilgrims and Native Americans held America's first Thanksgiving.

Massachusetts went on to become a thriving center for industry and trade. Although it did not depend on slave labor the way the Southern colonies did, it was a major center for the slave trade, which helped to build the fortunes of many Massachusetts millionaires. Africans were shipped into Massachusetts both from Africa itself and by way of the West Indies. Massachusetts also included a free black population made up of former slaves who had either won their freedom or who had escaped from their owners.

Ironically, it was one of these escaped slaves, Crispus Attucks, who was the first to die in America's own fight for freedom. Attucks was the leader of a group of colonists who started arguing with some British soldiers in Boston on March 5, 1770. The soldiers shot five American civilians—including Attucks—and the event became known as the Boston Massacre.

Massachusetts continued to be an important leader in America's battle for independence. In 1773 Boston patriots organized the Boston Tea Party, a raid on British ships in which tea was dumped into Boston Harbor to protest new taxes passed by the British parliament. Two years later, in 1775 the first battles of the Revolutionary War were fought between Minutemen and British soldiers at the Massachusetts towns of Concord and Lexington.

Many heroes of the War for Independence lived and fought in Massachusetts.

Clara Barton, founder of the American Red Cross

One of the most fascinating was Deborah Sampson, a former indentured servant who dressed as a man and went off to fight in disguise. She served honorably from 1782 until she was discovered in 1783. Later she married, went on a lecture tour to talk about her experiences, and eventually received a full military pension for her army service.

Astronomer Maria Mitchell (1818-1889)

FROM SEA POWER TO BRAIN POWER

Massachusetts has always relied on the sea. In its early days it was a major whaling center, while Boston ship-yards built the world-famous "Yankee Clippers." Massachusetts is still home to a major fishing industry, supplying the nation with fish, scallops, lobster, and squid. And the seacoast resorts of Nantucket, Martha's Vineyard, and Cape Cod are popular East Coast vacation spots.

In the nineteenth and early twentieth centuries, rural Americans and immigrant workers—Italian, Portuguese, Irish, and Greek—built Massachusetts' textile factories. African American engineer Jan Ernst Matzeliger invented the machine that revolutionized the shoe industry.

Now those industries have moved South and overseas, while Massachusetts has moved on to electronic and computer manufacture. The Boston area, drawing on the brainpower of such universities as Harvard and Massachusetts Institute of Technology, is also a center for medical and biotechnical research. Immigrant workers—now primarily from Asia, Eastern Europe, and the Caribbean—still provide vital labor to the new economy.

Fascinating Facts

MASSACHUSETTS HAD THE FIRST …
- college—Harvard—founded in Cambridge in 1636
- college for women—Mount Holyoke—founded in South Hadley, 1837
- public school system—founded in 1647
- large municipal public library—Boston Public Library—founded in 1852
- lighthouse—1716
- medical inoculation against smallpox in North America—1721
- printing press—1847
- subway—1897
- basketball game—1892

PRESIDENTS BORN IN MASSACHUSETTS INCLUDE:
- John Adams, (1735-1826), 2nd President
- John Quincy Adams (1767-1848), 6th President
- John F. Kennedy (1917-1963), 35th President
- George Bush (1924-), 41st President

DID YOU KNOW… that John Quincy Adams was the only President's son also to be elected President? His father was John Adams.

OTHER FAMOUS PEOPLE BORN IN MASSACHUSETTS:
- patriot of the American Revolution, diplomat, author, publisher, scientist, inventor Benjamin Frankin, Boston (1706-1790)
- essayist Ralph Waldo Emerson, born in Boston (1803-1882)
- patriot, writer, wife and mother of presidents, Abigail Adams, (1744-1818)
- novelist Nathaniel Hawthorne, born in Salem (1804-1864)
- poet Emily Dickinson, Amherst (1836-1886)
- poet e. e. cummings, Cambridge (1894-1962)
- writer and illustrator Theodor Geisel—Dr. Seuss (1904-1991)

IT USED TO BE ILLEGAL IN MASSACHUSETTS:
- to keep a dachshund as a pet dog
- to show movies that lasted more than twenty minutes
- to eat peanuts in church
- to put tomatoes in clam chowder

Michigan

The Basics

POPULATION: 9,938,444
8th most populous state
AREA: 96,705 square miles
11th largest state
STATE CAPITAL: Lansing
STATE BIRD: Robin (American robin)
STATE FLOWER: Apple blossom
STATE TREE: White pine
NICKNAMES: The Wolverine State, Great Lakes State, Lake State, Lady of the Lake, Auto State
STATE MOTTO: *Si Quaeris Peninsulam Amoenam, Circumspice* (Latin for "If you seek a pleasant peninsula, look around you")
SPORTS TEAMS: Detroit Tigers, baseball; Detroit Lions, football; Detroit Pistons, basketball; Detroit Red Wings, hockey
STATE FISH: Brook trout
STATE STONE: Petoskey stone
STATE GEM: Isle Royal greenstone (chlorastrolite)
STATE SONG: "Michigan, My Michigan," words by Giles Kavanagh, music by H. O'Reilly Clint
STATE LANDMARK: Historic Fort Wayne, Detroit
NATIONAL PARKS: Isle Royal; Pictured Rocks National Lakeshore; Sleeping Bear Dunes National Lake Shore
HISTORIC PARKS: Greenfield Village, Dearborn—built by Henry Ford, includes model of Edison's laboratory and Wright brothers' bicycle shop; Antique Auto Village, Frankenmuth, 1920s main street; Dutch Village, Holland
STATE PARK: Porcupine Mountains

Y ou might say Michigan has a split personality. The Detroit area is one of the largest metropolitan areas in the country. Yet in rural Michigan you could drive for miles without coming to a single town. In one day, you can travel from the noise of Motor City's auto factories to the quiet woods around Lake Superior.

MACKINAC AND MOTOWN   Michigan was created out of two separate peninsulas which can explain its "split personality." No land links the Upper and Lower Peninsulas and the two regions have different climates, landscapes, and economies. Yet together they make up one state—Michigan.

The Lower Peninsula is shaped like a mitten. It has a typical midwestern climate—mild and humid. And its landscape has rolling hills and flat plains. Almost all of Michigan's industry, agriculture, and population are concentrated on the Lower Peninsula. The Upper Peninsula, on the other hand has a harsh, cold, northern climate. Its mountainous, heavily forested terrain is rich in minerals, but it is a sparsely populated, rural area. Between the peninsulas are the Straits of Mackinac (pronounced mack-i-NAW, from the French). Almost half of Michigan's area is fresh water: 11,000 inland lakes and

19th century store in Greenfield Village

36,000 miles of rivers. Boating and fishing are popular pastimes here.

Michigan's largest city is Detroit, which produces over one-fourth of the nation's autos, trucks, and tractors. Nearly half of Michigan's people live in the Detroit area, which is home to over 150 ethnic groups, including almost 900,000 African Americans and 400,000 Polish Americans. The largest North American communities of Bulgarians, Belgians, and Arabs live in this state, adding to its cultural riches.

Music lovers know Detroit as the home of Motown (short for motor town), the record label and musical style made popular by Berry Gordy, Jr. When Gordy went into the music business in the late 1950s, there were many popular African-American singers and musicians, but virtually nobody of color behind the scenes. Gordy wasn't even a rich man; he was a former worker on an auto assembly line. Yet he brought to prominence such superstars as Smokey Robinson, the Four Tops, and the Temptations. Although Gordy took Motown out of the Motor City in 1971, you can visit Motown Museum at his old studio, still with his sign, Hitsville, USA.

FROM FORD TO FLINT The first U.S. auto factory was the Olds Motor Works, founded in 1900 in Detroit. From this small beginning came an industry that affected the entire U.S. economy, as well as the lives of millions of workers in and out of the auto business.

When Henry Ford started the Ford Motor Company, also in Detroit, in 1903, cars were luxuries that only the rich could afford. But by 1908 Ford was offering his Model T for only $850—an affordable price for many families. Ford had discovered a revolutionary new way of making cars. Previously, workers had assembled cars in groups, which took 14 hours. Ford figured out that if you gave each worker a very small task, such as tightening one screw, and if you put car parts on automatic conveyor belts that moved quickly past workers, you could make cars more cheaply and quickly—in only 93 minutes. (Today it takes only one hour to make a car.) This assembly-line process was quickly adopted by industries nationwide, changing the way most Americans worked.

Yet this way of working was hard, often dangerous, and frequently poorly paid. Now, though, workers were all together in a single, giant factory. Looking around, they realized that they had a new kind of power—the power to stop work, or strike. On December 30, 1936, thousands of workers at the GM plant in Flint began a sit-down strike; they sat down, at their machines, and refused to work until the company improved their wages and working conditions. They also refused to leave the factory, so that no one else could come in and do their jobs.

The strike quickly spread to other factories. Outside the plants, women's auxiliaries organized demonstrations to win support for the workers and their union, the United Auto Workers. When the strike succeeded, workers in other cities and industries took up this tactic. Once again, the Michigan auto industry had been a national leader.

AUTO UPS AND DOWN Michigan is one of the nation's top six manufacturing states. For almost a century, "manufacturing" has meant "auto-making" in Michigan. When Japanese cars took some of the U.S. market, Michigan's economy suffered and millions of people lost their jobs. Even when U.S. auto production shot up between 1986 and 1990, Michigan's economy was still on shaky ground.

Michigan factories also make machine tools, appliances, light machinery, pharmaceuticals, plastics, clothing, and paper. Grand Rapids has maintained a tradition of fine furniture manufacturing since 1859.

Iron and copper mining on the Upper Peninsula is an important source of income. Oil, natural gas, and salt are key Michigan products. Agriculture, on the other hand, is a very small part of the state's economy.

Detroit native, Ralph Bunche (1904-1971) won the Nobel Peace Prize in 1950.

Fascinating Facts

HOW MICHIGAN GOT ITS NAME:
Two theories:
• from the Chippewa words *michi gama,* meaning "great lake"
• from the Chippewa *majigan,* meaning "clearing," referring to an open area on the west side of the Lower Peninsula

MICHIGAN IS THE ONLY STATE...
• in the lower 48 states where Canada is *south* of the United States
• to have four of the five great lakes as borders—Erie, Huron, Michigan, Superior
• to be formed of two peninsulas

MICHIGAN HAD THE FIRST:
• concrete highway—1909
• university established by a state

DID YOU KNOW THAT... Michigan's shoreline is 3,121 miles—longer than the Atlantic coast from Maine to Florida.

MICHIGAN HALLS OF FAME:
• Afro-American Sports Hall of Fame, Detroit
• National Ski Hall of Fame, Ishpeming

MICHIGAN IS TOPS IN:
• car and truck production
• red tart cherries
• dry beans
• cucumbers for pickles
• baby food
• carpet sweepers
• U.S. copper reserve
• million-ton ports
• variety of trees in the U.S.

FAMOUS MICHIGAN NAMES:
• Antoine Cadillac, founded Detroit, 1701
• Pontiac, chief of the Ottawas
• Henry Ford, first Detroit automaker

PRESIDENT WHO LIVED IN MICHIGAN:
• Gerald Ford (1913-), 38th President

IT USED TO BE ILLEGAL IN MICHIGAN:
• to hitch a crocodile to a fire hydrant
• for a woman to lift her skirt more than six inches to avoid a puddle
• for a married couple not to live together

Minnesota

The Basics

POPULATION: 4,919,479
21st most populous state
AREA: 86,943 square miles
12th largest state
STATE CAPITAL: St. Paul
STATE BIRD: Common loon
STATE FLOWER: Pink-and-white lady's slipper
STATE TREE: Norway pine (also called Red pine, Canadian red pine, Hard pine)
NICKNAMES: The North Star State, the Gopher State, Land of 10,000 Lakes, the Bread and Butter State
STATE MOTTO: *L'Etoile du Nord* (French for "The North Star")
SPORTS TEAMS: Minnesota Twins, baseball; Minnesota Vikings, football; Minnesota Timberwolves, basketball; Minnesota North Stars, hockey
STATE FISH: Walleye
STATE GRAIN: Wild rice
STATE MUSHROOM: Morel
STATE GEM: Lake Superior agate
STATE DRINK: Milk
STATE SONG: "Hail! Minnesota," words by Truman E. Rickard and Arthur E. Upson, music by Truman E. Rickard
STATE LANDMARKS: Fort Snelling, St. Paul; Grand Portage National Monument—1768 fur-trading post
NATIONAL PARK: Voyageurs,
STATE PARK: Lake Itasca State Park
STATE FESTIVALS: Defeat of Jesse James Days, Northfield (September); Eelpout Festival, Walker (February); International Rolle Bolle Tournament, Marshall (August); John Beargrease Sled Dog Marathon, Duluth (January); Laura Ingalls Wilder Pageant, Tracy (July)

Minnesota winters are bitter cold

32nd state to enter the Union, May 11, 1858

Minnesota is a land of harsh winters and hot, humid summers; of quiet, self-sufficient Scandinavians with a strong sense of community; of isolated farms and tiny prairie towns and a metropolitan area with more theater for its size than any urban area outside of New York.

LAND OF 22,000 LAKES Minnesota is our northernmost state—except for Alaska—and the winters show it. Temperatures of -40 degrees Fahrenheit—lower if you count wind chill—are not unusual.

Two ethnic groups have done the most to shape the state's ways. Chippewa (Ojibway) still live in northern Minnesota. Their strong relationship to the land affects Minnesotans all over the state. And Scandinavians—Danes, Swedes, Norwegians, and Finns—bring Minnesota their strong religious traditions (Lutheran and Catholic), their attachment to farm life, and their sense of civic responsibility.

A buffalo in Itasca State Park

Minnesota has over 22,000 lakes. With the state's many rivers, they make up over 4,000 square miles of water—almost 5 percent of the state's area. Three great river systems begin in Minnesota: the Rainy and Red Rivers run north to Hudson Bay; the St. Louis and Pigeon Rivers run east to Lake Superior and the St. Lawrence Seaway; and the Mississippi River runs south from Lake Itasca down to the Gulf of Mexico. These waterways have made Minneapolis, St. Paul, and Duluth, major centers of trade.

LITTLE TOWN ON THE PRAIRIE Northeastern Minnesota is a land of lakes and forests. Outside of Bemidji you can see the giant statues of legendary lumberjack Paul Bunyan and his blue ox, Babe. Nearby is the Iron Range, one of the world's great sources of iron ore. Northwestern Minnesota, on the other hand, is farm country. Its flat, fertile land is perfect for growing wheat, corn, soybeans, and sugar beets. Southeastern Minnesota is hilly green country, where dairy cattle graze. The southeastern town of Rochester has gained worldwide renown for the medical research done at the Mayo Clinic, started by Dr. William W. Mayo in 1855. In southwestern Minnesota is New Ulm, home of Wanda Gag, who in 1928 wrote *Millions of Cats.* Laura Ingalls Wilder grew up in the nearby town of Walnut Grove, and used it as the setting for *On the Banks of Plum Creek*, the first book in her famous *Little House* series. Further west is Pipestone, whose red rock is found in the sacred quarry of the Omaha and Yankton Indians.

The Twin Cities of Minneapolis and St. Paul are Minnesota's largest city and its capital, respectively. Here there are many professional and ameteur theaters, professional symphonies and chamber orchestras, and a growing film community. The suburb of Bloomington—Minnesota's third largest city—boasts the Mall of America. With over 400 stores, it's the largest shopping complex in the world.

INDIAN UPRISINGS AND LABOR WARS Minnesota was first explored by the French voyageurs (explorers): Pierre Esprit Radisson, Daniel Greysolon, Sieur de Lhut (Duluth), and many others who have given their names to Minnesota cities and landmarks. By 1763, however, the British had won eastern Minnesota, which, in 1783, they ceded to the United States. In 1803 President Thomas Jefferson acquired western Minnesota when he signed the Louisiana Purchase. In 1819 settlers created the first European community in Minnesota at Fort St. Anthony (now Fort Snelling, near Minneapolis).

It's no accident that the first European dwelling was a fort, far from the first; the Europeans were at odds with Minnesota's native peoples. The Ojibway and Sioux ceded more and more of their land. By 1862 the Sioux were completely dependent on U.S. government support. They were starving but a government official was supposed to have said, "Let them eat grass." This provoked the famous Sioux uprising of 1862 in which the official was found dead with his mouth stuffed with grass and 485 other white people were killed. In retaliation, U.S. troops took 2,000 prisoners and executed 37 Sioux, the largest official execution in U.S. history. The other Sioux were expelled from the state.

Laura Ingalls Wilder wrote the Little House series.

Another major uprising in Minnesota's history was the Teamsters' Strike of 1934, which provoked one of the nation's two general strikes. (A general strike is when all workers in a city go on strike. The other general strike was in San Francisco.) Four years earlier, Minnesotans had elected the first governor from a third party (neither Democrat nor Republican), the Farmer-Labor Party. The liberal tradition remained strong in Minnesota throughout the twentieth century. The state gave the nation two liberal vice-presidents, Hubert H. Humphrey and Walter Mondale.

TACONITE AND HIGH TECH Dairy products, wheat, and iron ore (taconite) are some Minnesota resources important to the state's economy. But equally important are its human resources, the men and women who work in the growing high-tech industry centered in the Twin Cities. Processed foods, office supplies, metal, paper, and printing are also important industries in this state that relies upon manufacturing.

Mississippi

The Basics

POPULATION: 2,844,658
31st most populous state
AREA: 48,434 square miles
32nd largest state
STATE CAPITAL: Jackson
STATE BIRD: Mockingbird
STATE FLOWER: Magnolia
STATE TREE: Southern magnolia
NICKNAMES: The Magnolia State, the Eagle State, the Border-Eagle State, the Bayou State, the Mud-Cat State
STATE MOTTO: *Virtute et armis* (Latin for "By valor and arms")
STATE WATER MAMMAL: Bottlenosed dolphin
STATE FISH: Largemouth bass
STATE INSECT: Honeybee
STATE SHELL: Oyster shell
STATE FOSSIL: Prehistoric whale
STATE DRINK: Milk
STATE SONG: "Go, Mississippi," words and music by Houston Davis
STATE PLEDGE OF ALLEGIANCE: "I salute the flag of Mississippi and the sovereign state for which it stands, with pride in her history and achievements and with confidence in her future under the guidance of Almighty God."
STATE LANDMARKS: Old Spanish Fort and Singing River, Pascagoula
HISTORICAL PARKS: Florewood River Plantation, Greenwood—shows how people lived on a cotton plantation; John Ford House, near Sandy Hook—early 1800s frontier home
STATE FESTIVAL: Anniversary of the Landing of d'Iberville, Ocean Springs (April)

50

Rosalie in Natchez, was built in 1820   **20th state to enter the Union, December 10, 1817**

I f you want a glimpse of the Old South, Mississippi is the place to visit. You can still see white fields of cotton, smell magnolia blossoms, and ride steamboats up and down the Mississippi River. For a look at the New South, you can also visit Mississippi, just to see how much it has changed in the past forty years.

MISSISSIPPI MUD   Have you ever had "Mississippi mud cake"? That dark, gooey, chocolatey cake is named after the rich, black mud of the Mississippi Delta, the 65-mile-wide strip along Mississippi's western border, between the Mississippi and the Yazoo Rivers. It's some of the richest farmland in the world. Moving eastward, you'll find the hilly bluffs of central Mississippi. Farther south are the Pine Hills shading into the meadowlands and coastal plains along the Gulf of Mexico. Mississippi is warm and humid, with a year-round growing season.

Ida B. Wells-Barnett (1862-1931), a distinguished journalist, was born in Holly Springs.

In the old days of flatboats and barges, goods were floated down the Mississippi—but people had to take roads to go back *up*. They used the Natchez Trace, which followed an old Indian trail. Today you can drive north on the Natchez Trace Parkway, from Natchez up to Tupelo.

Natchez is the home of more than 500 mansions built before the Civil War. Twice a year, during the Natchez Pilgrimages, costumed guides will help you tour these homes. Farther north is Jackson, the state capital and largest city. When Union General William T. Sherman occupied the state in 1863, during the Civil War, his headquarters were in Jackson.

Up at Tupelo, you can see the two-room house where Elvis Presley was born—now a major state attraction. Along the Natchez Trace, you can also see an old Choctaw village and the nation's second largest petrified forest.

THE CIVILIZED TRIBES AND THE CIVIL WAR   Before the Europeans arrived in Mississippi, it was home to almost 30,000 Natchez, Choctaw, and Chickasaw. Mississippi was explored by the Spanish in the sixteenth century and settled in 1699 by the French. By 1763 the British had taken most of the state. It became American territory in 1798, though, and its people fought against the British in the War of 1812. The Choctaw fought with the Americans in the last battle of that war. But in the 1830s they and the rest of the Five Civilized Tribes were forced out of their homelands and into Indian territory in Oklahoma and

Lincoln's sunken gardens attract visitors to its fountains and paths.

"stakes" for five years. Nebraska was soon flooded with homesteaders—but there weren't enough trees to build houses for them all. So the pioneers built sod huts using huge blocks of earth from the prairie itself, held together by the roots of prairie grasses still growing in the fertile ground. Later, Nebraskans planted trees to help hold the soil in place, even creating the Nebraska National Forest at Halsey—the only national forest completely planted by the people.

The first homestead in the nation was claimed by Daniel and Agnes Freeman near Beatrice. There you can visit the Homestead National Monument to Agnes Freeman, True Pioneer Mother. Freeman lived in a one-room house, miles from any neighbor. There she raised six children, baked biscuits in a wood stove, made friends with neighboring Otoe Indians, and learned enough medicine from her doctor husband to get her own state license as a physician. One day a visiting niece asked her how she bore the loneliness. "It wasn't easy at first," Freeman answered, "but now it's my home."

You can learn more about pioneer life at Omaha's Great Plains Black Museum. Even today, there are barely 60,000 African Americans in the five states of Nebraska, Montana, Wyoming, and the Dakotas. Yet black pioneers and cowboys are an important part of the history of the West. At this museum you can find out about Mary Fields, who ran a stagecoach stop in Cascade, Montana, or Aunt Sally Campbell, who mined gold in Deadwood, South Dakota.

Willa Cather grew up in this small Red Cloud home.

THE BUSINESS OF AGRICULTURE Agriculture is the main source of income for this overwhelmingly rural state. Beef cattle graze on ranches in the west, while dairy cattle browse the Platte River Valley. The state also supports huge farms in corn, wheat, oats, rye, barley, sugarbeets, potatoes, beans, alfalfa, and sorghum. What little industry exists is based on agriculture: meatpacking, dairy processing, and agricultural machinery. Omaha is also a major insurance and telemarketing center.

Fascinating Facts

HOW NEBRASKA GOT ITS NAME: The Omahas called it *Nibthaska,* and the Otoes *Nibrathka.* Both were talking about the "flat river" that runs through the state and gave Nebraska its name. The French called the river *Platte,* which means "flat" in French, but kept the native name for the state.

HOW NEBRASKA GOT ITS NICKNAMES: The University of Nebraska football team is called the Cornhuskers. When there's a home football game, the stadium at Lincoln actually becomes "the third largest city in the state." The "bug-eating state" refers to Nebraska's many insect-eating bull bats.

PRESIDENT BORN IN NEBRASKA:
• Gerald R. Ford (1913-), 38th President

OTHER FAMOUS PEOPLE BORN IN NEBRASKA:
• Dancer Fred Astaire, Omaha (1899-1987)
• Actor Henry Fonda, Grand Island (1905-1982)
• Actor Marlon Brando, Omaha (1924-)
• Leader Malcolm X, Omaha (1925-1965)

NEBRASKA HOLIDAY: In 1872, there were very few trees in Nebraska. So newspaper publisher J. Sterling Morton asked people in his state to set aside a special tree-planting day. Arbor Day became a nationwide holiday!

NEBRASKA HAS THE NATION'S ONLY:
• *unicameral* (one-house) state legislature. That means there are no state senators, only representatives. Some people think this makes Nebraska more democratic, since its elected officials are more directly accountable to smaller numbers of people.

NEBRASKA HAD THE FIRST:
• homestead—claimed by Daniel and Agnes Freeman—near Beatrice

IT USED TO BE ILLEGAL IN NEBRASKA:
• to picnic in the same place twice within a 30-day period
• to sneeze in public
• for a mother to curl her daughter's hair without a state license

Nevada

The Basics

POPULATION: 1,998,257
35th most populous state
AREA: 110,567 square miles
7th largest state
STATE CAPITAL: Carson City
STATE BIRD: Mountain bluebird
STATE FLOWER: Sagebrush
STATE TREE: Single-leaf piñon (also called Nut pine, Pinyon, Gray pine, Nevada nut pine, and Single-leaf pinyon pine)
NICKNAMES: Silver State, Sagebrush State, Sage State, Battle Born State, Mining State
STATE MOTTO: All for our Country
STATE ANIMAL: Desert bighorn sheep
STATE FISH: Lohonta cutthroat trout
STATE METAL: Silver
STATE FOSSIL: Icthyosaur
STATE GRASS: Indian rice grass
STATE COLORS: Silver and blue
STATE SONG: "Home Means Nevada," words and music by Bertha Raffeto
NATIONAL PARK: Great Basin, near Baker, site of the Bristlecone Pines, over 2,000 years old—among the oldest living things on earth
STATE PARKS: Washoe Lake State Recreation Area, near Carson City, with views of the Sierra Nevada, known for fishing and horseback riding; Valley of Fire State Park, near Las Vegas, featuring rock formations and Pueblo petroglyphs (picture-writing)
STATE THEME PARK: Ponderosa Ranch and Western Theme Park, Crystal Bay—based on the TV series *Bonanza*

Desert sand sculptures

36th state to enter the Union, October 31, 1864

Nevada is a state with few people—but a lot of famous places. The gambling cities of Las Vegas, Reno, and Lake Tahoe are "the playground of the nation." Gigantic Hoover Dam and human-created Lake Mead are impressive sights. And the Nevada desert—dry, deserted, yet full of wildlife—is a landmark of the American West.

DESERT LAND Nevada's eerie, lovely landscape is primarily desert, for this state lies in the center of the Great Basin, a desert plateau between the Sierra Nevada and the Rocky Mountains. The 5,000-foot-high plateau is crisscrossed by valleys—most deeply, by Death Valley (mostly in California). This sparsely settled state is too dry to farm, so it has primarily been used to graze cattle, horses, and sheep.

Professional rodeo riders compete for millions of dollars in prizes.

Until recently, Las Vegas, Reno, and Lake Tahoe were the only places in the United States where widespread gambling was legal. Las Vegas, Spanish for "the meadows," is the biggest of these cities and the state's major metropolis. Although gambling was legal here by the 1930s, Las Vegas as we know it was created after World War II when the gangster Benjamin "Bugsy" Siegel decided to build a huge resort in what was then a small town. Siegel's Flamingo Hotel failed—but the idea of a gambling resort area took off and today, Las Vegas has nine of the ten largest hotels in the world.

Las Vegas offers many curious sights to the tourist: the Union Pacific train inside the Plaza Hotel; the 61-pound solid gold nugget at the Gold Nugget casino; and the one million dollars in cash displayed at Binion's Horseshoe Casino. You can also visit the Guinness World of Records Museum. The Imperial Palace Auto Collection features more than 300 antique cars, owned by such famous people as Adolf Hitler and gangster Al Capone. Las Vegas is also the site of the National Finals Rodeo.

Reno is also a key gambling city, known as the "Biggest Little City in the World." Some 24 miles away is Virginia City, an old mining town that has been preserved and restored. When gold and silver were discovered in Nevada in 1859, the rush of settlers to the state caused Virginia City to grow to 20,000 almost overnight, second only to San Francisco as a key western city. By 1863 this former mining town had luxury homes, a fancy opera house, six churches—and 110 saloons! It also had the only elevator between Chicago and the West Coast. You can visit many of these spots today.

BUILDING THE SILVER STATE Nevada was the last western state to be explored by Europeans, for it seemed to offer nothing but desert wilderness. The Mono Panamint, Utes, Western Shoshone, Washo, and Paiute lived in Nevada, but few settlers wished to do so.

One famous Washo resident was basketmaker Dat-So-La-Lee (1826-1925), whose designs have been called the most exquisite in the world. She made more than 300 baskets, each with 100,000 stitches portraying legends, sacred shapes, and Washo symbols. If you visit Carson City, you can see many of her beautiful creations in the Nevada State Museum.

Prairie dogs are often seen in the desert.

Thousands of prospectors crossed Nevada on their way to the California gold rush. By 1859 settlers came to Nevada, first for gold, then for silver. The Great Comstock Lode—named for the prospector who found it—yielded some $293 million by 1882. President Abraham Lincoln said that Nevada's riches had "made it possible for the government to…continue this terrible war for the Union." Lincoln was also eager for Nevada to become a state by 1864, so that its senators could vote for the 13th Amendment, which abolished slavery.

By the 1880s most of the old mining towns had become ghost towns. Later there were other gold and silver strikes (discoveries), but today Nevada's riches come more from tourists' pockets than from the ground.

GOLD AND GRAINS Tourism is certainly the mainstay of Nevada's economy, causing this state's population to increase more than 550 percent between 1950 and 1988. Other industries include the manufacturing of gambling equipment and mining. Nevada is first in mining U.S. gold (56 percent of all U.S. production), second in mining silver, and the only state to mine mercury.

There is also some agricultural activity, thanks to the dam. Constructed on the Colorado River in the 1930s, the Hoover Dam has made irrigation possible, so that farms can grow alfalfa, potatoes, hay, barley, and wheat. This dam, which also produces electricity, contains as much steel as the Empire State Building and enough concrete to pave a two-lane highway from Los Angeles to Miami. To build the dam, concrete had to be poured continually for two years. Lake Mead became one of the largest man-made lakes in the world when the dam was completed. It was filled by the tremendous flow of water from the Colorado River.

Hoover Dam

Most of the land in Nevada is owned not by miners or ranchers, but by the U.S. government. It was in this state that the first underground tests of atomic weapons were conducted in the 1950s, and the state is still a major site for atomic development.

New Hampshire

The Basics

POPULATION: 1,235,786
41st most populous state
AREA: 9,351 square miles
46th largest state
STATE CAPITAL: Concord
STATE BIRD: Purple finch
STATE FLOWER: Purple lilac
STATE TREE: White birch (also known as Canoe birch, Silver birch, Paper birch, Large white birch)
NICKNAMES: The Granite State, the White Mountain State, the Switzerland of America, Mother of Rivers
STATE MOTTO: Live Free or Die
STATE ANIMAL: White-tailed deer
STATE INSECT: Ladybug
STATE REPTILE: Red-spotted newt
STATE SONG: "Old New Hampshire," words by John F. Homes, music by Maurice Hoffman; "New Hampshire, My New Hampshire," words by Julius Richelson, music by Walter P. Smith
STATE LANDMARKS: Franconia Rock, the natural profile of "The Old Man of the Mountain" (featured in Nathaniel Hawthorne's story "The Great Stone Face"), Profile Mountain, White Mountains; Franklin Pierce Homestead, Hillsboro
HISTORIC PARKS: America's Stonehenge, Salem; Canterbury Shaker Village, Concord; Six Gun City, Jefferson; Strawberry Banke, 10-acre village museum, with buildings from 1695 to 1820, Portsmouth

Colonial buildings in Harrisville

9th state to enter the Union, June 21, 1788

If you visit New Hampshire's White Mountains, you can still see the notches carved by the glaciers millions of years ago. Yet the glacial soil is too rocky to be good for farming. Though it is a rural state with forests covering 80 percent of its territory, New Hampshire depends on manufacturing for its livelihood.

LAND OF THE SMILING WATER New Hampshire divides into three regions. To the north and west are the White Mountains, the highest in New England. Central New Hampshire is full of lakes, most notably Lake Winnepesaukee, an Indian word for "Smiling Water." This region features hardwood forests and three of New Hampshire's major cities: Manchester, Nashua, and Concord. Also in central New Hampshire is Dartmouth, originally Moor's Indian Charity School and today an Ivy League college. To the southeast are New Hampshire's coastal lowlands. The 18-mile coastline is the shortest in New England, ending in Portsmouth, a busy seaport and one of New Hampshire's major cities.

Home of statesman and orator Daniel Webster, Franklin

Owls nest and hunt in New Hampshire's many forests. The owls also stand on one leg while sleeping.

THE STATE THAT MADE THE NATION The territory that is now New Hampshire was first inhabited by the Asmokeag, Nashua, Ossipee, Pennacook, Pequawket, Piscataqua, Squamscot, and Winnipesaukee, who gave their name to many of the state's cities and waterways. The first European in the area was probably the English sea captain Martin Pring, who in 1603 sailed up the Piscataqua River and landed near what today is Portsmouth. French explorer Samuel de Champlain followed in 1605 and after him came English captain John Smith in 1614. The first settlers, immigrants from England, established towns at Portsmouth and Dover in 1623.

Relations between native peoples and the new settlers were often violent. In 1627 the Indian

State House, Concord

leader Passaconaway (Child of the Bear) united 17 Indian nations into the Pennacook Confederacy, hoping to bring peace with the "palefaces." But by 1675 Indian leader King Philip began to resist the European invasion with a series of raids on farmhouses and villages. The French and Indian War led to more raids which continued until the Indians were finally defeated in 1759.

Meanwhile, English colonists—many from Massachusetts—settled along the New Hampshire coast. In 1629 Captain John Mason of the British Royal Navy was granted the land, which he named after his childhood home, England's Hampshire county.

For a time New Hampshire was part of Massachusetts, then "the Dominion of New England," but eventually it became independent. Independence was important to New Hampshirites, so much so that on January 5, 1776, they formed their own independent republic, seven months before the Declaration of Independence was signed. But until New Hampshire signed the Constitution the United States could not formally come into existence. When it became the ninth state to sign, in 1788, New Hampshire truly became "the state that made a nation."

THE FORTUNE OF AMOS FORTUNE One of New Hampshire's most famous residents was Amos Fortune, an African prince who was enslaved at an early age and brought to Massachusetts. Fortune received his freedom at age sixty—and moved to New Hampshire to begin a new life. In Jaffrey, he started a tanning business, founded a library, trained both black and white apprentices, and became a leading citizen. When he died in 1801, he left money to support the local school. The money is still used for the Amos Fortune Forum, which brings speakers to give talks each summer.

TEXTILE MILLS AND MAPLE SUGAR New Hampshire had some of America's first factories—and America's first women's strike. The women at Cocheco Manufacturing Company wanted to oppose their wage cut—from 58 cents a day to 53. They worked under harsh rules: a twelve-and-a-half-cent fine for arriving one second late and no talking at the machines. More than 300 workers paraded through the streets in December 1828—but by January 1, they had to go back to work for fear of losing their jobs.

Today New Hampshire relies less on textile mills than on high-tech industries. Many computer and software companies are attracted by the state's low taxes and have relocated from Boston. The state continues to mine granite, used in monuments and public buildings. Poultry and dairy farms sell eggs and milk to tourist hotels. And the state's hardwood forests supply maple syrup for the nation's pancakes.

New Jersey

The Basics

POPULATION: 8,414,350
9th most populous state
AREA: 8,722 square miles
47th largest state
STATE CAPITAL: Trenton
STATE BIRD: Eastern goldfinch
STATE FLOWER: Meadow violet
(purple violet)
STATE TREE: Red oak and dogwood
NICKNAMES: The Garden State, Cockpit
of the Revolution, the Clam State, the
Camden and Amboy State, the Jersey
Blue State, the Pathway of the Revolution
STATE MOTTO: Liberty and Prosperity
SPORTS TEAMS: Giants, Jets, football;
New Jersey Nets, basketball; New Jersey
Devils, hockey
STATE ANIMAL: Horse
STATE INSECT: Honeybee
STATE COLORS: Buff and blue
STATE SONG: "New Jersey Loyalty"
(unofficial)
STATE LANDMARKS: Grover Cleveland
Birthplace, Caldwell; Thomas A. Edison
National Historic Site, West Orange—
the inventor's workshop
NATIONAL PARK: Morristown National
Historical Park—includes General
George Washington's headquarters
during the winter of 1779-1780 and Fort
Nonsense
HISTORIC SITES: Batsto—a colonial
village; Clinton Historical Museum
Village, Clinton; Fosterfields Historical
Farm, Morristown; Historic Allaire
Village, Allaire State Park; Historic Cold
Spring Village; Cape May; Historic
Towne of Smithville, Absecon; Victorian
Wheaton Village, Millville; Waterloo
Village Restoration, Stanhope

This mid-Atlantic state is right in the center of the manufacturing belt that stretches from Washington, D.C., to Canada. Although it's one of our smallest states, and our most densely populated, it seems there is room for some of everything: farms and factories, superhighways and dirt roads, mountains and beaches, port cities and fishing villages. Some 90 percent of the people in this highly urban state live in cities and towns, many of which are actually suburbs of New York and Philadelphia.

Mother deer and fawn

SUNTANNING ON THE JERSEY SHORE New Jersey is almost completely bounded by water. It shares Hudson River ports with New York and Delaware River ports with Pennsylvania. Along the Atlantic coast is the famous Jersey Shore: 127 miles of sandy beaches dotted with vacation resorts and amusement parks. Young Bruce Springsteen used to perform in the Asbury Park area, and he still sings about the Jersey Shore. Farther south on the Shore is Atlantic City, a major East Coast gambling center. In nearby Ocean City, check out the Hermit Crab Race and Miss Crustacean Contest, and the Miscellaneous Suntanning Tournament, both in August.

Most of southern Jersey is coastal plain, suitable for farming. Along the Hudson River, across from New York, you can see the sheer cliffs of the Palisades. New Jersey's Kittatinny Mountains —part of the Appalachians—are in the state's northwest corner. Cutting deeply across the Kittatinnies is the Delaware Water Gap.

Absecon lighthouse at Graveyard inlet

New Jersey's towns have been home to many famous figures. The great American poet Walt Whitman lived in Camden— which is also the home of Campbell's Soup Headquarters. (See their collection of soup tureens!)

Princeton, home of Princeton University, is where physicist Albert Einstein worked. It was also the birthplace of Paul Robeson—actor, singer, and civil rights activist. Woodrow Wilson, America's president during World War I, was first a professor and then the president of Princeton University, and later the governor of New Jersey.

Mount Laurel was the birthplace of Alice Paul, who worked first for women's right to vote and then—unsuccessfully—for an Equal Rights Amendment to the Constitution that was meant to guarantee women full legal equality. Paul might have been inspired to know about the 172 women of Vineland, who in 1868 cast their ballots in a presidential election—although they would not have the legal right to do so until 1920. (The ballots were kept in a separate box and not included in the official count.) You can still see her farmhouse, Paulsdale, on Hooton Road.

In Red Bank, you can visit the T. Thomas Fortune House. In the 1880s Fortune founded the influential newspaper *New York Age.* In its pages, he argued for integrating public schools and expanding civil rights.

Perhaps the most famous place in New Jersey's history is Trenton, where General George Washington and his men crossed the ice-clogged Delaware on Christmas Night, 1776. You may have seen the famous painting *Washington Crossing the Delaware*—this is where it happened! You can still visit Trenton's Old Barracks, where Washington's men surprised the sleeping Hessians—and if you visit on Christmas, you can see the crossing reenacted at Crossing State Park.

Rhodes Scholar, basketball star, Senator, Bill Bradley (1943-)

THE GARDEN STATE GETS ITS NAME When the first Europeans arrived in New Jersey, they found a native people called the Lenni-Lanape. Early Swedish settlers bought much of the present state from these people in 1640. Dutch settlers had also come to New Jersey, and by 1655 they had forced the Swedes out. The British, in turn, took the land from the Dutch in 1664 and named the town of Elizabeth after their queen. When the colony was given to British settlers Sir John Berkeley and Sir George Cartaret, they named it after Jersey, the island in the English channel where Carteret had been born and had been lieutenant governor.

Almost 100 Revolutionary War battles were fought in New Jersey, including the Battle of Monmouth on June 28, 1778, near Freehold. The battle was waged with the help of Molly Hays, who carried water to the men as they fought. She got her famous nickname as the soldiers called for "Molly Pitcher." When her husband, an artilleryman, was shot, Molly loaded the cannon in his place and fought to the battle's end.

New Jersey's farms were of key importance in supplying soldiers with the food they needed to fight the war. New Jersey became known as the Garden State, since its gardens helped to win our independence.

A LEADER IN FARMS AND FACTORIES Farms occupy less than 20 percent of New Jersey's land, yet the fruit and vegetables grown here help feed all the city dwellers in Philadelphia and New York. New Jersey tomatoes, corn, strawberries, and peaches are especially famous. New Jersey also produces fish and shellfish—bluefish, clams, flounder, and lobster.

This industrial state is a leader in chemical production and the manufacture of medicine. Electric and electronic equipment, machinery, and printing are also important, as are New Jersey's oil refineries.

Fascinating Facts

NEW JERSEY HAD THE WORLD'S FIRST:
- professional baseball game—Hoboken—1846
- intercollegiate football game—New Brunswick—between Rutgers and Princeton
- four-lane highway—between Elizabeth and Newark
- Miss America Contest—Atlantic City—1921

NEW JERSEY INVENTIONS:
- telegraph—Samuel Morse
- lightbulb, phonograph, movie camera—Thomas A. Edison
- submarine—John P. Holland
- Standard Time—William F. Allen

PRESIDENT BORN IN NEW JERSEY:
- Grover Cleveland (1837-1908), 22nd and 24th President

OTHER FAMOUS PEOPLE BORN IN NEW JERSEY:
- Politician Aaron Burr, Newark (1756-1836)
- Author James Fenimore Cooper, Burlington (1789-1851)
- Author Stephen Crane, Newark (1871-1900)
- Poet William Carlos Williams, Rutherford (1883-1963)
- Scholar, actor, singer Paul Robeson, Princeton (1898-1976)
- Jazz great William "Count" Basie, Red Bank (1904-1984)
- Actress Meryl Streep, Summit (1949-)

NEW JERSEY IS TOPS IN:
- variety of manufactured products
- flag-making
- chemical production
- jewelry—national jewelry center is Newark

BEFORE HOLLYWOOD... New Jersey was the motion picture capital of the world until about 1916. That's because Thomas A. Edison pioneered the development of movie equipment in his laboratory at Menlo Park.

IT USED TO BE ILLEGAL IN NEW JERSEY:
- to delay or detain a homing pigeon

New Mexico

12th century Anasazi village

47th state to enter the Union, January 6, 1912

The Basics

POPULATION: 1,819,046
36th most populous state
AREA: 121,598 square miles
5th largest state
STATE CAPITAL: Santa Fe
STATE BIRD: Roadrunner (also called Chaparral bird)
STATE FLOWER: Yucca flower
STATE TREE: Piñon
NICKNAMES: Land of Enchantment, the Cactus State, the Spanish State
STATE MOTTO: *Crescit Eundo* (Latin for "It grows as it goes")
STATE ANIMAL: New Mexico black bear
STATE GRASS: Blue grama grass
STATE FOSSIL: Coelophysis
STATE GEM: Turquoise
STATE SONG: "O Fair New Mexico," words and music by Elizabeth Garrett; *Asi Es Nuevo Mejico*," words and music by Almadeo Lucero
STATE LANDMARKS: Palace of the Governors, Santa Fe; Taos Pueblo; Puye Cliff Dwellings, Santa Clara Pueblo—740-room Indian structure
NATIONAL PARKS: Carlsbad Caverns; White Sands National Monument.
STATE PARK: Valley of Fires, near Carrizozo—1,500-year-old lava flow
STATE FESTIVALS: International Balloon Fiesta, Albuquerque (October); Piñata Festival, Tucumcari (June); Whole Enchilada Fiesta, Las Cruces (October)
STATE PLEDGE OF ALLEGIANCE: In English, "I salute the flag of the state of New Mexico, the Zia Indian symbol of perfect friendship among united cultures." In Spanish, *"Saludo la bandera del estado de Nuevo Mejico, el simbolo zia de amistad perfecta, entre culturas unidas."*

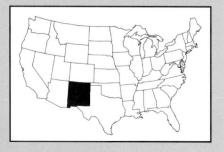

New Mexico is home to many different Indian nations and pueblos, each with its own feast days, customs, and tribal governments. And New Mexico is a kind of living record of Spanish and Mexican history in the United States. Visitors to this southwestern desert state will find that it is truly a Land of Enchantment.

PUEBLO, APACHE, NAVAJO Eastern New Mexico is part of the Great Plains—flat, endless prairie. The central part of the state is occupied by the Rocky Mountains. And to the west is the Colorado Plateau, high, dry grasslands. To outsiders this land might appear harsh, if beautiful, but to the many native peoples who live here, the land is rewarding.

Cheyenne perform the Sky Dance.

There are 18 separate pueblos (Indian villages) in New Mexico, each governed by its own people, each with its own historic buildings. The Laguna pueblo consists of six villages spread over several acres. It's famous for its pottery. The Acoma pueblo is near the Enchanted Mesa, a huge monolith towering 400 feet above the plains. The Cochiti pueblo is known for its ceremonial dances and drumming, and for its storyteller dolls. The pueblo at Isleta includes an old Mission from Spanish colonial days—and nightly bingo games! At the Jemez pueblo, you can see baskets woven from yucca leaves, as well as another old Mission, of San Juan de Jemez. The largest pueblo is that of the Zuni, who are famous for their turqoise-and-silver jewelry.

Also in New Mexico is part of the Navajo reservation, home to the largest Native American group in the United States. This 16-million-acre reservation stretches into Arizona and Utah as well. And New Mexico is the site of the Jicarilla Apache and Mescalero Apache reservations.

A LAND OF LIVING HISTORY Both Indian and Spanish influences can be felt in Santa Fe, the U.S.'s oldest continuously inhabited city. The oldest house in Santa Fe was built by the Alaco Pueblo in A.D. 1200. When the Spanish came in 1540, they added adobe bricks and a fireplace.

Visiting Albuquerque, you might take one of the town's famous hot-air balloon rides. Or you can take a four-hour drive northwest and visit the Aztec Ruins National Monument, one of the largest Native American ruins on the continent. This 500-room dwelling was misnamed by the nineteenth century people who discovered it. They believed they had found Aztec ruins, not realizing that the Aztecs were active much further south, in Mexico. This was a Pueblo ruin. Not too far away, at the Petroglyph National Monument, you can see over 17,000 ancient rock drawings along a 17-mile natural wall, probably created around A.D. 1300.

Other famous landmarks in New Mexico include the artist Georgia O'Keeffe's house and studio at Abiquiú and Mabel Dodge Luhan's salon at Taos. Mabel Dodge once ran a salon (a kind of open house) in New York City, welcoming artists and writers for many evenings of conversation. Then she married the Taos Pueblo Indian Antonio Lujan (later Luhan) and moved to Taos. She continued to invite artists and writers to her new salon, including O'Keeffe and the English novelist D.H. Lawrence.

For a taste of the Old West, take a look in Lincoln at Mountain Pride, the stagecoach driven by Sadie Orchard. As you look, imagine riding in the rickety carriage over the rocky mountain roads of New Mexico. And don't miss the Carlsbad Caverns in the southeastern part of the state. Most of its 77 underground rooms aren't open to the public, but the caves that you can visit feature rock sculptures in delicate, fantastic shapes. At night, millions of bats fly out of the cave opening, like a huge column of smoke in the sky.

ALONG THE SANTA FE TRAIL The Golden Age of the Pueblo civilization was probably 950-1200. But there were still many highly developed native peoples living in New Mexico when the Spanish first arrived in the 1500s. Soon Spanish settlers brought cattle and sheep into the region and founded missions to convert the Indians to Christianity.

Ruins at Chaco Canyon National Monument

In 1680 the Pueblos drove out the Spanish. But by 1692 the Spanish had regained control. In 1821 the first caravan of Americans drove their wagons from Missouri to Santa Fe along the Santa Fe trail. Although Mexico governed New Mexico for a time, the United States eventually gained control of this land—and continued to push native peoples onto reservations. In 1886 Apache leader Geronimo led an uprising when his people were exiled to Arizona—but they were defeated.

Today native peoples still live on the lands that were set aside for them. But in New Mexico, more than any other state, Indians have managed to maintain their culture, their language, and their government.

URANIUM AND SHEEP FARMS New Mexico's sheep and cattle ranches are extremely important to the state. But its true wealth is under the ground, not on the plains. Uranium, oil, copper, zinc, potash, gold, silver, and lead are all key resources in New Mexico. And the state's natural beauty is a foundation for thriving tourism.

New York

The Basics

POPULATION: 18,976,457
3rd most populous state
AREA: 54,471 square miles
27th largest state
STATE CAPITAL: Albany
STATE BIRD: Bluebird
STATE FLOWER: Rose
STATE TREE: Sugar maple
NICKNAMES: The Empire State, the Excelsior State, the Knickerbocker State
STATE MOTTO: *Excelsior* (Latin for "Ever upward")
SPORTS TEAMS: New York Mets, New York Yankees, baseball; Buffalo Bills, football; New York Knicks, basketball; New York Rangers, New York Islanders, Buffalo Sabres, hockey
STATE ANIMAL: American beaver
STATE FISH: Brook trout or Speckled trout
STATE INSECT: Ladybug
STATE FOSSIL: *Eurypterus remipes*
STATE GEM: Garnet
STATE BAKED GOOD: Apple muffin
STATE DRINK: Milk
STATE SONG: "I Love New York," words and music by Steve Karmen
STATE LANDMARK: U.S. Military Academy at West Point
NATIONAL PARK: Saratoga National Historical Park
STATE FESTIVALS: Alpo International Dog Sled Races, Saranac Lake (January); Fort Ticonderoga Muzzle Loading Rifle Shoot, Ticonderoga (May, September); The Hill Cumora Scottish Pageant, Palmyra (July-August); Inner Tube Regatta, Wellsville (Memorial Day weekend); Toy Festival, East (August)

New York is a state of wild contrasts. At the southeastern tip of the state is New York City, one of the largest, most diverse urban areas in the world. Stretching out into the Atlantic, Long Island, with 1,723 square miles, is the largest island on the East Coast. Further upstate is some of the nation's most beautiful countryside—dramatic mountains, peaceful orchards, lush vineyards.

FROM LEATHERSTOCKING COUNTRY TO NIAGARA FALLS Eastern New York State is dominated by mountains. The Catskills are only a few hours' drive north of New York City and were once known as The Borscht Belt—full of resort hotels catering to Jewish New Yorkers (who ate borscht and other Eastern European foods). Today most of these resorts are closed, and the Catskills are home to many craftspeople. Farther north are the Adirondacks, an older, higher mountain range, site of the luxury resorts of Lake Placid and Lake George.

Tucked in among the mountains are the Hudson and Mohawk River Valleys. Here you'll find Sunnyside, Washington Irving's estate, where he lived while writing his tales of old New York, *The Legend of Sleepy Hollow* and *Rip Van Winkle*. Here, too, are President Franklin Delano Roosevelt's home at Hyde Park, and Eleanor Roosevelt's Val-kill.

Farther west are the Appalachian Mountains, and beyond them, the Finger Lakes region—Leatherstocking country of James Fenimore Cooper. This part of New York is quintessential rural America. Cooperstown is the legendary home of America's first baseball game. Its Baseball Hall of Fame includes an exhibit on women's professional teams. The female teams began in 1943, while male players were off at war, and continued until 1954.

The World Trade Center towers over the Brooklyn Bridge.

Also in this region is Harriet Tubman's home at Auburn. From the late 1850s until the Civil War, this was Tubman's base of operations as she returned to the South to bring slaves to freedom. Women's history was made at Seneca Falls in 1848, when a group of female abolitionists convened America's first women's rights convention. The Women's Hall of Fame is there now, in the midst of a park. Nearby, in Rochester, Susan B. Anthony wrote *History of Woman Suffrage*.

At the western end of the state is Niagara Falls. America's most famous waterfall is actually three falls in two countries: American and Bridal Veil Falls in New York and Horseshoe Falls in Ontario, Canada.

AMERICA'S LARGEST CITY New York City is the largest city in the western hemisphere and the trade capital of the world. For hundreds of years it's been home to immigrants from almost every culture and nationality on earth. In 1990 over one fifth of New York State's population was foreign-born, and nearly one fourth spoke languages other than English at home. Most of these diverse peoples were living in New York City.

Niagara Falls

Even a casual walk through the city is like taking a tour of two hundred years of American history. At the Fraunces Tavern, for example, General George Washington held a farewell dinner for the officers with whom he'd fought in the Revolutionary War. Washington chose the tavern because it was owned by his friend, Samuel Fraunces, an African American of West Indian descent who had opened the tavern in 1762. The rebellious Sons of Liberty had often met here. And when Washington became President, he made Fraunces his first Steward, in charge of getting supplies for the people entertained by the Washingtons.

New York City's Lower East Side recalls the Jews, Italians, Czechs, Poles, and Ukrainians who came to the city in the 1890s and early 1900s to work in the growing garment and construction industries. These workers started some of America's first unions. Their sons and daughters became some of our country's finest writers and artists.

Farther uptown, in Harlem, African Americans in the 1920s were also creating new art and literature, the so-called Harlem Renaissance. And for many decades thereafter, America's "classical music"—jazz—was developed in clubs throughout the city. You can still visit the homes of such artists as jazz trumpeter Louis Armstrong and poet Claude McKay.

New York continues to attract new generations of immigrants from around the world and around the nation. Both new and native New Yorkers create the city's unique energy, as well as building its industries: tourism, publishing, finance, theater, trade, and real estate.

Labor leader, Samuel Gompers (1850-1924) immigrated to America when he was 13.

UPSTATE, DOWNSTATE Rural New York is dairy country, producing cheese, butter, and milk, as well as truck vegetables, grapes, and orchard fruits. Mineral wealth comes from New York's stores of stone, gravel, and sand. Along the Hudson and Mohawk Rivers are New York's industrial cities—Albany, Troy, Schenectady, Utica, Rome, Rochester, and Buffalo. These river towns first developed when goods were being shipped from New York along the the Erie Canal to the Great Lakes. They also have their own factories, producing machinery, electrical products, chemicals, aircraft, and photographic equipment.

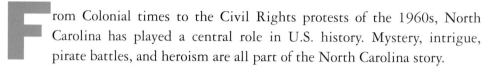

North Carolina

The Basics

POPULATION: 8,049,313
11th most populous state
AREA: 53,821 square miles
28th largest state
STATE CAPITAL: Raleigh
STATE BIRD: Cardinal (Red bird, Kentucky cardinal)
STATE FLOWER: Dogwood
STATE TREE: Longleafed pine (Southern pine, Longleaf yellow pine, Pitch pine, Hard pine, Heart pine, Turpentine pine, Rosemary pine, Brown pine, Fat pine, Longstraw pine, Longleafed pitch pine)
NICKNAMES: The Tarheel State, the Old North State, the Turpentine State
STATE MOTTO: *Esse quam videri* (Latin for "To be rather than to seem")
SPORTS TEAM: Charlotte Hornets, basketball
STATE MAMMAL: Gray squirrel
STATE INSECT: Honeybee
STATE REPTILE: Eastern box turtle
STATE SALTWATER FISH: Channel bass or red drum
STATE ROCK: Granite
STATE SHELL: Scotch bonnet
STATE STONE: Emerald
STATE BEVERAGE: Milk
STATE COLORS: Red and blue
STATE SONG: "The Old North State," traditional
STATE MUSICAL TOAST: "A Toast to North Carolina"
STATE LANDMARKS: Andrew Johnson Birthplace, Raleigh; James K. Polk Birthplace, Pineville
NATIONAL PARKS: Cape Hatteras National Seashore; Cape Lookout National Seashore; Great Smoky Mountains National Park

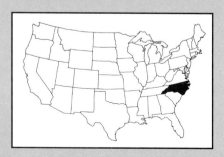

From Colonial times to the Civil Rights protests of the 1960s, North Carolina has played a central role in U.S. history. Mystery, intrigue, pirate battles, and heroism are all part of the North Carolina story.

SMOKY MOUNTAINS AND TOBACCO COUNTRY You can divide North Carolina into three areas. Along the coast are the Outer Banks, a long string of sandy islands running along the coast, and the dangerous waters of Cape Hatteras, Cape Lookout, and Cape Fear. This was the Graveyard of the Atlantic because of the many ships wrecked here. In the 1700s, pirates like Captain Kidd and Blackbeard (Edward Teach) buried their treasure on these islands. It's vacationland now and home to many types of sea birds.

At Kitty Hawk, the Wright Brothers first developed an airplane that could really fly. A museum shows their achievements, along with the Wright Brothers National Memorial.

The state's heartland is the Piedmont Plateau, an industrial region of forested hills where most of the state's people live in cities: the Research Triangle of Raleigh, Durham, and Chapel Hill; and the triad of Greensboro, Winston-Salem, and High Point. This is tobacco country. You can also visit such

Old Fire Engine Museum in New Bern

historic sites as the 1774 Hezekiah Alexander Homesite in Charlotte, where costumed guides show you colonial customs.

Farther west are the state's Appalachian ranges: the Great Smoky Mountains (with the most-visited national park in the country, shared with Tennessee); as well as the Blue Ridge, Black, and Unaka Mountains.

MYSTERIES AND REBELLIONS The very first English colony in America was Sir Walter Raleigh's settlement at Roanoke Island, begun in 1585. The first wave of settlers faced starvation and returned to England. But in 1587 another group arrived. Virginia Dare, the first English child in North America, was born. The colony seemed secure. But when a new boat from England arrived in Roanoke three years later, they found only the word "CROATOAN" carved on a tree. The Lost Colony had disappeared.

The English settled North Carolina again in the 1650s, and in 1677 it became the site of North America's first rebellion against foreign rule. Colonists resented the royal governor's taxes on their trade, so John Culpeper led them in the uprising known as Culpeper's Rebellion. They put the governor in jail and ran the colony themselves until 1683.

In 1768 a group of backcountry farmers called the Regulators threatened another rebellion against British taxes. They were defeated at the 1771 Battle of Alamance Creek—which some have called the first battle of the Revolution. In 1774, the year after the Boston Tea Party, 51 Edenton women signed a petition boycotting tea; a

Biltmore in Asheville is the largest private house in America—152 rooms.

teapot-shaped monument honors their rebellion. And in 1775, a year before the Declaration of Independence, the citizens of Mecklenberg County declared their independence from the British with the Mecklenberg Resolutions.

With such a history, it's not surprising that North Carolina was the first colony to vote for independence at the Continental Congress. North Carolina refused to ratify the Constitution, however, until the Bill of Rights guaranteed the freedom they had come to expect.

FROM SLAVERY'S WRONGS TO CIVIL RIGHTS One of the most famous tales of slavery is Harriet Ann Jacobs' *Incidents in the Life of a Slave Girl*. Jacobs was a slave in the house of Edenton plantation owner Dr. James Norcom, who "told me I was his property; that I must be subject to his will in all things." Unwilling to submit, Jacobs escaped to hide in a tiny space—"a living coffin"—under her grandmother's front porch. She stayed there nearly seven years, until she won her freedom.

Over a hundred years later, Greensboro was the site of one of the most important actions in the Civil Rights movement. On February 1, 1960, four young African-American men ordered coffee at the whites-only Woolworth lunch counter. The black students politely refused to leave until they were served—sparking a protest that spread throughout the South. It also gave birth to a new organization, the Student Nonviolent Coordinating Committee (known as SNCC, or "snick"). Thirty years later, the four men returned for an anniversary celebration of integration. They were served by the very same woman who had refused them before.

Kitty Hawk—site of the Wright Brothers first flight on December 17, 1903

TOBACCO FARMS AND TEXTILE MILLS
North Carolina's economy is both agricultural and industrial—but in this state the two are closely linked. The state produces tobacco and cigarettes, cotton and textiles, lumber and paper. Only Texas has more farms than this fertile state, which also produces corn, soybeans, peanuts, and sweet potatoes, as well as chickens, hogs, and dairy products. At the Research Triangle, scientists develop electronic equipment and figure out how the latest technological discoveries can be useful to industry.

North Dakota

The Basics

POPULATION: 642,200
47th most populous state
AREA: 70,704 square miles
19th largest state
STATE CAPITAL: Bismarck
STATE BIRD: Meadowlark
STATE FLOWER: Wild prairie rose
STATE TREE: American elm
NICKNAMES: The Sioux State, the Flickertail State, Land of the Dakotas, the Peace Garden state
STATE MOTTO: Liberty and Union Now and Forever, One and Inseparable
STATE FISH: Northern pike
STATE FOSSIL: Teredo petrified wood
STATE DRINK: Milk
STATE GRASS: Western wheat grass
STATE SONG: "North Dakota Hymn," words by James W. Foley, music by C.S. Putnam
STATE MARCH: "Spirit of the Land" by James D. Ployhar
STATE ART GALLERY: University of North Dakota Art Gallery, Grand Forks
NATIONAL HISTORIC SITES: Fort Union Trading Post; Knife River Indian Villages, near Stanton, preserving the Hidatsa and Mandan Indian earth lodges—circular mud and timber structures
NATIONAL PARKS: Theodore Roosevelt National Park, Medora; International Peace Garden, shared with Canada, established in 1941 to commemorate the longest undefended border in the world
NATIONAL TRAIL SYSTEMS: Lewis and Clark National Historic Trail; North Country National Scenic Trail
STATE FESTIVALS: Potato Bowl Weekend, Grand Forks (September); Steam Threshers Show, Carrington (September)

Mandan Indian Village

39th or 40th state to enter the Union, November 2, 1889

North Dakota's fertile prairies and sometimes deadly winters have drawn pioneers who are fond of the "wide open spaces." The land is so flat that the 19-story state capitol building in Bismarck is visible for miles. In the 1880s President Theodore Roosevelt spent three years ranching in this Great Plains state and fell in love with its beauties and its challenges. "I would never have been President," he said later, "if it had not been for my experiences in North Dakota."

FROM THE RED RIVER TO THE BADLANDS Eastern North Dakota has some of the world's best farmland, especially in the fertile Red River Valley. The rich black soil of the Central Lowlands stretches westward to Bismarck, the state capital. Western North Dakota is more arid and less hospitable to farms, particularly in the Badlands near the Montana border. Here you can see the eroded landscape carved by a river that dried up millions of years ago—cliffs, valleys, buttes, and table mesas in fantastic shapes. Here, too,

Four Eyes Theater, Medora

you can visit Theodore Roosevelt National Park where bison, wild horses, mule deer, pronghorn antelope, and bighorn sheep still roam freely.

North Dakota's largest city, Fargo, has fewer than 75,000 people, and its next three principal cities—Bismarck, Grand Forks, and Minot—have fewer than 45,000 each. Although this is a rural state, over half the population lives in cities and towns.

In the nineteenth century North Dakota was settled by Norwegian immigrants who were used to farming a cold northern land. They were joined by settlers from Iceland, Germany, and Czechoslovakia. As a result, many people in the state share the same religion: some one-half of the population is Lutheran, and one-third is Catholic.

EXPLORING THE DAKOTA TERRITORY The first recorded European expedition to this state was by Pierre Gaultier de Varennes, Sieur (lord) de la Verendrye. The land he claimed for France in 1738 was already inhabited by Arapaho, Assiniboine, Cheyenne, Hidatsa, Mandan, and Sioux.

The monument to the Pioneer Family is on the state capitol grounds in Bismarck.

Most of North Dakota was bought by the United States in the Louisiana Purchase and was explored by Lewis and Clark in 1804-1806. It was at their winter quarters near Washburn, North Dakota, that they hired their Shoshone guide and translator, Sacagawea.

The Dakota territory saw few settlers until 1863 when the Homestead Act offered pioneers 160 acres of free land after five years of farming. Railroads and the U.S. government continued to offer incentives to European and U.S. settlers, despite opposition from native peoples. By 1881, however, Indians had been forced onto reservations, and North Dakota's European population skyrocketed from 37,000 in 1880 to 152,000 in 1885. By 1890 some 43 percent of the state's residents were foreign-born—one-eighth of them from Norway.

FARMERS FIGHT BACK In 1915 many North Dakota farmers were angry. They had some of the biggest and most productive farms in the country. Yet they were poor, while the grain elevators which bought their grain and the railroads that shipped it were getting rich. To fight back, farmers created the Non-Partisan League, which ran candidates in local and state elections. For a time, League-elected officials—including Governor Lynn J. Frazier—were remarkably successful. They created the only state-owned bank in the country, to make low-interest loans to farmers. They started a state-owned grain mill and grain elevator in Grand Forks, to guarantee farmers fair prices. They established social programs to benefit farmers and poor people, many of which still exist today. Although the League's effectiveness petered out by 1922, many people in North Dakota still remember the Non-Partisan League.

BONANZA FARMS AND OIL WELLS North Dakota has more people working on farms than anywhere else in the U.S. Wheat, potatoes, sugarbeets, flax, barley, sunflowers, and soybeans are all important to this state's agricultural economy. However, family farms are in danger here as elsewhere, and more farmers have lost their land

Lakota Sioux in traditional dress at the Whitman Ranch

in North Dakota than in any other state.

The first lignite coal was mined here in 1884, and the first oil gushed forth in 1951. Coal and oil, as well as uranium, are still key North Dakota products.

Ohio

Rock and Roll Hall of Fame, Cleveland

17th state to enter the Union, March 1, 1803

The Basics

POPULATION: 11,353,140
7th most populous state
AREA: 44,828 square miles
34th largest state
STATE CAPITAL: Columbus
STATE BIRD: Cardinal (Red bird, Kentucky cardinal)
STATE FLOWER: Scarlet carnation
STATE TREE: Buckeye (Ohio buckeye, Fetid buckeye, Stinking buckeye, American horse chestnut)
NICKNAMES: The Buckeye State, the Mother of Modern Presidents
STATE MOTTO: With God, All Things are Possible
SPORTS TEAMS: Cincinnati Reds and Cleveland Indians, baseball; Cincinnati Bengals and Cleveland Browns, football; Cleveland Cavaliers, basketball
STATE INSECT: Ladybug
STATE FOSSIL: Trilobite
STATE GEM: Ohio flint
STATE DRINK: Tomato juice
STATE SONG: "Beautiful Ohio," words by Ballard MacDonald, music by Mary Earl
STATE LANDMARKS: Perry's Victory and International Peace Memorial, Put-in-Bay; William Howard Taft birthplace, Cincinnati
STATE HISTORIC SITES: Adena State Memorial, Chillicothe—1807 stone house; Gardens of Zoar, near New Philadelphia—1817 settlement where men and women had equal rights
STATE NATIONAL PARKS: Hopewell Culture National Historic Park, near Columbus; Cuyahoga Valley National Recreation Area

Ohio is one of our richest states—in resources, location, and people. It has rich deposits of clay, coal, and gas. It is located just west of the Appalachians, between Lake Erie and the Ohio River, giving it access to East and West, North and South, land and water. And its people benefit from the state's 43 colleges and universities—second only to Pennsylvania in the number of higher educational institutions.

PORTS AND FARMS Ohio's northern border is formed by Lake Erie, with its flat plains and its port cities of Toledo and Cleveland. Ohio's southern border is the Ohio River, with the hilly, elevated land of the Central Plains and the major city of Cincinnati. Ohio's heartland is in the heart of the Central Plains, a land of farms and small cities, as well as the state capital, Columbus. And eastern Ohio is the western end of the Allegheny Plateau, a rugged land of rivers and bluffs. No wonder the state has taken the name Ohio—"large" or "beautiful" in Iroquois.

Nobel Prize-winning author Toni Morrison was born in Lorain

BUCKEYE CITIES Some two-thirds of Ohioans live in cities, urban areas that represent the rich history of this urban state. Akron, for example, besides being the first home of the B.F. Goodrich Tire Company, was also the site of a famous convention for women's rights in 1852. There Sojourner Truth gave her famous "Ain't I a Woman?" speech.

Columbus, Ohio's largest city and state capital, is the headquarters of many big companies. Here, in 1886, Samuel Gompers helped found the American Federation of Trades and Labor, ancestor of today's AFL-CIO. And nearby, outside the town of Chillicothe, is the Hopewell Cultural National Historical Park, or Mound City, an Indian burial site used by the Hopewell Indians from about 200 B.C. to A.D. 500.

Cincinnati is the site of the Stowe House, where the young Harriet Beecher moved when she was 21. Four years later she married Calvin E. Stowe, and had five children—but she never stopped writing. In the 1830s she traveled across the Ohio River to the slave state of Kentucky. What she saw became material for her book, *Uncle Tom's Cabin.*

Cleveland was once infamous for water pollution—its Cuyahoga River actually caught fire in the 1970s because of all the toxic waste in the water, and Lake Erie was known as a "dead lake." Since then, Cleveland has made a remarkable recovery, and Lake Erie has recovered so much that you can now eat fish caught in it. Cleveland is also notable for its Art Museum and world-famous clinic.

Visitors to Dayton can take a tour of Dayton's Aviation Trail, starting at the Wright Brothers Bicycle Shop, where airplane inventors Orville and Wilbur Wright got their start. Or they can visit the Paul Laurence Dunbar House, home of the brilliant African-American poet.

For space buffs there is the International Women's Air and Space Museum at Centerville or the Neil Armstrong Air and Space Museum at Wapakoneta. Nature lovers can visit Kelleys Island, where millions of years ago glaciers cut deep, rippling grooves into the rocks on the Erie shore.

The All-American Soapbox Derby is held in Akron each year.

THE GROWTH OF AN INDUSTRIAL STATE Ohio was the first of the organized territories to be carved out of the Northwest Territory, and one of the first of those territories to try to become a state. In its key position just west of the more settled United States, Ohio was one of the first areas to experience the westward movement that followed the Revolutionary War. Gradually Ohio became the center of a network of canals, railroads, and finally, highways, which were used to bring raw materials into Ohio and carry industrial products out.

Sharp-shooter Annie Oakley (1860-1926) was born in Darke County.

Each Ohio urban center developed its own industrial specialty. Cleveland became the world's largest iron ore port. Aircraft and machinery are made in Columbus, and Cincinnati has been a port city since riverboat days. Later, jet engines were made there. Dayton was the national center for cash registers. In fact, Dayton native James Ritty invented "Ritty's incorruptible cashier" and then founded the National Cash Register company in 1879. Toledo is known for making scales and glass, while Akron is famous as one of the world's greatest rubber centers.

Ohio has rich resources of its own: limestone, sandstone, lime, salt, coal, oil, and natural gas. America's first billionaire, John D. Rockefeller, started his Standard Oil Company in Cleveland. Cleveland is also a steel town, as are many of the smaller cities around it, including Youngstown and Lorain.

Agriculture in Ohio produces corn, oats, tomatoes, grapes, tobacco, and hay. The state is second in the production of hothouse vegetables.

Fascinating Facts

OHIO FIRSTS:
• First U.S. college to enroll both men and women—Oberlin—1837
• First U.S. electric street railway—Cleveland—1884
• First professional baseball team, Cincinnati Red Stockings

PRESIDENTS BORN IN OHIO:
• Ulysses Simpson Grant (1822-1885), 18th President
• Rutherford B. Hayes (1822-1893), 19th President
• James Garfield (1831-1881), 20th President
• Benjamin Harrison (1833-1901), 23rd President
• William McKinley (1843-1901), 25th President
• William Howard Taft (1857-1930), 27th President
• Warren G. Harding (1865-1923), 29th President

FAMOUS PEOPLE BORN IN OHIO:
• General William T. Sherman, Lancaster (1820-1891)
• Inventor Thomas A. Edison, Milan (1847-1931)
• Director Steven Spielberg, Cincinnati, (1947-)

OHIO ASTRONAUTS:
• John J. Glenn, Jr., first American to orbit the earth
• Neil Armstrong, first man on the moon
• Judith Resnik, one of the first women astronauts, killed in the *Challenger* shuttle explosion

OHIO HALLS OF FAME:
• College Football Hall of Fame, Mason
• National Aviation Hall of Fame, Dayton
• Pro Football Hall of Fame, Canton
• Rock and Roll Hall of Fame, Cleveland
• Trapshooting Hall of Fame, Vandalia

OHIO IS TOPS IN:
• baseballs and footballs • pretzels
• metal toys • firefighting equipment
• machine tools • soap
• rubber products • ice cream cones
• crackerjack (candy-coated popcorn)

Oklahoma

The Basics

POPULATION: 3,450,654
27th most populous state
AREA: 69,903 square miles
20th largest state
STATE CAPITAL: Oklahoma City
STATE BIRD: Scissor-tailed flycatcher
STATE FLOWER: Mistletoe
STATE TREE: Redbud (also called Judas tree, Red Judas tree, Salad-tree, Canadian Judas tree)
NICKNAMES: The Sooner State, the Boomer State
STATE MOTTO: *Labor Omnia Vincit* (Latin for "Labor conquers all things")
STATE ANIMAL: American buffalo
STATE FISH: White bass
STATE INSECT: Honeybee
STATE REPTILE: Mountain boomer lizard
STATE ROCK: Barite rose (rose rock)
STATE COLORS: Green and white
STATE POEM: "Howdy Folks" by David Randolph Milsten
STATE SONG: "Oklahoma," words by Oscar Hammerstein II, music by Richard Rodgers
STATE FESTIVALS: World's Championship Watermelon Seed Spitting Contest; Chocolate Festival, Norman (February); Kiamichi Owa Chito Festival, Broken Bow (June); Pelican Festival, Grand Lake (September)
HALLS OF FAME: National Cowboy Hall of Fame, Oklahoma City; International Photography Hall of Fame, Oklahoma City; National Softball Hall of Fame, Oklahoma City; Rodeo Cowboy Hall of Fame, Oklahoma City; National Hall of Fame for Famous American Indians, Anadarko; National Wrestling Hall of Fame, Stillwater

Roundup on a dairy farm

46th state to enter the Union, November 16, 1907

FROM THE PANHANDLE TO THE OZARKS Oklahoma has two major climates. The state is dry along the panhandle and in the southwest. There you'll see oceans of grass and blue granite mountains. There, too, every little town has a saddle shop, a testament to the state's living cowboy heritage. In the east, on the other hand, the climate is humid and subtropical. The Ouachita Mountains can be found in the southeast, while the Ozark Mountains are in the northeast.

The largest city in northeast Oklahoma is Tulsa, "the Oil Capital of the World." Nearby is the Tallgrass Prairie Reserve, a 52,000-acre unbroken prairie of tall, waving grass; roaming herds of bison; and old cowboy bunkhouses. You can also find bison and 40 other species of wild animals roaming the Woolaroc Wildlife Preserve (visitors have

Oklahoma City skyline

to stay in their cars!). And if you want to see 1,200 wild horses running across the prairie, visit the Prairie Wild Horse Refuge.

The Oklahoma City area is rich in museums and historic centers where you can see how people lived in the Old West. A cowboy monument in front of the Capitol building reminds Oklahomans of their frontier heritage.

BROKEN PROMISES ON THE TRAIL OF TEARS Before Europeans came to North America, Comanche, Osage, and other native peoples lived in Oklahoma. In 1803, when President Thomas Jefferson bought Oklahoma as part of the Louisiana Purchase, he believed that Indians could always be relegated to the western part of the new territory. Oklahoma became a place to forcefully relocate native peoples when U.S. farmers and railroads took their land. As early as 1809, the Delaware, Sac, and Fox were deported to Oklahoma. In 1830 Congress made it official, designating Oklahoma as Indian Territory.

The deportations continued. From 1831 to 1833, 20,000 Choctaw were moved to Oklahoma. Both the journey and the new life were arduous. By 1843 there were only 12,000 Choctaw left. In 1838, 15,000 Cherokee were relocated, forced to make the grueling trip along the Trail of Tears. The experience cost

4,000 Cherokee their lives. In 1842 the Seminole were defeated in Florida, and they, too, were relocated. The Creek and Chickasaw had also been moved to Oklahoma.

Once in Oklahoma, each tribe was given national sovereignty over its government, land, and schools. Many native people became farmers—some even had slaves, like farmers in the South. In 1861 when pro-slavery Southerners seceded from the Union, the Indian nations sided with the Confederacy. (When the war ended, however, African Americans were welcomed into Indian nations as equal citizens.)

In 1869 the U.S. Army established Fort Sill Military Reservation to insure military control over Indian nations. (In 1909 the famous Apache warrior Geronimo was killed at Fort Sill.) Throughout the 1870s, 25 more Indian nations were forced into Oklahoma, while Indian lands were gradually decreased. In 1889 Oklahoma was

Humorist Will Rogers (1879-1935) was born in Oolagah when Oklahoma was still Indian Territory.

first opened to white settlers—who instantly swarmed in to take the free land being offered. In 1893 the Dawes Commission liquidated Indian tribal government.

Wichita grass home

Indian nations had been working together, forming their own Confederation. In 1905 they tried to form a new state, Sequoyah, but Congress rejected their plea for statehood. An Oklahoma Territory had already been established, so the Indian Territory joined with it. Together, the two territories became admitted to the nation as the state of Oklahoma, whose state seal honors the five nations. Oklahoma is still Indian country, where native culture and languages are still alive.

DUST BOWL DAYS In the 1930s the United States was shaken by a Great Depression, in which almost one-third of all workers lost their jobs. In addition, the nation was struck by drought. Oklahoma's dry soil simply blew away, creating what people called a Dust Bowl. Many white Oklahoma residents struck out for California, where they hoped to find new jobs and new lives. Many of these "Okies," however, ended up as migrant laborers, going from farm to farm as work became available. The Oklahoma-born folksinger Woody Guthrie wrote many songs about the Dust Bowl days.

BLACK GOLD AND CATTLE RANCHES The mainstay of Oklahoma's economy is oil. There's so much oil in Oklahoma, some people have found oil wells in their backyards! Natural gas and coal are also plentiful in this state. In the dry western half of the state, farmers grow wheat, hay, and rye. In the humid eastern half, sorghum, peanuts, and cotton flourish. Ranches in the west also raise cattle, sheep, horses, and turkeys. The state also manufactures machinery, plastic, and rubber.

Turner Falls in the Arbuckle Mountains

Fascinating Facts

DID YOU KNOW THAT... One of Oklahoma's oil wells pumps oil right from under the Capitol building in Oklahoma City.

HOW OKLAHOMA GOT ITS NAME: The Choctaw word *okla* means "people," while *humma* means "red." Missionary Reverend Allan Wright named this territory to which "red people" were relocated in the nineteenth century.

HOW OKLAHOMA GOT ITS NICKNAMES: On April 22, 1889, a pistol was fired to mark the day that Oklahoma Territory was opened to white settlers. Some 50,000 settlers waited for that pistol "boom" and then rushed into the area to claim *homesteads*—free land for those who would farm it for five years. These settlers were called *boomers*. Some homesteaders, however, "jumped the gun" and entered the territory *sooner*.

DID YOU KNOW THAT... In the 1920s Tulsa had more millionaires than any other U.S. city.

OKLAHOMA MINERAL WEALTH:
• first in helium
• fourth in oil and natural gas

DID YOU KNOW THAT... America's deepest hole is a 31,441-foot-deep natural gas well in Washita County.

OKLAHOMA HAD THE NATION'S FIRST:
• parking meter—Oklahoma City

FAMOUS PEOPLE BORN IN OKLAHOMA:
• Folksinger Woody Guthrie, Okemah (1912-1967)
• Novelist Ralph Ellison, Oklahoma City (1914-1994)

IT USED TO BE ILLEGAL IN OKLAHOMA:
• to get a fish drunk
• to catch whales in Oklahoma waters
• to eavesdrop

DID YOU KNOW THAT: More languages are spoken in Oklahoma than in Europe. That's because that state is home to 55 Indian nations, each with a language or dialect of its own.

Oregon

The Basics

POPULATION: 3,421,399
28th most populous state
AREA: 98,386 square miles
9th largest state
STATE CAPITAL: Salem
STATE BIRD: Western meadowlark
STATE FLOWER: Oregon grape
STATE TREE: Douglas fir
NICKNAMES: The Beaver State, the Web-Foot State, the Hard-Case State
STATE MOTTO: The Union; *Alis Volat Propriis* (Latin for "She flies with her own wings") is on the state seal
SPORTS TEAM: Portland Trail Blazers, basketball
STATE ANIMAL: American beaver
STATE FISH: Chinook salmon
STATE INSECT: Swallowtail butterfly
STATE ROCK: Thunderegg
STATE HOSTESS: Miss Oregon
STATE SONG: "Oregon, My Oregon," words by J.A. Buchanan, music by Henry B. Murtagh
STATE LANDMARKS: Painted Hills National Monument; John Day Fossil Beds National Monument; Fort Clatsop National Memorial, near Astoria (1805-6 winter camp of Lewis and Clark); Oregon Caves National Monument (caves on four levels); Sea Lion Caves, near Florence (home of hundreds of sea lions)
STATE HISTORIC SITE: Million Hill Village, Salem
NATIONAL PARKS: Crater Lake, near Medford; Newbery National Volcanic Monument, near Bend; Mt. Hood National Forest, near Gresham; Kalmiopsis Wilderness in Siskiyou National Forest, near Ashland

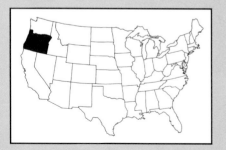

Residents of Oregon tend to be mavericks—people who go their own way no matter what anybody thinks. Why else would the University of Oregon choose the "killer duck" as its mascot? Oregon's "pioneer spirit" has a more serious side, too. Long before others realized how important the environment was, Oregon passed laws to protect its land and water.

ROLL ON, COLUMBIA   This Pacific Northwestern state is full of spectacular scenery: 400 miles of white sandy beaches—all public—marked by twisted rock formations, lonely lighthouses, and tiny port towns. At Gold Beach, where the Rogue River meets the ocean and temperatures are milder, you can see lilies, daffodils, and even palm trees. Cape Arago is a great place for spotting whales and sea lions, while at South Slough National Estuarine Reserve you can find bald eagles and black bears.

The Chinook used canoes like this to fish the Columbia River.

Farther inland are the Coastal Mountains, and farther still are the Cascade Mountains, so called for the many waterfalls that cascade down their rugged peaks. Most Oregonians live between these two ranges, in the Willamette Valley, which contains all of Oregon's major cities—Portland, Eugene, and Salem. East of the Cascades is the Columbia Plateau, which features a drier, harsher climate.

Oregon's northern border with Washington is formed by the mighty Columbia River. Early settlers tried to sail west on this river, but the current was too strong for their rafts and flatboats. Today that power is harnessed by the Columbia Dam, which provides one-third of the hydroelectric potential of the continental United States. Salmon swim upstream to lay and fertilize their eggs, but they can't swim through the dam. So the dam builders added fish ladders, a step-like series of pools that allow the salmon to make their way upstream.

ON THE OREGON TRAIL   The land we now call Oregon was once home to over 100,000 Indians, including Shoshone, Bannock, Paiute, and Nez Percé. Conflicts began almost as soon as European explorers tried to claim the land. Then for a time the 1805-6 expedition of Lewis and Clark created more peaceful relations. (You can still visit Fort Clatsop, winter home of the explorers and their Shoshone translator, Sacagawea.)

The area that is now Oregon was claimed by Russia, Spain, and England. But the first permanent white settlement here was started in 1811 by an American corporation, John Jacob Astor's Pacific Fur Company, which called their new town Astoria. The Spanish and Russians withdrew their claim, and the British and Americans eventually agreed to share the land.

The first immigration to Oregon began in 1842 along the Oregon Trail. The trail was the major means of entering the state until the railroads came in the 1870s. When gold was discovered in the Rogue River Valley, in 1853, thousands of California miners poured into the state—and sparked a bloody war with local Indians. Within 15 years the Umatilla, Walal, Cayuse, and Paiute were defeated and sent onto reservations.

The water of Crater Lake is so clear that sunlight penetrates to a depth of 400 feet.

Battles between Indians and European Americans continued throughout the Civil War, when federal troops were busy fighting elsewhere. After the war, though, U.S. forces returned and tried to force Chief Joseph and the Nez Percé off their land. Joseph resisted, then tried to lead his people into Canada. But in 1877 they too were defeated and moved to a reservation.

THE OREGON SYSTEM   In the early twentieth century, Oregon's state legislature adopted many laws that made their government more democratic. These were called the Oregon system. Although many states have such laws today, they were very unusual for their time. In 1902 Oregon approved initiative (voters can initiate putting a measure on the ballot) and referendums (legislators can put an issue on the ballot for voters to decide directly). In 1904 it established primary elections, so that voters could choose which candidates

Oregon's Pacific coastline is one of the most beautiful in the world.

should run in the general election. The state also authorized recall, a way for voters to vote someone out of office before a regular election.

Later, Oregon was the first state to pass an enforceable law to protect working women and children—thanks to the hard work of crusader Caroline Gleason. In 1955 the state mandated that women should receive equal pay for equal work. And in the 1970s, the state prohibited nonrefundable bottles and cans and outlawed aerosol sprays.

TREES AND TOURISTS   Some 12 million tourists visit Oregon each year to hunt, fish, and ski. Lumber is another key state industry as is the production of electricity. In recent years there has been a great deal of controversy between the lumber industry, which wants to cut down and sell Oregon's trees, and environmentalists, who want to preserve the forests and protect the species that live there.

On the coast, wild and farmed salmon and trout are caught and sold to fish canneries along the Columbia River. Although there is not much dairy farming in the state, Tillamook Valley is famous for its cheddar cheese. Western Oregon farms grow fruit and vegetables. Eastern Oregon specializes in wheat, corn, and cattle.

Fascinating Facts

OREGON IS TOPS IN:
- U.S. lumber and plywood production
- nickel—the only state to mine this product
- seeds
- filbert nuts
- peppermint oil
- blackberries, boysenberries, raspberries

OREGON DEPTHS:
- The deepest lake in the United States is Crater Lake, created when the ancient volcano Mount Mazama exploded, making a crater at the mountain's summit. The lake is nearly half a mile deep—1,932 feet.
- The Snake River canyon is the deepest in the country.

HOW OREGON GOT ITS NAME: No one knows for sure. Four theories:
- from the French-Canadian *ouragan*, "hurricane" or "storm"
- from the Columbia River, called the River of Storms (*ouragans*) by Canadian fur traders
- from the Spanish *orejon*, meaning "big-ear," applied to Indian peoples in the region
- from the Spanish *oregano*, the wild sage plant common in the area

DID YOU KNOW THAT... Oregon contains the only major city named by a coin toss. Amos Lovejoy of Boston and Francis Pettygrove of Portland, Maine, each wanted to name a city after his hometown. Pettygrove won—and the city was named Portland, Oregon.

FAMOUS PEOPLE BORN IN OREGON:
- Radical journalist John Reed, Portland (1887-1920)
- Pulitzer Prize-winning poet Phyllis McGinley, Ontario (1905-1978)
- Chemist Linus Pauling, twice honored Nobel Prize winner, Portland (1901-1994)

DID YOU KNOW THAT... The geographic center of the whole U.S.—if Guam and American Samoa are included—is in Oregon's China Cap Mountains.

IT USED TO BE ILLEGAL IN OREGON:
- for a dead person to serve on a jury

Pennsylvania

The Basics

POPULATION: 12,281,054
6th most populous state
AREA: 46,058 square miles
33rd largest state
STATE CAPITAL: Harrisburg
STATE BIRD: Ruffled grouse
STATE FLOWER: Mountain laurel
STATE TREE: Hemlock (Eastern hemlock, Canadian hemlock, hemlock spruce, spruce pine, New England hemlock, spruce)
NICKNAMES: The Keystone State, the Quaker State
SPORTS TEAMS: Pittsburgh Pirates, Philadelphia Phillies, baseball; Pittsburgh Steelers, Philadelphia Eagles, football; Philadelphia 76ers, basketball; Philadelphia Flyers, Pittsburgh Penguins, hockey
STATE MOTTO: Virtue, Liberty, and Independence
STATE ANIMAL: White-tailed deer
STATE DOG: Great Dane
STATE FISH: Brook trout
STATE INSECT: Firefly
STATE BEAUTIFICATION AND CONSERVATION PLANT: Penngift crownvetch
STATE FOSSIL: Trilobite
STATE DRINK: Milk
STATE COLORS: Blue and gold
STATE SLOGAN: "You've got a friend in Pennsylvania."
STATE LANDMARK: Valley Forge National Historical Park; Gettysburg
STATE FESTIVALS: Chocolate Festival, Hershey (February); St. Ubaldo Day, Scranton (Memorial Day weekend); Das Awkscht Fescht Ethnic Festival, Allentown (August); Mifflin County Goose Day Celebration, Lewiston (September)

Pennsylvania was the birthplace of the nation and the home of its first government. When you think of Pennsylvania, think of historic Philadelphia, the City of Brotherly Love…Pittsburgh, the steel town… the rolling hills and Allegheny mountains of Pennsylvania's rugged countryside…and the Amish, a traditional people, driving their horse-drawn buggies down country lanes in Pennsylvania Dutch country.

APPALACHIAN HIGHLAND COUNTRY   Most of this rectangular state is part of the Appalachian Highlands, a region of plateaus and valleys with two parallel

Dr. Benjamin Rush, noted patriot and physician

mountain ranges—the Alleghenies and the Appalachians—running northeast to southwest across the state. In the southeastern corner of the state, around Philadelphia, is a small section of Atlantic coastal plain, shading into the agricultural region of the eastern Piedmont.

Pennsylvania is the only mid-Atlantic state that doesn't touch the ocean. But Philadelphia is a major port on the Delaware, one of Pennsylvania's four major rivers. The other key waterways in the state are the Susquehanna, the Allegheny, the Ohio, and the Monongahela.

Most Pennsylvania residents live in cities and towns, including some 1.6 million in Philadelphia, the nation's fifth-largest city (after New York, Los Angeles, Chicago, and Houston). Philadelphia is a treasure trove of historical landmarks, including Independence Hall, where the Declaration of Independence and the Constitution were signed.

Another Philadelphia landmark is the Betsy Ross House, former home of Elizabeth Griscom Ross. According to a popular myth, it was Ross, a seamstress, who made the first American flag. While no proof exists, in 1777, the marine committee of the Continental Congress did pass a resolution calling for a flag on June 14. We celebrate this as Flag Day.

The Underground Railroad stopped frequently in Philadelphia, and you can still see the house of the Quaker Samuel Johnson who not only harbored runaway slaves, but also let abolitionists use his house for meetings. Harriet Tubman once spoke there. Also in Philadelphia are the homes of Frances Ellen Watkins Harper, a nineteenth-century poet, suffragist, and crusader for civil rights; and Henry Ossawa Tanner, considered the finest African-American painter of his generation.

About 65 miles west of Philadelphia is Pennsylvania Dutch country, which is named not for the Dutch but for the German peoples who came here in the nineteenth century for religious reasons. ("Dutch" comes from the word Deutsch, which means German.) The Amish still preserve their traditional way of life, avoiding all modern conveniences, such as electricity and automobiles. They even use buttons instead of zippers.

Baseball fans might catch the Little League World Series at Williamsport.

Singer Marian Anderson

Chocolate-lovers can visit Hershey, home of the largest chocolate factory in the world. The streets of Hershey have names like Cocoa Avenue, and the streetlights are shaped like Hershey's kisses!

VALLEY FORGE AND GETTYSBURG Pennsylvania was founded by William Penn, a Friend, or Quaker, who believed in freedom and equality for all. When Penn and his colonists arrived in 1682, they set about establishing peaceful relations with the Indians. They passed the first laws guaranteeing jury trials and other liberties that later became part of the U.S. Constitution. In 1774 the First Constitutional Congress was held in Philadelphia, followed by the second Congress in 1775-1776. Present at both Congresses was Pennsylvania's famous inventor and scientist, Benjamin Franklin, who would later be ambassador to France from the new United States.

Pennsylvania is also the site of Valley Forge, where General George Washington and his men passed a harsh winter before finally winning the War of Independence. And it's the only Northern state in which a critical Civil War battle took place. On July 1-3, 1863, the Battle of Gettysburg became a turning point in the war. If you visit Gettysburg you can see the battlefield. You can also visit the house of Jennie Wade, the 20-year-old woman who baked bread for the Union troops. When Confederate troops asked her to leave, she refused. She was shot on the third day of battle by a stray bullet, the only civilian to be fatally shot. Four months later, on November 19, President Lincoln gave his famous Gettysburg Address in this town.

Independence Hall

STEEL TOWNS AND DAIRY FARMS The nation's first steel mill was in Pennsylvania, and the Pittsburgh region is still our national center of steel production. The giant steel corporations have eliminated many jobs, but western Pennsylvania is still an industrial region. Cement, lime, petroleum, heavy machinery, and processed foods are other key industries for this state.

Pennsylvania farming produces eggs, cattle, and dairy products, along with buckwheat, corn, tobacco, vegetables, orchard fruits, grapes, and mushrooms. Other riches of the earth include iron ore and anthracite coal, much of which is used in local industry. Another Pennsylvania product is Christmas trees—this state is one of the leading growers.

Fascinating Facts

PENNSYLVANIA HAD THE NATION'S FIRST:
- circulating library—1731
- medical college—1765
- oil well—Titusville—1859
- fire department
- art museum—Pennsylvania Academy of the Fine Arts—1805
- natural history museum
- hospital—The Pennsylvania Hospital
- chamber of commerce
- steam locomotive on rails
- permanent commercial radio station—KDKA, Pittsburgh—1920

DID YOU KNOW THAT... Pennsylvania is actually not a state but a commonwealth. It does not have towns but boroughs.

PENNSYLVANIA IS TOPS IN:
- hard coal or anthracite—all the nation's hard coal is mined here
- pig iron
- steel

HOW PENNSYLVANIA GOT ITS NAME:
Colony founder William Penn wanted to call the land Sylvania, Latin for woods or woodland. King Charles II, who granted Penn the land, insisted on calling it *Penn's woods*—Pennsylvania.

PRESIDENT BORN IN PENNSYLVANIA:
- James Buchanan (1791-1868), 15th President

OTHER FAMOUS PEOPLE BORN IN PENNSYLVANIA:
- Writer Louisa May Alcott, Germantown (1832-1888)
- Writer Stephen Vincent Benét, Bethlehem (1898-1943)
- Singer Marian Anderson, Philadelphia (1902-1993)
- Actor Bill Cosby, Philadelphia (1937-)

DID YOU KNOW THAT... The carp crowd so closely together in Lake Pymantuning that ducks can walk across their backs.

IT USED TO BE ILLEGAL IN PENNSYLVANIA:
- to talk loudly at picnics

Rhode Island

The Basics

POPULATION: 1,048,319
43rd most populous state
AREA: 1,545 square miles
Smallest state
STATE CAPITAL: Providence
STATE BIRD: Rhode Island Red
(a chicken)
STATE FLOWER: Violet
STATE TREE: Red Maple
NICKNAMES: Little Rhody, the Smallest
State, Ocean State, Land of Roger
Williams, the Plantation State
STATE MOTTO: Hope
STATE MINERAL: Bowenite
STATE ROCK: Cumberlandite
STATE COLORS: Blue, white, and gold
STATE SONG: "Rhode Island," words
and music by T. Clarke Brown
**STATE AMERICAN FOLK ART
SYMBOL:** Charles I. D. Loof Carousel
STATE LANDMARKS: Old Colony
House, headquarters of Colonial and state
governments, 1739, Newport; Touro
Synagogue, oldest U.S. synagogue, 1763,
Newport; Trinity Church, 1724,
Newport; Redwood Library, oldest U.S.
library in continuous use, 1748, Newport;
Capitol Building, with the largest
unsupported dome in the United States,
Providence; First Baptist Church, 1639,
oldest church in America, Providence
STATE HISTORIC MUSEUM: Slater Mill,
Pawtucket, one of the first textile mills in
North America, founded in 1793, now a
museum
STATE FESTIVAL: Hot-Air Balloon
Festival, Kingston (July or August)

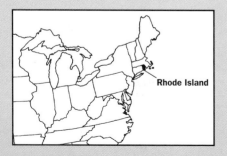

Rhode Island

Rhode Island is one of the six New England states. The original Rhode Island, also called Aquidneck Island, is the largest island in the Narragansett Bay. But today's state of Rhode Island also includes the land that surrounds that bay, as well as Connecticut Island, Prudence Island, and Block Island.

SANDBARS AND SALT MARSH The Narragansett Bay cuts up from Rhode Island Sound as far north as Providence, the state's capital and largest city. West of the bay is flat, rocky soil, not good for farming.

Mainland Rhode Island's coastline is rocky and marked by sandbars, sometimes blending into salt marsh. But the island beaches are broad and sandy, making this a popular area for swimming and sailing.

MANY PEOPLES, MANY LANGUAGES Although only about a million people live in Rhode Island, the state is remarkable for its diversity. In the state's early days, Narragansett and Wampanoag lived there. In Colonial times, French Huguenots (an outcast Protestant minority), English Quakers, and Portuguese Sephardic Jews came to Rhode Island in search of the colony's famed religious freedom. In the 1820s, laborers came to work in Rhode Island's new industries: primarily Irish Catholics, but also French Canadians, Portuguese, Cape Verdeans, Italians,

John Carter Brown House, built in 1786, Providence

and Poles. Later they were joined by Ukrainians, Lithuanians, Armenians, Syrians, Greeks, and Germans. Most recently, immigrants came from the Portuguese islands, Latin America, and Southeast Asia, as well as from the U.S. South. In 1990 almost 10 percent of all Rhode Islanders were foreign-born, with one-fourth of those coming from Portugal. A full 17 percent spoke some language other than English at home, including Portuguese, Spanish, French, Italian, Polish, Mon-Khmer (Cambodian), German, Chinese, Thai (Laotian), and Armenian.

IN SEARCH OF RELIGIOUS FREEDOM The founder of Rhode Island was Roger Williams, who came with his followers from Massachusetts in 1636. Williams's group had been expelled by the Puritans, in part for religious differences, in part because they criticized their fellow English for taking land from the Indians.

Williams made peaceful arrangements with the Indians in his region, and in 1639 he and his followers founded the First Baptist Church.

Another free thinker who came to Rhode Island was Anne Hutchinson, and her husband, who founded the town of Pocasset (now Portsmouth). The state's tradition of religious freedom attracted Quakers, Jews, Seventh Day Adventists, and others who could not worship freely elsewhere.

Williams had had good relations with the Indians he knew, but by 1652 Wampanoag leader

Newport State House

King Philip had started a war with the European colonists, trying to regain the lands his people had lost. Philip was captured and killed in 1676, ending Indian power in the region.

Princess Red Wing at Tomaquag Indian Museum

Rhode Island passed the first law against slavery in North America on May 18, 1652, and for actually abolishing slavery in 1784. This was especially striking because much of Rhode Island's early economy was based on the infamous "triangle trade." Rhode Island merchants would trade rum for slaves in Africa, trade slaves for molasses in the West Indies, and then make rum out of molasses back in Rhode Island.

Rhode Islanders greatly prized independence, and they were the first to resist British taxation in 1769. When the British ship *Gaspee* came to collect taxes in 1772, Rhode Islanders actually set it on fire. On March 2, 1775, Providence residents had their own "tea party," throwing tea from British ships into Narragansett Bay. One Providence man actually crossed out the word "tea" in every sign in the city! On May 4, 1776—two months before the other 12 colonies—Rhode Island declared its indpendence from the British, calling itself the "first free republic in the New World." It was the last colony to join

Touro Synagogue, the oldest in the U.S., was founded in 1763.

the new United States, however, waiting until the Bill of Rights was added before it would ratify the Constitution.

THE COSTUME JEWELRY CAPITAL OF THE WORLD The U.S. industrial revolution began in Rhode Island with the textile mills of Samuel Slater and Moses Brown. Half the state's economy once relied on textiles. Now costume jewelry and electronics are more important industries. Rhode Island also produces machinery, rubber and plastic goods, and silverware.

Although Rhode Island is a small state with poor farmland, it is famous for developing the Rhode Island Red, a chicken that lays lots of eggs. The state is considered the birthplace of the modern poultry industry and eggs are still big business in Rhode Island.

South Carolina

The Basics

POPULATION: 4,012,012
26th most populous state
AREA: 32,008 square miles
40th largest state
STATE CAPITAL: Columbia
STATE BIRD: Carolina wren
STATE FLOWER: Yellow jasmine
STATE TREE: Palmetto (also called Sabal palmetto, Cabbage palm, Cabbage palmetto, Tree palmetto, Bank's palmetto)
NICKNAMES: The Palmetto State, the Rice State, the Swamp State, Keystone of the South Atlantic Seaboard, the Iodine State
STATE MOTTO: *Animis Opibusque Parati* (Latin for "Prepared in mind and resources") and *Dum Spiro Spero* (Latin for "While I breathe, I hope")
STATE ANIMAL: White-tailed deer
STATE FISH: Striped bass
STATE STONE: Blue granite
STATE SHELL: Lettered olive
STATE GEM: Amethyst
STATE FRUIT: Peach
STATE DRINK: Milk
STATE DANCE: The Shag
STATE SONGS: "Carolina," words by Henry Timrod, music by Anne Custis Burgess; "Carolina on My Mind," traditional
STATE LANDMARKS: Andrew Jackson State Park, near Lancaster—birthplace of the President; President Woodrow Wilson's boyhood home, Columbia
HISTORIC PARK: Historic District, Cheraw
STATE FESTIVAL: Spoleto USA, Charleston (May-June)
STATE PLEDGE: "I salute the flag of South Carolina and pledge to the Palmetto State love, loyalty, and faith."

S outh Carolina's warm, humid climate and its miles of sandy beaches have made it one of America's top vacation spots. On the Grand Strand, from the state's northeast border to Georgetown, South Carolina offers a lively family resort area featuring golf, camping, malls, and live entertainment. The aristocratic Low Country—including the barrier islands of Hilton Head, Edisto, and Fripp—offers a more exclusive and genteel vacation area. No wonder tourism is a key industry here!

AT THE HEART OF PLANTATION COUNTRY   South Carolina's coastal lowlands, with their marshy ground and subtropical climate, extend inland for up to 150 miles. Most of the state, however, is the Piedmont plain, a hilly country that rises gradually westward until, at the extreme western end of the state, you reach the Blue Ridge range of the Appalachians.

House on Tradd Street, one of the oldest streets in America

South Carolina's most distinctive city is Charleston. Although this gracious city was badly damaged during the Civil War, many of its eighteenth- and nineteenth-century mansions have been restored, and many of its lovely cypress and magnolia gardens are open to the public. At the Charleston City Hall you can see a portrait of the young George Washington, before false teeth changed the shape of his face—and without his white wig! Charleston is also the site of the Old Slave Mart Museum, located in an old warehouse used to house slaves who were about to be auctioned. From Colonial times until 1930, South Carolina had more black residents than white, because local plantations had held so many African-American slaves to till huge fields of indigo, rice, and cotton. Charleston was also one of the most active slave-trading ports, receiving ships directly from Gambia and the Gold Coast.

WINNING THE WAR OF INDEPENDENCE   North and South Carolina weren't separated until 1712, and the two states share a heritage of independence. In 1719, South Carolinians overthrew the king-appointed Lords Proprietors that governed them and elected their own governor instead. During the Revolutionary War, backwoods guerillas as well as trained soldiers fought the British. Francis Morgan, the Swamp Fox, founded one of the most famous guerilla bands. The first decisive American victory, at Fort Moultrie, was won in South Carolina, as was the Battle of King's Mountain, the turning point of the war.

REBELLIONS AND SECESSION

South Carolina has had a long history of slave rebellions, starting in Stono River in 1739. At that time the Spanish were occupying Florida. They sent a message north saying

Aerial view of Charleston

that slaves who reached St. Augustine would be given freedom. A slave leader, Cato, organized 100 people to break into a weapons storehouse and begin a trek southward to liberty. His band killed 21 people—and was caught within five hours. Some 44 rebels were executed—and the colony passed a law making it illegal to teach slaves to read.

Another African-American leader, the minister Denmark Vesey, planned a general black uprising and the seizing of Charleston for mid-July 1822—but he never lived that long. A thousand slaves and four white men were involved

Epworth House (1717) in Beaufort

in the plan, and one of the slaves betrayed the plan to the authorities. Vesey and 34 others were hanged on July 2, and the state passed a law restricting the number of black people allowed to gather at one time. Since Vesey had been a free man, the state also made it nearly impossible for slaves to purchase their freedom.

White citizens of South Carolina were also rebellious. They strongly supported slavery and feared that when President Abraham Lincoln was elected, slavery would become illegal. So in 1860, they were the first state to secede from the Union. And on April 12, 1861, South Carolinians fired the first shot of the Civil War on Fort Sumter in Charleston Harbor.

TEXTILES AND TOURISM

South Carolina takes second place only to North Carolina as a producer of textiles. Wool, rayon, nylon, orlon—and cotton from homegrown plants—are all produced in this state. In recent years, however, industry has grown to include the manufacture of chemicals, plastics, and rubber. BMW, the German auto maker, has one of its largest plants here.

South Carolina also depends on tourism, particularly to beautiful, historic Charleston, and in the resort areas of Hilton Head Island and Myrtle Beach. Tobacco, soybeans, corn, peaches, and lumber are also major products, as well as furniture made from local wood.

South Dakota

The Basics

POPULATION: 754,844
46th most populous state
AREA: 77,121 square miles
17th largest state
STATE CAPITAL: Pierre
STATE BIRD: Ring-necked pheasant
STATE FLOWER: American pasqueflower
STATE TREE: Black Hills spruce
NICKNAMES: The Sunshine State, the Coyote State, the Artesian State
STATE MOTTO: Under God the People Rule
STATE ANIMAL: Coyote
STATE FISH: Walleye
STATE INSECT: Honeybee
STATE GRASS: Western wheat grass
STATE MINERAL: Rose quartz
STATE STONE: Fairborn agate
STATE FOSSIL: Triceratops
STATE GEM: Fairburn agate
STATE COLORS: Blue and gold
STATE GREETING: *"How Kola"* (Souix greeting that means "Hello, friend."
STATE SONG: "Hail! South Dakota," words and music by Deecort Hammitt
STATE LANDMARKS: Badlands National Park; Black Hills National Forest (shared with Wyoming); Crazy Horse Memorial—a statue of the Dakota leader carved into a mountain; Jewel Cave National Monument—a cave of beautiful crystals; Mount Rushmore National Memorial—the heads of Washington, Jefferson, Lincoln, and Theodore Roosevelt carved into a mountain; Custer State Park, where the bison still roam

South Dakota is a land rich in both nature and culture. It has some of the most extraordinary geographical features in the United States. And it has a rich heritage of Indian nations who still speak their languages, practice their religion, and keep their traditions alive.

THE BADLANDS AND THE BLACK HILLS South Dakota is a flat prairie state. To the southwest lie the Badlands—colored rocks in strange shapes, the result of millions of years of the earth's erosion. To the west are the Black Hills, sacred to the Dakota people and prized by other Americans for their rich stores of gold and oil. Most of the rest of South Dakota is either farmland or grazing land that supports huge ranches of cattle and sheep. The geographic center of the United States is near the small South Dakota town of Castle Rock.

Millions of years of erosion have produced the spectacular landscape of Badlands National Park.

INDIAN WARS, PAST AND PRESENT For thousands of years the region now known as South Dakota was inhabited by the Dakota, a vast nation including many different peoples, among them the Oglala, the Lakota, and the Teton. Dakota means "friend" or "ally." Ojibwa, however, referred to the nation as Sioux from an insult meaning Snake People. The name became common among other Native Americans.

The first Europeans came to South Dakota in 1743. French explorers Louis-Joseph and Francois Verendrye were looking for a route to the Pacific. French fur traders came soon after. President Thomas Jefferson bought the state as part of the Louisiana Purchase in 1803, and in 1804-1806 Lewis and Clark explored the area with the help of their translator and guide, the Shoshone Indian Sacagawea. (Although Sacagawea's final resting place is unknown, there is a monument in Mobridge claiming that "Sakakawea" died there.)

Gradually farmers and ranchers began to settle the land that the Dakota still regarded as their nation. U.S. Army troops moved in, so that the first permanent settlement was Fort Pierre (later it became Pierre, South Dakota's capital city).

After the Civil War the newly reunited United States was tired of fighting. The U.S. and Dakota made peace with an 1868 treaty that placed the region

State Capitol in Pierre

under Indian rule. Then, in 1874 gold was discovered in the Black Hills and U.S. troops again tried to seize the land. The Sioux fought back but were finally defeated after the 1890 uprising at Wounded Knee. They were relocated onto reservations throughout the state, where many Sioux continue to live today.

The Sioux people, however, have never forgotten the many injustices of the United States government. Many are still working through the United Nations and the U.S. courts to win recognition for the 1868 treaty. Others began a lawsuit in the U.S. Court system in 1922, trying to set economic compensation. Demonstrations erupted in the 1970s, including a second uprising at Wounded Knee. In 1979, $105 million was awarded as compensation for lost land, but many issues have been left unaddressed. Indian political activity continues today for treaty rights as well as for preserving the Dakota language and culture.

DANCE HALLS ON THE PRAIRIE If you visit South Dakota today you can still see the traces of this state's Wild West heritage. In Deadwood, for example, Main Street is lined with replicas of the saloons and dance halls that made this gold rush boomtown famous throughout the 1870s. Here Wild Bill Hickock was shot during a poker game. Here, too, "Poker Alice" Tubbs—who gambled her way across the mining camps of the West—used to smoke her big cigars while winning thousands of dollars at cards.

Another famous South Dakota landmark can be found in De Smet. This town is the original "little town on the prairie" featured in six of the Laura Ingalls Wilder series. Laura's parents were the first white family to settle in the area, in 1879, and you can still visit some of the houses where the Ingalls lived.

RICHES ON AND UNDER THE EARTH Before the Europeans arrived, the Plains Indians of South Dakota survived by killing the buffalo and bison that abounded in the region. When the railroads wanted to move into the state in the 1870s, they hired hunters like

Sioux Indians at Sitting Bull Crystal Cave

"Buffalo Bill" Cody to kill the buffalo so that South Dakota became a land of farms and ranches. Cattle and sheep are still important products in South Dakota today. The state also produces wheat, corn, and other grains.

South Dakota is primarily an agricultural, rural state. Most of its manufacturing is food processing, in very small factories with fewer than 50 workers. However, tourism, and, recently, telemarketing are also important industries.

Fascinating Facts

MOUNT RUSHMORE FACT:
• The largest sculptures in the world are these presidents' heads. They average 60 feet tall—six stories—and Lincoln's mouth is 22 feet wide.

FAMOUS SOUTH DAKOTANS:
• Crazy Horse, leader of the Oglala Sioux nation. In 1876 he and fellow leaders Sitting Bull and Gall defeated General George Custer at the Battle of Little Bighorn, but eventually had to surrender. He was stabbed to death trying to escape from prison in 1877.
• Sitting Bull, another Dakota leader. He and his followers fled to Canada after defeating Custer. Later he appeared in Buffalo Bill's Wild West Show and was killed while allegedly resisting arrest in 1890.
• Calamity Jane, a frontierswoman whose real name was Martha Jane Cannary. She got her name by saying that to offend her was to "court calamity" (ask for a disaster).
• Wild Bill Hickok (James Butler Hickok), American frontier marshal who fought outlaws in Kansas.
• Senator George McGovern, the 1972 Democratic Presidential candidate.

DID YOU KNOW THAT... South Dakota was once home to tiny three-toed horses and saber-toothed tigers. Their fossilized bones were discovered in the White River Badlands and can now be seen in museums around the world. Scientists also think the ancient camel originated here.

SOUTH DAKOTA IS TOPS IN...
• geese
• gold mines—the largest working gold mine in the Americas is the Homestake Mine in Lead (rhymes with "fed"), South Dakota. It has produced more gold than any other single mine in the world.

DID YOU KNOW THAT... South Dakota and North Dakota are the only two states to enter the Union on the same day.

IT USED TO BE ILLEGAL IN SOUTH DAKOTA:
• for an 80-year-old woman to stop in the street to talk to a young married man.

Tennessee

The Basics

POPULATION: 5,689,283
16th most populous state
AREA: 42,146 square miles
36th largest state
STATE CAPITAL: Nashville
STATE BIRD: Mockingbird
STATE FLOWER: Iris
STATE WILDFLOWER: Passionflower
STATE TREE: Tulip poplar
NICKNAMES: The Volunteer State, Big Bend State, Mother of Southwestern Statesmen, Hog State, Hominy State
STATE MOTTO: Agriculture and Commerce
STATE WILD ANIMAL: Raccoon
STATE INSECTS: Firefly, ladybug
STATE ROCK: Limestone
STATE GEM: Tennessee pearl
STATE RAILROAD MUSEUM: Tennessee Valley Railroad Museum
STATE FINE ART: Porcelain painting
STATE FOLK DANCE: Square dance
STATE SONGS: "My Homeland, Tennessee," words and music by Nell Grayson Taylor and Roy Lamont; "When It's Iris Time in Tennessee," words and music by Willa Mae Waid; "My Tennessee," words and music by Francis Hannah Traum; "The Tennesee Waltz," words and music by Redd Stewart and Pee Wee King; "Rocky Top," words and music by Boudleaux and Felice Bryant
STATE POEM: "Oh Tennessee, My Tennessee," by Admiral William Lawrence
STATE LANDMARKS: The Hermitage, east of Nashville—home of President Andrew Jackson; Home of President James K. Polk, Columbia; Home and Tailor Shop of President Andrew Johnson, Greenville
STATE NATIONAL PARKS: Great Smoky Mountains National Park, near Gatlinburg; Chickamauga-Chattanooga military park

When you think Tennessee, think music. The Grand Ole Opry in Nashville; Beale Street in Memphis, birthplace of the blues; Memphis's Sun Studio, birthplace of rock and roll, where Elvis Presley, Jerry Lee Lewis, B.B. King, and Roy Orbison launched their careers—these historic sites contribute to a living Tennessee heritage of American music.

THREE STARS—THREE STATES The three stars on Tennessee's flag refer to the three parts of the state. In east Tennessee are the Great Smoky Mountains, with hills so steep that farmers have to harvest their crops on sleds. Here, too, is the Tennessee River Valley, between the Blue Ridge and Cumberland Mountains. East Tennessee's Chattanooga is located at the meeting point of three ancient Indian trails. The city's "Blue Goose Hollow" is the birthplace of

Elvis Presley, rock star (1935-1977)

blues singer Bessie Smith. As a little girl, she sang outside her broken-down shack, until she was discovered in 1912 by the great Ma Rainey.

Central Tennessee is the land of the Cumberland foothills, a rolling, hilly country where sheep, cattle, and horses graze. This is the "bluegrass basin" and the home of the famous Tennessee walking horse. In central Tennessee is Nashville, where the longest-running radio show in the country is still broadcast live each week from the Grand Ole Opry.

West Tennessee is bounded by the Tennessee and Mississippi Rivers. Its level, fertile land is planted with cotton fields. Memphis, the state's largest city, looks out over the Mississippi.

Near Memphis you can visit the Chucalissa Archaeological Museum, a reconstruction of a Native American village that stood on the banks of the Mississippi from 1000 to 1500. At the C.H. Nash Museum, you can see contemporary Choctaw craftspeople making jewelry, weapons, and pottery.

STRUGGLES OF A STATE Tennessee had to struggle more than most to become a state. In 1663 it was part of the Carolina colony. But in 1772 settlers on the Watauga River formed the Watauga Association to be free of the British Royal Colony and create "a homespun government." Nonetheless, in 1777, they were annexed as North Carolina's Washington County.

Tennessee's patriots would not give up. In 1784 the pioneers between the mountains and the Mississippi formed the State of Franklin (named for Ben

Tennessee walking horse

Franklin) and applied to the Continental Congress for entry into the Union. Neither the Congress nor North Carolina would recognize the "Frank-linites," but they had their own governor and legislature until 1788 when they joined North Carolina once again. In 1789 North Carolina ceded the land to the federal government, which created the "Territory of the United States South of the Ohio River." Finally, in 1796, Tennessee had enough people to become a state.

Unlike most other Southern states, Tennessee was sharply divided on the issue of slavery. It was the last state to secede from the Union in 1861, largely because East Tennessee was antislavery and pro-Union. During the Civil War some 186,000 men from Tennessee signed up as Confederate soldiers—but over 30,000 fought for the Union. Tennessee was the only state to free slaves by popular vote, on February 25, 1865, and it was the first state to rejoin the Union in 1866.

DEATH OF A LEADER In February 1968 the Memphis garbage collectors—almost all African American—had had enough. They refused to continue working for low pay, in unsafe conditions, and subject to racial insults from white supervisors. But Memphis city government refused to budge. The strike had gone on for weeks when civil rights leader Martin Luther King, Jr., was invited down to help. On April 3, King marched with the strikers, wearing a badge with the slogan of the strike: "I am a man." That night he spoke to cheering crowds. The next day he was assassinated by James Earl Ray while standing on the balcony of the Lorraine Motel. Riots broke out nationwide after his death. The motel was turned into a museum to honor Dr. King.

SOUVENIR PROGRAM

THE GRAND OLE OPRY
THE MOTHER CHURCH OF COUNTRY MUSIC

COTTON AND COUNTRY MUSIC For years, Tennessee was a major cotton state. Gradually, though, the soil wore out, and floods washed away the topsoil. Tennessee's economy suffered. Then, in 1933, the Tennessee Valley Authority, a government agency, built dams throughout the valley, bringing hydroelectric power and economic revitalization to the region. Now Tennessee has a growing industrial sector, manufacturing chemicals and machinery. Cottonseed oil is made in Memphis, where cotton is still traded. Soybeans, wheat, and tobacco have become more important crops, however. Tourism is another key industry, as is music recording and publishing.

Fascinating Facts

HOW TENNESSEE GOT ITS NAME: The Cherokee Indians called two villages on what is now the Little Tennessee River *Tanasi*. No one now knows what the word means, but it was used to name both the river and the region.

HOW TENNESSEE GOT ITS NICKNAMES: Tennessee volunteer troops fought bravely under Tennessee native Andrew Jackson in the Battle of New Orleans in the War of 1812—so the state became "The Volunteer State." "The Big Bend State" refers to the Tennessee River; "the Mother of Southwestern Statesmen" refers to the two American presidents born there.

THEY LIVED IN TENNESSEE:
• Andrew Jackson (1767-1845), 7th President
• Andrew Johnson (1808-1875), 17th President

DAVY CROCKETT:
• born in Great Smoky Mountains, 1786
• soldier and Indian scout
• elected to Congress three times
• motto: "Be sure you're right, then go ahead."

DID YOU KNOW THAT... The state's biggest lake, Reelfoot, near Tiptonville, was formed by an earthquake in 1811.

TENNESSEE HAS THE WORLD'S LARGEST:
• cotton market—Memphis
• underground lake—the Lost Sea, in Craighead Cavern

TENNESSEE IS TOPS IN:
• U.S. alumimun production
• greatest variety of birds in the U.S.

IT USED TO BE ILLEGAL IN TENNESSEE:
• for a motorist to drive unless he or she had warned the public one week in advance with a notice in the newspapers
• to take a fish off another person's hook

Texas

The Alamo

The Basics

POPULATION: 20,851,820
2nd most populous state
AREA: 268,601 square miles
2nd largest state
STATE CAPITAL: Austin
STATE BIRD: Mockingbird
STATE FLOWER: Bluebonnet
STATE TREE: Pecan
NICKNAMES: The Lone Star State, the Beef State, the Banner State
STATE MOTTO: Friendship
SPORTS TEAMS: Houston Astros, Texas Rangers, baseball; Dallas Cowboys, Houston Oilers, football; Dallas Mavericks, Houston Rockets, San Antonio Spurs, basketball
STATE DISH: Chili
STATE GEM: Topaz
STATE GRASS: Sideoats grama
STATE STONE: Petrified pinewood
STATE SONG: "Texas, Our Texas," words and music by William J. Marsh and Gladys Yoakum Wright
STATE LANDMARK: Alamo
NATIONAL PARKS: Big Bend, near Alpine; Guadalupe Mountains, near El Paso; Padre Island National Seashore, near Corpus Christi—untouched since Indian times; Aransas National Wildlife Refuge, near Tivoli—winter ground of whooping cranes
STATE PLEDGE OF ALLEGIANCE: "Honor the Texas Flag; I pledge allegiance to thee, Texas, one and indivisible."
TEXAS FESTIVALS: Goat Cookoff and Goat Roping, Sonora (May); Great Mosquito Festival, Brazosport (July); Rattlesnake Roundup, Big Spring (March)

When you think Texas, think BIG! You could fit 220 Rhode Islands into Texas, which is second only to Alaska in size. Texas is so big that it has different climates—subtropical along the Gulf Coast, cold as an Illinois winter up north. In fact, Texas is so big, it's the only state with permission to turn itself into five states if its people choose!

FROM BEAUMONT TO EL PASO Eastern Texas is more like the South than the West: piney woods, rolling hills, and vast fields of cotton. In this region is Beaumont, home of the Babe Didrikson Memorial Museum. Didrikson (later Zaharias), a Beaumont native, was a 1932 Olympic Gold medalist who became one of the world's outstanding golfers. Although she died in 1956 of cancer, at age 45, she remains an inspiration to women athletes.

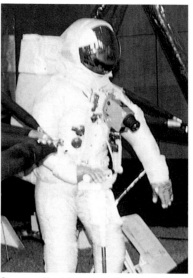

Spacesuit at Johnson Space Center

Houston is in the fertile crescent of the Gulf Coast plain, watered by many rivers and by complex irrigation systems. Here, grapefruit, pecans, and peanuts grow. Houston is Texas's largest city. Its mix of new buildings and boarded-up homes reflects the boom and then the bust in the 1980s oil market. Houston is also known for its famous covered Astrodome and for NASA's Johnson Space Center.

Farther northwest is hill country, which turns into the Great Plains, a deserted, windswept area. And west of the Pecos River, all the way to El Paso, is desert, marked by tumbleweed and sagebrush.

The famous cities Dallas and Fort Worth are in northeast Texas. Dallas is in the heart of oil and cotton country. It's glitzy and ritzy, although folks tend to go to bed early and go to church on Sunday. Fort Worth is more down-to-earth, though Dallasites call it a "cow town." It's true that Fort Worth is Texas's cattle capital, with an Old West history second to none. Just southeast of here was the hideout of Butch Cassidy (Robert Leroy Parker) and the Sundance Kid (Harry Longbaugh). The two used to come into the rowdy section of Fort Worth, known as "Hell's Half Acre."

If you want to see rural Texas, though, you'd better visit Big Bend National Park, where millions of years of erosion have carved out deep canyons and weird rock formations. Here are black bears, mountain lions, coyotes, javelinas, and jackrabbits, along with over 430 species of birds. Nearby is the Rio Grande, the

Congresswoman Barbara Jordan (1936-1995)

"big river" that many see as the heart of Texas. For 800 miles this river forms the border between the United States and Mexico.

REMEMBER THE ALAMO This southwestern state has been shaped by its Wild West heritage, and by its mix of Chicano, African-American, and Anglo cultures. First to enter the state were the Spanish explorers—Fernando Vasquez de Coronado, Hernando de Soto, and others—who were looking for the golden cities they mistakenly believed had been built here. The first permanent European settlement was at Ysleta, in 1682. By 1731 the Spanish had erected dozens of missions and forts. They wanted to subdue the Indians militarily, and they wanted to convert them to Christianity.

In 1821 Mexico won its own independence from Spain. Although there were already U.S. citizens living in Texas, Mexico claimed the land and even tried to stop immigration in 1830, fearing that too many Anglos would change the area's culture and political loyalties. In fact, American colonists did revolt. In the Texas Revolution of 1835, they took San Antonio. In 1836, 187 Texas volunteers holed up in a fort known as the Alamo, resisting for 13 days the siege of Mexico's dictator, Santa Anna. Everyone at the Alamo was killed, including Davy Crockett and Jim Bowie (five survivors were killed as prisoners later). But Texas leader Sam Houston rallied his troops with the cry, "Remember the Alamo!" and went on to win independence for Texas.

Tigua Indian drummer in El Paso

From 1836 to 1845 Texas was its own independent Republic. During this time, it drove the Cherokee people into Mexico and expelled other native peoples. Finally Texas became part of the United States.

Then, in 1861, states that supported slavery seceded from the Union. Texas seceded too and joined the Confederacy. Not until 1870 was Texas to belong to the United States, once and for all.

BLACK GOLD In 1901 the famous Spindletop gusher, near Beaumont, exploded through the earth. This amazing oil well produced a record 100,000 barrels of petroleum each day. The oil industry has been good to Texas, creating a group of millionaires and a boom economy. Natural gas, coal, salt, sulfur, and other minerals are also important to Texas. Cotton is the state's main cash crop. Cattle are another key product. In 1902 the Chicago packing companies of Swift and Armour set up stockyards in Fort Worth—and shipped the meat in brand-new refrigerator cars.

The space program has brought new industry to Texas. The Johnson Space Center in Houston monitors and controls U.S. manned space flights. Aerospace equipment is manufactured in Dallas.

Fascinating Facts

HOW TEXAS GOT ITS NAME: The Caddo Indian word *Texas* or *Teysha* means "Hello, friend." The name is also spelled *Texias, Tejas,* and *Teysas.*

DID YOU KNOW THAT... Texas has had six national flags flying over it: those of Spain, France, Mexico, the Republic of Texas, the Confederacy, and the United States. (That's where the original Six Flags amusement park got its name!)

TEXAS HALLS OF FAME:
• National Cowgirl Hall of Fame, Hereford
• Texas Rangers Hall of Fame, Waco

TEXAS FIRST:
• First woman to manage a circus—Mollie Bailey, Mollie A. Bailey Show—late 1800s

TEXAS IS TOPS IN:
• amount of farmland farmed
• sheep and cattle
• rice, cotton, spinach
• oil (almost half of U.S. production)
• natural gas (almost half of U.S. production)
• salt, magnesium, sulfur, helium
• asphalt
• kinds of wildflowers and reptiles
• drive-in theaters

TEXAS HAS THE BIGGEST:
• ranch—King Ranch—bigger than Rhode Island!
• state capitol building
• state fair—Dallas—October
• rose-growing center—near Tyler
• battle monument—Houston
• urban bat colony—Austin

TEXAS HAD THE NATION'S MOST:
• rainfall—43 inches at Alvin, July 25-26, 1979

PRESIDENTS BORN IN TEXAS:
• Dwight D. Eisenhower (1890-1969), 34th President
• Lyndon B. Johnson (1908-1973), 36th President

Utah

The Basics

POPULATION: 2,233,169
34th most populous state
AREA: 84,904 square miles
13th largest state
STATE CAPITAL: Salt Lake City
STATE BIRD: California gull
STATE FLOWER: Sego lily
STATE TREE: Blue spruce (also called Colorado blue spruce, balsam, Colorado spruce, Prickly spruce, White spruce, Silver spruce, Parry's spruce)
NICKNAMES: The Beehive State, the Mormon State, the Land of the Saints, the Salt Lake State
STATE MOTTO: Industry
SPORTS TEAM: Utah Jazz, basketball
STATE EMBLEM: Beehive
STATE ANIMAL: Elk
STATE FISH: Rainbow trout
STATE INSECT: Honeybee
STATE GEM: Topaz
STATE SONG: "Utah, We Love Thee," words and music by Evan Stephens
STATE LANDMARK: Golden Spike National Historic Site, Promontory—where railroad tracks from east and west met in 1869
NATIONAL PARKS: Bryce Canyon, Zion, Arches, Canyonlands, Capitol Reefs
NATIONAL MONUMENTS: Dinosaur National Monument, Jensen; Timpanogos Cave, American Fork; Natural Bridges National Monument, Lake Power
STATE PARKS: Goblin Valley State Park, Green River—wind-eroded sandstone "goblins"; This Is The Place State Park, Salt Lake City, recreates 1850s township of early Mormons
STATE FESTIVAL: Deseret Vagabond Days, Kanab (July)

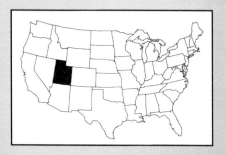

Bryce Canyon

45th state to enter the Union, January 4, 1896

Utah has a beauty unlike that of any other state. Where else could you find a desert with seagulls and pelicans, or a collection of weird, brilliantly colored sandstone shapes rising out of the dusty ground? This western, rural, Rocky Mountains state is known for its luxury ski resorts and for the influence of its Mormon founders.

ROCKY MOUNTAIN DESERT Southern Utah is famous for the spectacular red deserts of the Colorado Plateau, along with strangely colored canyons, bizarrely shaped rock formations, and petrified forests. The landscape has been etched by Ice Age glaciers and the erosion from flash floods.

There are many dinosaur fossils at Dinosaur National Monument near Vernal.

In northeastern Utah are the Wasatch and Uinta Mountains. And to the west is the Great Salt Lake Desert, with the famous lake that was once an inland sea. Water flows into the lake but has nowhere to drain. So it just evaporates, leaving salt and minerals behind.

Utah was once home to many native peoples. An 83-room Anasazi village is now the site of Anasazi State Park in southern Utah. The dwellings were probably built between A.D. 1129 and 1169 by people from the Kayenta Anasazi region of northeastern Arizona. Anasazi and Fremont rock art can also be seen in several Utah state parks.

THIS IS THE PLACE So said Mormon leader Brigham Young, who with a party of 143 men and three women, arrived at what is now Salt Lake City in 1847. The Mormons had left their prosperous communities in Ohio, Missouri, and Illinois for a place where they would be left alone to practice their religion. Young chose Utah because he thought no one else would want it.

Of course, many native peoples lived in Utah. When Young arrived, he found Paiutes, Shoshones, Gosiute, and Ute. Navajo arrived in the 1860s. But by 1868 Indians had been forced off their land onto reservations.

Meanwhile, the Mormons were facing the difficult task of growing food in the hot, dry climate. They developed a complex system of irrigation channels that made the desert bloom and led Utah to be known as "the cradle of American irrigation." Mormons feared starvation when a swarm of crickets threatened to eat the entire crop of 1847—but in 1848 a flock of seagulls miraculously appeared to eat the insects and save the crops. That's why Utah now has the world's only monument to a bird.

In 1849 thousands of prospectors were heading to California for the gold rush. Mormons prospered as they supplied these pioneers on their journey. From 1855 to 1860, 8,000 Mormons arrived in Utah from Europe. Over 3,000 had walked from the railroad station in Iowa to Salt Lake City, pushing their possessions on handcarts. They founded towns in Utah, Idaho, and Nevada—including Las Vegas!

State Capitol, Salt Lake City

Utah kept applying for statehood, but the Mormon practice of polygamy—one husband having many wives—was frowned on by Congress. In 1857, 2,500 Army troops entered the state to install a governor to replace Brigham Young. Mormons responded with the Utah War, killing 120 emigrants on their way to California. In 1858, the area won amnesty—but not statehood. In the 1880s and 1890s, over 1,000 Mormons were fined or imprisoned as the government continued to oppose polygamy. Finally Mormons themselves outlawed this practice, and after 46 years of being a territory, Utah's seventh application for statehood was accepted.

In the twentieth century the Mormons—officially, the Church of Jesus Christ of Latter-Day Saints—refused to ordain African Americans as priests. Yet at least three black pioneers were among Brigham Young's original party, and several black converts came to the area over the years. At least one African-American man, Elijah Abel, served as a priest until his death in 1884. In 1978 Joseph Freeman, Jr. was ordained as the first modern African-American Mormon priest.

The Mormon Tabernacle

TABERNACLES AND BEEHIVES Visitors to Salt Lake City can see many historical and religious monuments that are still in use today: the Salt Lake Tabernacle, home of the Mormon Tabernacle Choir; the six-spired Salt Lake Temple; and the Beehive House, where Brigham Young lived with his many wives and children. Next door was Lion House, where another seven wives resided. (The rest were dispersed around the state.) In the same neighborhood was the home of Ann Eliza Webb Young, who made history in 1873 by moving out of her cottage into a hotel and demanding a divorce from Young. She became a nationwide crusader against polygamy.

RICHES UNDER THE EARTH Copper and coal are key Utah products, as well as gold, silver, lead, zinc, uranium, magnesium, molybdenum, and petroleum. Soft western woods—fir, pine, and spruce—support Utah's timber and paper industries. Manufacturing in the state is primarily making metals and food processing. There is some high-tech industry near Provo, and the West's largest steel plant is near that town. Tourism, centered in the ski resort at Park City, is also an important Utah industry.

Vermont

The Basics

POPULATION: 608,827
49th most populous state
AREA: 9,615 square miles
45th largest state
STATE CAPITAL: Montpelier
STATE BIRD: Hermit thrush
STATE FLOWER: Red clover
STATE TREE: Sugar maple (also called Hard maple, Rock maple, Black maple)
NICKNAMES: The Green Mountain State
STATE MOTTO: Freedom and Unity
STATE ANIMAL: Morgan horse
STATE COLD-WATER FISH: Brook trout
STATE WARM-WATER FISH: Walleye pike
STATE INSECT: Honeybee
STATE SOIL: Tunbridge soil series
STATE DRINK: Milk
STATE SONG: "Hail, Vermont!" words and music by Josephine Hovey Perry
STATE LANDMARKS: Calvin Coolidge Historic Site, Plymouth Notch; Chester Alan Arthur Historic Site, near Fairfield
NATIONAL PARK: Green Mountain National Forest
HISTORIC PARKS: Candle Mill Village, Arlington; Shelburne Museum, Shelburne—37 early American buildings and a side-wheeler steamship; Peter Matteson Tavern, Shaftsbury—200-year-old stagecoach tavern; Green Mountain Railroad, Bellows Falls—26-mile scenic train ride; Hyde log cabin, built in 1738, on Grand Isle
STATE FESTIVALS: Bay Day, St. Albans (July 4 weekend); Wurstfest, Stratton Mountain (Labor Day weekend); Vermont Maple Festival, Franklin County (April)

Vermont

Nature-lovers have many reasons to enjoy Vermont. This rural state is famous for its brilliant fall foliage, its green mountains, its miles of ski trails, and its 400 lakes.

GREEN MOUNTAINS AND POETRY Vermont is the most sparsely populated state east of the Mississippi. Only 23 percent of its people live in cities. It's our most rural state, with the smallest state capital. Although Vermont is the only New England state with no seacoast, it is bounded by two major bodies of water—Lake Champlain and the Connecticut River.

The Green Mountains—part of the Appalachians—run down the state from Canada to Massachusetts. These mountains are among the oldest in the nation, nearly half a billion years old. A few hundred million years ago the tallest mountain, Mt. Mansfield, was 12,000 feet high. Now, thanks to erosion, it's only 4,393 feet.

County courthouse in Newfane

Although Vermont's cities are small, they are rich in history and culture. Bennington, for example, is the home of Bennington College and was once the home of the abolitionist William Lloyd Garrison. Garrison published his famous newspaper, *The Liberator*, in Massachusetts, but he got his start in Vermont publishing *The Journal of the Time,* which you can see in the Bennington Museum.

Middlebury is the site of Middlebury College as well as the former home of poet laureate Robert Frost, who spent 23 summers at his farm in the area. Visitors can walk along the Robert Frost Wayside Trail, reading bits of Frost's nature poetry posted along the way. Vermont seems to attract famous writers. Russian Nobel Prize-winning novelist Alexander Solzhenitsyn settled there after emigrating from the Soviet Union in the 1970s. He returned to his native land only after the fall of Communism. Other well-known Vermont cities include Burlington, Rutland, Barre, and the famous ski resort of Stowe.

THE GREEN MOUNTAIN BOYS When French explorer Samuel de Champlain first set foot in Vermont in 1609, it was peopled by the Abenaki, Mohican, Pennacook, and Iroquois. Champlain claimed the land for France and named Lake Champlain after himself.

Over one hundred years later, British soldiers established the first permanent

European settlement at Fort Drummer (now Brattleboro). Despite attacks from the French and the Indians, the English retained control of the territory. However, two American colonies both claimed Vermont's land. In 1741 England's King George II granted the land to New Hampshire, but in 1764 King George III granted much the same land to New York. In 1770 Vermonter Ethan Allen founded the Green Mountain Boys to chase New York settlers away. In May 1775 he and his "boys" won further fame by taking Fort Ticonderoga from the British during the Revolutionary War.

Poultney Historical Society

When the 13 colonies signed the Declaration of Independence in 1776, Vermont was not among them because neither New York nor New Hampshire considered it a separate colony. In 1777, however, Vermont declared its own independence from the British as a separate nation called New Connecticut. Finally, in 1790, the competing land claims were resolved. In 1791 Vermont became the first state *after* the original 13 colonies to join the Union.

A DEMOCRATIC TRADITION   From the beginning, Vermont stood for democracy and equal rights for all. In 1777 its "national" constitution declared that slavery was illegal—the first North American government to do so. Moreover, Vermont was the first government to call for "universal suffrage"—

18th century round barn in Irasburg

voting rights for all. (Up to this time, states would only permit property owners to vote.) Of course, "universal" suffrage did not include voting rights for Indians, African Americans, or women, but the measure was quite radical for its time.

The basic unit of Vermont government is the town meeting. When an important issue comes up, all the townspeople assemble at town hall, discuss the issue, and come to a decision together. The New England town meeting is a democratic ideal that has inspired people around the world.

MARBLE AND MAPLE SYRUP   Although Vermont's soil is poor, farming is more important here than in other New England states. Dairy farms and apple orchards are most suitable for the state's hilly land. Of course, Vermont's most famous agricultural product is maple syrup.

Vermont's lush forests cover 70 percent of the state, providing lumber and supporting wood-processing and paper industries as well. Vermont's quarries have made it a leader in granite, marble, slate, talc, and asbestos. (You can see Vermont granite in the United Nations building in New York.) The state has many factories near its small cities, making tools, machinery, electronic equipment, measuring instruments, stuffed toys, and quilts. Rutland and St. Johnsbury make scales, while Brattleboro is famous for making organ pipes.

Fascinating Facts

HOW VERMONT GOT ITS NAME: In 1647 Samuel de Champlain named the region *Verd Mont*, or "Green Mountain." *Verd* is the old spelling of the French word for green.) The name took its present form in 1777, when the area was an independent nation, New Connecticut. Vermont became the official name in 1790.

DID YOU KNOW THAT: The people of Vermont were so enraged at the Nazis that in 1941 they declared war on Germany—two months before the United States did!

PRESIDENTS BORN IN VERMONT:
• Chester Alan Arthur (1829-1886), 21st President
• Calvin Coolidge (1872-1933), 30th President

VERMONT HAS THE WORLD'S LARGEST:
• granite quarry, near Barre

VERMONT HAD THE NATION'S FIRST:
• marble quarry—Manchester—1785
• canal—Bellows Falls—1802
• ski tow—Woodstock—1933
• patent issued in the United States

VERMONT IS TOPS IN:
• maple syrup

VERMONT HAS THE ONLY:
• breed of horse produced in the U.S., the Morgan horse, developed in the late 1700s by schoolteacher Justin Morgan

DID YOU KNOW THAT... British author Rudyard Kipling wrote *The Jungle Book* and *Captains Courageous* in Brattleboro, where he lived for four years.

DID YOU KNOW THAT... At the Haskell Opera House at Derby Line, the audience sits in the U.S. but the singers are in Canada. Once, a U.S. police officer had to sit in the audience and watch a wanted criminal perform on stage.

IT USED TO BE ILLEGAL IN VERMONT:
• to paint a horse

Virginia

The Basics

POPULATION: 7,078,515
12th most populous state
AREA: 42,777 square miles
35th largest state
STATE CAPITAL: Richmond
STATE BIRD: Cardinal (also called Red bird, Kentucky cardinal)
STATE FLOWER: Dogwood flower
STATE TREE: Dogwood (also called Flowering dogwood, Boxwood, False box-dogwood and New England boxwood.
NICKNAMES: The Old Dominion, the Mother of Presidents, the Mother of States, the Mother of Statesmen, the Cavalier State
STATE MOTTO: *Sic semper tyrannis* (Latin for "Thus always to tyrants")
STATE DOG: American foxhound
STATE SHELL: Oyster shell
STATE DRINK: Milk
STATE SONG EMERITUS: "Carry Me Back to Old Virginia," words and music by James B. Bland
STATE LANDMARKS: Monticello, home of Thomas Jefferson; Mount Vernon, home of George Washington; Yorktown, where the English surrendered to George Washington; Robert E. Lee's birthplace, Stratford Hall, near Montross, and his grave at Lexington; Arlington National Cemetery
HISTORIC SITES: Jamestown, replicas of 1607 fort and ships; Williamsburg, replica of 200-year-old colonial village
NATIONAL PARK: Shenandoah
STATE FESTIVALS: Chili Cookoff, Roanoke (May); Pony Penning, Chincoteague (July); Pork, Peanut and Pine Festival, Surry (July); Virginia Poultry Festival, Harrisonburg (May)

If you had to pick just one state whose history was intertwined with the early history of the United States, that state would be Virginia. Four of the first five American presidents were born in Virginia. The decisive battle of the Revolutionary War was fought at Yorktown. The ending of the Civil War—Confederate General Robert E. Lee's surrender to Union commander Ulysses S. Grant—took place in the Virginia town of Appomattox. To tour Virginia is to take a tour of our nation's history.

FROM TIDEWATER TO THE APPALACHIANS
This rural mid-Atlantic state can be divided into three sections. Its eastern Atlantic coast is a low-lying area where several rivers—the Potomac, Rappahannock, York, and James—empty into the Chesapeake Bay. This Tidewater region was once covered by ocean. Farther west, the central Piedmont region is a fertile land of rolling hills. And still farther west are the Appalachian mountains, the Blue Ridge Range, and the Shenandoah Valley.

1791 lighthouse at Cape Henry

In Tidewater is the so-called Historic Triangle: Williamsburg, Jamestown, and Yorktown. All year long at Williamsburg, costumed interpreters and craftspeople re-create a colonial village, down to the authentic taverns serving foods of the times. Near Jamestown, the first permanent English settlement, you can see another living history re-creation, and in the harbor you can see replicas of the ships that first brought the colonists to America: the *Godspeed, Discovery,* and *Susan Constant.* At the Yorktown Victory Center you can see a re-created Continental Army encampment and a working tobacco farm.

In northern Virginia is the most visited house museum in the nation: Mount Vernon, the home of George Washington. In the Piedmont region is Monticello, Thomas Jefferson's estate, full of such Jeffersonian inventions as a two-pen contraption for copying letters as he wrote them. Just outside Washington, D.C. is the Arlington National Cemetery, final resting place of thousands of American soldiers. It is also the site of the Tomb of the Unknown Soldier and the eternal flame lit in memory of President John F. Kennedy.

POCAHONTAS AND JOHN SMITH Sir Walter Raleigh was the first European to colonize Virginia—which he named after his sovereign, Elizabeth, known as the "Virgin Queen." In 1607 the first English colonists established themselves at Jamestown, but they faced hard times in this unknown land. Pocahontas, daughter of the Indian emperor Powhatan, was only ten when the English arrived. She taught them how to grow tobacco, corn, and peanuts and helped to save the life of their leader, John Smith. Later she married another settler, John Rolfe, and went to England with him.

Tomb of the Unknown Soldier in Arlington Cemetery

TWO TRADITIONS Virginia is a land of both democratic and aristocratic traditions. In 1619, for example, Virginians formed the House of Burgesses, the first democratically elected legislature in the world. Yet in the same year, people in this southern state began to own slaves.

Throughout the Revolutionary years Virginia was a leader in the fight for independence. It was at the Virginia Convention of 1775 that Virginia politician Patrick Henry cried "Give me liberty, or give me death!" Virginia's Thomas Jefferson wrote the Declaration of Independence; the state's James Madison wrote the Constitution. Virginia's own bill of rights was the model for the national document. And of course, Virginia's George Washington first led American armies to victory and then became the nation's first president.

In 1861 Virginia became a leader of another nation: the Confederacy. Richmond was the Confederacy's final capital, while native son Robert E. Lee was the Confederacy's commander in chief.

African Americans in Virginia also followed two traditions: rebellion and compromise. Nat Turner, a Virginia slave, led an 1831 uprising in Southampton County that lasted for three days. While he and his 60 followers failed to end slavery, they did shatter the myth that slaves were happy with their lot. Another famous Virginian, Booker T. Washington, had a very different approach to improving the lives of African Americans. Washington was born into slavery on a tobacco farm near Roanoke. In the years after the Civil War he rose to become one of the most influential black politicians this country has ever known. Washington believed that African Americans should improve themselves by working as skilled laborers. That way, they could gradually acquire the money and respectability that would win them acceptance into American society. Washington's ideas were controversial among both black and white people of his time. A living history museum now marks his birthplace.

Robert E. Lee at age 33

SHIPYARDS AND DAIRY FARMS Manufacturing is a key part of Virginia's economy, mainly shipbuilding, although the state also produces paper, clothing, chemicals, light machinery, and processed stone. Dairy products, chickens, turkeys, and hogs are also important, as are tobacco, wheat, orchard fruits, peanuts, and fish from the Chesapeake Bay. Suburbs of Washington, D.C., are Virginia's most populated area, and a great deal of income comes into the state from people employed in our nation's capital.

Fascinating Facts

PRESIDENTS BORN IN VIRGINIA:
- George Washington (1732-1799), 1st President
- Thomas Jefferson (1743-1826), 3rd President
- James Madison (1751-1836), 4th President
- James Monroe (1758-1831), 5th President
- William Henry Harrison (1773-1841), 9th President
- John Tyler (1790-1850), 10th President
- Zachary Taylor (1784-1850), 12th President
- Woodrow Wilson (1856-1924), 28th President

OTHER FAMOUS PEOPLE BORN IN VIRGINIA:
- Explorer Meriwether Lewis, Albemarle County (1774-1809)
- Writer Willa Cather, Winchester (1873-1947)

VIRGINIA HAS THE WORLD'S LARGEST:
- naval station—Norfolk Naval Station
- Naval Air Station

VIRGINIA HAD THE NATION'S FIRST:
- manufacturing—a glass factory—1608
- democratically elected legislature—the House of Burgesses—1619
- canal—7 miles between Richmond and Westham—1790
- reaper—1831

VIRGINIA HAS THE NATION'S OLDEST CONTINUOUS:
- daily newspaper—the Alexandria *Gazette*
- sporting event—the annual jousting tournament near Staunton

DID YOU KNOW THAT...
All or part of Illinois, Indiana, Kentucky, Michigan, Minnesota, Ohio, West Virginia, and Wisconsin were once carved out of the original Virginia colony....Before the Revolutionary war, in Virginia you could pay your taxes in tobacco!

IT USED TO BE ILLEGAL IN VIRGINIA:
- to have a bathtub in the house

Washington

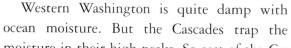

Mt. Rainier National Park

42nd state to enter the Union, November 11, 1889

The Basics

POPULATION: 5,894,121
15th most populous state

AREA: 71,302 square miles
18th largest state

STATE CAPITAL: Olympia

STATE BIRD: Willow goldfinch

STATE FLOWER: Pink rhododendron
(Coast rhododendron, Rhododendron)

STATE TREE: Western hemlock (West
coast hemlock, Pacific hemlock, Hemlock
spruce, California hemlock spruce,
Western hemlock fir, Prince Albert's fir,
Alaskan pine)

NICKNAMES: The Evergreen State, the
Chinook State

STATE MOTTO: *Alki* (an Indian word for
"By and by")

SPORTS TEAMS: Seattle Mariners,
baseball; Seattle Seahawks, football;
Seattle SuperSonics, basketball

STATE FISH: Steelhead trout

STATE GEM: Petrified wood

STATE DANCE: Square dance

STATE SONG: "Washington, My Home,"
words and music by Helen Davis

STATE LANDMARKS: Gingko Petrified
Forest, near Ephrata; Grand Coulee Dam

NATIONAL PARKS: Mount Rainier, near
Enumclaw; North Cascades, near
Bellingham; Olympic, near Port Angeles;
Columbia River National Scenic Area;
Dungeness National Wildlife Refuge

HISTORIC PARKS: Fort Vancouver
National Historic Site—1825 fur trading
post; Klondike Gold Rush National
Historical Park/Pioneer Park, Seattle

STATE PARK: Leadbetter Point State
Park, Ilwaco has over 100 species of birds.

Washington residents are particularly proud of their state's beauty: its rugged Alpine scenery, its glistening evergreen forests, and its sparkling lakes and rivers. Its largest city, Seattle, used to be a simple port town. However, in recent years it has become a sophisticated coastal city, particularly well-known for its elaborate coffee drinks. Its first gourmet coffee shop, Starbucks, opened in 1981. The 607-foot-high Space Needle has been a symbol of the city since it was constructed for the 1962 World's Fair.

WASHINGTON'S SPLIT PERSONALITY The Cascade Mountains run north to south, from Canada to Oregon, splitting Washington into two parts. West of the Cascades are coastal lowlands and evergreen forests. Northwest is the Olympic Peninsula, marked by the Olympic Mountains and the climate of a temperate rain forest. Further south is Puget Sound, the most populous part of the state and site of Washington's three principal cities: Seattle, Tacoma, and Olympia.

State Capitol at Olympia

Western Washington is quite damp with ocean moisture. But the Cascades trap the moisture in their high peaks. So east of the Cascades is a semi-desert region in which you can't see a tree for miles.

Washington is a favorite state of those who like to hunt, fish, and ski. The Columbia and Snake Rivers offer more than 40 types of fish. The Olympic Peninsula features the Hoh Rain Forest, the Sol Duc Hot Springs, and the spectacular views from Hurricane Ridge, a mile above sea level. An even more isolated spot is Long Beach Peninsula, where the Columbia River and the Pacific Ocean meet. Nearby is Oysterville, a town that prospered in 1854 when the shellfish abounded. Now the oysters have been fished to extinction and most townspeople have moved away, leaving their homes to be washed away by the tides. A small village still remains, though.

LOOKING FOR BOUNDARIES The borders of the Washington Territory changed several times between the first European explorers of the 1770s and Washington's entry into the Union in 1889. Both British explorer Captain George Vancouver and U.S. Captain Robert Gray tried to claim the land in 1792—while Cayuse, Colville, Nez Percé, Okanogan, Spokane, Yakima, Chinook, and Puyallup peoples were still living there.

Settlement was slow, as settlers feared attack by local native peoples. When gold was discovered in 1855, attempts were made to resettle Washington's western Indians but they bitterly resisted. Finally, in 1858 a confederacy of Yakima, Spokane, Coeur d'Alene, Nez Percé, and Palouse was defeated by federal troops and local militia. Washington's Indians were forced onto reservations.

Seattle skyline

Meanwhile, in 1848 the Oregon Territory had been formed, including Oregon, Washington, and parts of Idaho. In 1853 the Washington Territory was formed, leaving out Oregon but including parts of Idaho and Montana, and expanding in 1859 to Wyoming as well. This territory was to have been named the Territory of Columbia, after the river. But the U.S. already had a District of Columbia, so the name Washington was chosen, to honor the nation's first president. Finally, in 1863 Idaho Territory was formed, and Washington got its present boundaries.

GEORGE WASHINGTON AND GEORGE BUSH No, those names don't refer to two presidents. The George Washington Park in Centralia honors a former slave who escaped from Virginia, resisted the racial restrictions of slave-holding Missouri, and joined a wagon train on the Oregon Trail in 1850. Washington thrived in the lumber business and founded the town of Centerville, now called

Ferry on Puget Sound

Centralia. When he died in 1905 the town shut down for a day of mourning.

George Bush was born free but he, too, resented Missouri's racial restrictions. He came to the Oregon Territory in 1844—only to discover that African Americans were not allowed to own property there. He was so disgusted that he crossed into Washington, where he prospered as a farmer near Tumwater. Exhibits in the Henderson House Museum tell his story.

RICH RESOURCES Washington is blessed with abundant natural resources. But it has been a logging state for so many years now that environmentalists worry that the forests will become exhausted. Logging companies argue that if they cut down fewer trees, the economy will suffer. The argument continues—and so does the extensive logging.

Salmon, halibut, and other ocean fish are an important Washington resource. Seattle is one of the largest salmon markets in the world, selling fish from both Washington and Alaska. Farms in western Washington raise beef and dairy cattle, wheat, fruit, and vegetables.

Seattle's aircraft industry, particularly Boeing, has had financial challenges in recent years but a merger with Rockwell International bodes well for the area. And Microsoft, the computer software giant, has created many jobs in the state.

HOW WASHINGTON GOT ITS MOTTO:
When settlers landed at Alki Point—now Seattle—they called it "New York Alki." That meant that *Alki*—"by and by"—they hoped their town would someday be the New York of the West Coast.

WASHINGTON IS TOPS IN:
• apple production—world leader
• hops, rhubarb, edible peas, cherries
• vegetable seeds

WASHINGTON HAD THE FIRST:
• female symphony conductor in America, possibly in the world—Mary Davenport Engberg, who conducted the 85-member symphony orchestra in Bellingham in 1914
• Native American woman novelist, Mourning Dove, an Okanogan who wrote *Cogewea, the Half Breed* and *Coyote Stories*

THE SNOWIEST TOWN IN THE U.S.:
• Stampede Pass—431.9 inches/year

THE CLOUDIEST TOWN IN THE U.S.:
• Quillayute—241 cloudy days a year

DID YOU KNOW THAT... La Push is the westernmost town in the continental U.S. and Cape Alava the westernmost point.

HYDROELECTRIC FACTS:
• Washington furnishes 30 percent of our hydroelectric power.
• The Grand Coulee is the nation's largest concrete dam, completed in 1942.
• It has enough concrete to pave a four-lane highway from Seattle to New York.

THE LARGEST ORGANISM is a 1,500-acre fungus growing south of Mt. Adams.

IT USED TO BE ILLEGAL IN WASHINGTON:
• to hunt ducks from a rowboat unless you were sitting up and visible from the waist up

West Virginia

Coal miners are important to the state's economy   **35th state to enter the Union, June 20, 1863**

The Basics

POPULATION: 1,808,344
37th most populous state
AREA: 24,231 square miles
41st largest state
STATE CAPITAL: Charleston
STATE BIRD: Cardinal (Red bird, Kentucky cardinal)
STATE FLOWER: Big rhododendron
STATE TREE: Sugar maple (Hard maple, Rock maple, Black maple)
NICKNAMES: The Mountain State, the Switzerland of America, the Panhandle State
STATE MOTTO: *Montani Semper Liberi* (Latin for "Mountaineers are always free")
STATE ANIMAL: Black bear
STATE FISH: Brook trout
STATE FRUIT: Apple
STATE SONGS: "This Is My West Virginia," words and music by Iris Bell; "West Virginia, My Home Sweet Home," words and music by Julian G. Hearne; "The West Virginia Hills," words by David King, music by H.E. Engle
STATE LANDMARK: Harpers Ferry National Historical Park
NATIONAL PARK: Monongahela National Forest
HISTORIC PARKS: Beckley Exhibition Mine—with 1890s coal-car ride through mine; Cass Scenic Railroad—with old logging train ride to mountaintop; Watters Smith Memorial Park, near Clarksburg—200-year-old pioneer farm; West Virginia State Farm Museum, Point Pleasant
STATE FESTIVALS: Apple Butter Festival, Berkeley Springs (Columbus Day weekend); Webster Springs Wood-chopping Festival, Webster Springs (May)

West Virginia has given the nation two famous folk songs. "John Brown's Body" (whose tune was later used in "The Battle Hymn of the Republic") tells of the abolitionist who seized the arsenal at Harpers Ferry. "John Henry" describes the legendary railroad worker who died drilling a tunnel through a West Virginia mountain. Rugged individualism, mountainous terrain, and folk music still shape this historic state.

PANHANDLES AND PLATEAUS   West Virginia has the most irregular boundaries of any state in the Union. That's because it was created from another state—Virginia—without that state's consent. As a result, and also to resolve old boundary disputes, West Virginia has two panhandles, extending north and east. Most of the state is mountain country, dominated by the Appalachians. The Allegheny Plateau occupies the western two-thirds of the state, with the Appalachian Valley as the eastern third.

Most of West Virginia is too rocky for farming. The only level ground is bound in the valleys of the Ohio and Kanawha Rivers. So this rural state is highly industrial, relying on manufacturing and mining. Yet West Virginia has lovely unspoiled scenery, including 200 natural springs. One of them, Berkeley Springs, was George Washington's favorite vacation spot.

GRAVE CREEK MOUND: A LOST CIVILIZATION   The world's tallest burial mound is in West Virginia—the Grave Creek Mound on the bank of the Ohio River. The earthen mound is about 62 feet high and 240 feet in diameter. It was built by the Adena people over a hundred-year period, from 200 to 100 B.C. Originally the mound was surrounded by a moat some 910 feet long, 4 feet deep, and 40 feet wide. The earth taken from the moat was used to build the mound. Although the Adena people had neither wheels nor horses, they managed the amazing engineering feat of using three million bas-ketloads of earth to build a one-million-cubic-foot structure.

The Greenbriar Hotel

JOHN BROWN'S INSURRECTION John Brown was a white man who believed that black and white people were equal, and he hated slavery with a passion. By 1859 he was tired of trying to abolish slavery by legal means. He wanted to set off a revolt in which African-American slaves would rise up and end slavery by force. So on October 16, 1859, Brown and his team of 21 men—including five African Americans—seized the armory (weapons storehouse) at Harpers Ferry. Federal troops quickly moved to West Virginia (then still a part of Virginia) to put down the uprising. Instead of sparking a nationwide rebellion, Brown lost two of his sons and was later executed himself. Some abolitionists supported him. Others, like Frederick Douglass, were opposed. Slavery finally came to an end during the Civil War, with the Emancipation Proclamation of 1863.

Today you can visit the Harpers Ferry National Historic Park, where costumed guides demonstrate Colonial skills on the city's old cobblestone streets. The John Brown Wax Museum depicts the famous raid.

A DOUBLE SECESSION Until 1861 West Virginia was part of Virginia. But east and west had always been distinct cultures. East Virginia was an aristocratic agricultural region that depended on slavery to farm its large plantations. West Virginia was mountain country, occupied by workers who mined salt, cut timber, dug for coal—and opposed slavery. When Virginia wanted to secede from the Union in 1861, legislators from the west voted against it. So the west seceded from Virginia, called itself Kanawha, and asked to be readmitted to the Union. The first Union soldier killed in the Civil War was Baily Thornsberry Brown, of the 2nd West Virginia Volunteers. Some 36,530 West Virginians fought for the Union—although another 7,000 became Confederate soldiers. West Virginia was hotly contested territory during the War Between the States. One town, Romney, actually changed hands 56 times!

The arsenal at Harpers Ferry was built in 1740.

COAL COUNTRY More than half of West Virginia rests on rich seams of bituminous (soft) coal, and the state's economic history is full of stories of mine explosions, union battles, and, finally, mine closings. Of all the states, West Virginia lost the highest percentage of its population between 1980 and 1990. In 1985 it had the highest unemployment rate in the nation—showing how the once prosperous mines had declined.

Coal is still important to West Virginia's economy, as are natural gas, salt, clay, sand, and gravel. The manufacture of chemicals, rubber, metals, ceramics, glass, food products, and machinery are key elements as well. Although the Shenandoah Valley is an important apple-producing area, agriculture is far less important in this industrial state.

Wisconsin

Super Bowl Champion Green Bay Packers   **30th state to enter the Union, May 29, 1848**

The Basics

POPULATION: 5,363,675
18th most populous state
AREA: 65,499 square miles
23rd largest state
STATE CAPITAL: Madison
STATE BIRD: Robin (American robin)
STATE FLOWER: Wood violet
STATE TREE: Sugar maple (also called Hard maple, Rock maple, Black maple)
NICKNAMES: The Badger State, the Copper State
STATE MOTTO: Forward
SPORTS TEAMS: Milwaukee Brewers, baseball; Green Bay Packers, football; Milwaukee Bucks, basketball
STATE ANIMAL: Badger
STATE DOMESTIC ANIMAL: Dairy cow
STATE WILDLIFE ANIMAL: White-tailed deer
STATE FISH: Musekellunge or Muskie
STATE INSECT: Honeybee
STATE MINERAL: Galena
STATE ROCK: Red granite
STATE SOIL: Antigo silt loam
STATE SONG: "On, Wisconsin," words and music by William T. Purdy
STATE LANDMARKS: Wisconsin Dells—rocks cut into strange shapes by the Wisconsin River.
STATE HISTORIC SITES: Cave of the Mounds, near Blue Mounds; Circus World Museum, Baraboo—where the Ringling Brothers began; Stonefield Village, near Cassville—1890s crossroad village; Galloway House and Village, Fond du Lac; Historical Society Log Village and Museum, Reedsburg; Historyland, Hayward; Old Falls Village, Menominee Falls;
STATE PARK: Heritage Hill, Green Bay

Ice fishing on a frozen, northern lake…Dairy cattle grazing in a lush green pasture…Families riding the Wisconsin Ducks down the peaceful river at Wisconsin Dells… Hunters stalking deer in the deep north woods…Beer being bottled at the giant Milwaukee breweries….These are just some images of Wisconsin, in the heart of the Midwest.

GLACIER COUNTRY Wisconsin is almost completely surrounded by water: Lake Michigan to the east; the Menominee River to the northeast; Lake Superior to the north; and the St. Croix and Mississippi Rivers to the west. There's a lot of water in Wisconsin, too: 10,000 smaller rivers and streams, and over 8,500 lakes. You can boat and fish on ice in the winter, or just boat and fish on water in the summer.

You can still see the traces left by glaciers in Wisconsin millions of years ago. The northern part of the state has a granite bed and tends to be flat, forested land—glaciers flattened it as they slid southwards.

Ojibwa perform a traditional dance.

The southeastern part of the state, on the other hand, features rolling hills and choppy ridges. That's where the glacier tore up the land.

Wisconsin is primarily a rural state, but its major cities—Milwaukee, Madison, Green Bay, and Racine—are modern urban areas. They tend to combine a modern, glass-and-steel downtown area with neighborhoods of gracious nineteenth-century homes. Milwaukee is known for its many breweries, and for its summer of festivals by the lake. Madison is the state capital and is home to the University of Wisconsin.

WORLD LEADER FROM WISCONSIN One of Wisconsin's most famous residents was Golda Meir, whose family emigrated to Milwaukee from Kiev in the Russian Empire when she was only eight years old. Meir became a socialist and a Zionist—someone who believed in establishing a Jewish nation. From 1969 to 1974 she served as the prime minister of the Jewish state of Israel—a job she began at the age of seventy! The Milwaukee school she attended was renamed the Golda Meir School in her honor. On a 1969 visit, she told students, "It was here I first experienced a lack of prejudice."

HOMELAND Wisconsin got its name from the Chippewa word for the Wisconsin River, spelled Ouisconsin or Mesconsing in early reports. The word may be translated as grassy place, gathering of the waters, wild rice country, or homeland. Before the Europeans came, Wisconsin was home to many native peoples, including the Winnebago, Dakota, and Menominee. French explorers and fur traders first came to Wisconsin in the early 1600s. In the late 1600s new Indian peoples came to the state: Chippewa, Sac, Fox, Ottawa, Kickapoo, Miami, Illinois, and Potawatomie. For a while they lived peacefully with the Europeans, but during the French and Indian Wars there were conflicts.

One of 50 restored buildings on 576 acres in the Southern Kettle Moraine State Forest

In 1832 Chief Black Hawk fled Illinois and came to Wisconsin at the end of the Black Hawk War. At the Battle of Bad Axe, Black Hawk's people were defeated, and they were massacred as they tried to escape across the Mississippi. As in other states, Indians were gradually either driven out of Wisconsin or relocated onto reservations.

IMMIGRANTS AND PROGRESSIVES After Wisconsin became a state in 1848, many immigrants came to farm its fertile fields and pastures. Throughout the state you can find historical parks commemorating these early residents. In Southern Kettle Moraine State Forest, farm and village buildings have been gathered from across the state and restored to show German, Norwegian, Danish, and Finnish settlements. Near Madison you can visit Little Norway, as well as the Swiss Historical Village in New Glarus. This international heritage still shapes the state's culture today.

Hamlin Garland wrote about rural Wisconsin in the 19th century.

Another strong Wisconsin heritage is that of Governor Robert La Follette, part of the Progressive movement to take power away from big business and run government honestly. After La Follette's term, Wisconsin became a leader in social programs to help workers and their families, providing the first workers' compensation and pensions (1911); teachers' pensions (1911); mothers' pensions (1913); minimum wage (1913); old age pensions (1931); and unemployment insurance (1932).

CHEESE AND TREES Wisconsin is the leading dairy state, providing 40 percent of the nation's cheese and 20 percent of our butter. However, manufacturing is actually a bigger part of the state's economy. Wisconsin's forests cover almost half the state, providing the resources for the state paper industry. Factories near Lake Michigan also make tractors, auto engines, hardware, furniture, and beer.

Wyoming

Grand Tetons National Park

The Basics

POPULATION: 493,782
least populous state
AREA: 97,818 square miles
10th largest state
STATE CAPITAL: Cheyenne
STATE BIRD: Western meadowlark
STATE FLOWER: Indian paintbrush
STATE TREE: Plains cottonwood (also called the Cottonwood, Plains poplar)
NICKNAMES: The Equality State, Big Wyoming, the Cowboy State
STATE MOTTO: Equal Rights
STATE GEM: Jade
STATE SONG: "Wyoming," words by Charles E. Winter, music by George E. Knapp
STATE LANDMARK: Hell's Half Acre, central Wyoming,—320-acre depression filled with pits and caverns
HISTORIC SITES: Fort Laramie National Historic Site—a fort that helped win the West, still with 21 buildings; Fort Bridger—key stop on the Oregon Trail; Riverton Museum, Riverton; South Pass City, Lander—a gold camp near the Oregon trail; Wyoming Territorial Prison Park, Laramie—where outlaw Butch Cassidy once was in jail
HISTORICAL MUSEUMS: Buffalo Bill Historical Center, Cody; Plains Indian Museum, Cody; Winchester Museum, Cody; Wyoming Pioneer Museum, Douglas
NATIONAL PARKS: Grand Teton, near Jackson; Yellowstone, near Cody
STATE FESTIVAL: Frontier Days, Cheyenne—a rodeo that has been held each July since 1897; prizes are awarded for roping, bronco-riding, and *bulldogging* (throwing steers)

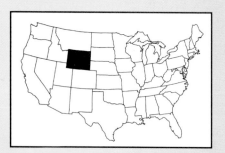

Wyoming is a land of fire and ice: from the hot springs of Yellowstone Park to the snowcapped Rockies. The western frontier of Wyoming is a solid wall of mountains, made up of more than a dozen ranges, including the Grand Tetons. Eastern Wyoming is part of the Great Plains: flat, rolling prairies marked by buttes (pronounced byoots), or towers of rock. This is an overwhelmingly rural state, whose principal cities—Casper, Cheyenne, and Laramie—have only about 50,000 people or less.

YELLOWSTONE FANTASIES When John Colter reported the first descriptions of what is now Yellowstone Park in a St. Louis newspaper in 1810, readers thought he was telling tall tales. How else to explain his fantastic stories of fuming mud pots, geysers, and waterfalls? We now know that Yellowstone's hot spots are caused by molten rock collected near the earth's surface, which heats snow and rainwater to boiling.

Yellowstone National Park still offers many fascinating sights. The Grand Canyon of the Yellowstone is 24 miles long and 1,200 feet deep, its red and ochre stone a brilliant contrast to the emerald forest above. True to its name, the geyser called Old Faithful erupts about once an hour, while the Steamboat Geyser shoots water 300 feet into the air. Elk, bison, and other wildlife roam the park, to visitors' delight.

Old Faithful is heated by molten rock beneath the earth's crust.

COWBOYS AND CATTLE WARS Wyoming is the only state to be formed out of the four principal U.S annexations: the Louisiana Purchase in 1803, the annexation of Texas in 1845, the cession of Oregon by the British in 1846, and the land taken at the end of the Mexican War in 1848. Before U.S. possession, Wyoming belonged to the Arapaho, Cheyenne, and Shoshone.

In the 1850s Wyoming was a place that settlers passed through to get to the California gold rush: more than 60,000 people crossed the state in 1850 alone. After the railroad was completed in 1869, however, ranchers, farmers, and coal miners began to come to the area. Wyoming was known for its Wild West rough-and-tumble cowboy atmosphere.

Wars with the Shoshone and Arapaho were finally settled by forcing them onto reservations in eastern Wyoming. Later the reservations were made smaller as more settlers came looking for land.

Like its neighbor Idaho, Wyoming depended on Chinese immigrants to work its mines, and like Idaho, it had a violent, often bloody labor history. In 1885, for example, 85 Chinese coal miners were killed and hundreds more chased out of town near Rock Spring. Federal troops were brought in to restore order—and remained for 14 years.

In 1892 another conflict shook the state: the Johnson County Cattle War. "Nesters"—big ranchers and farmers—hired gunmen to shoot "rustlers"—the small ranchers and homesteaders who they believed were stealing their cattle. From 1897 to 1901 the conflict was between sheep and cattle ranchers fighting over which animal would be allowed to graze Wyoming's plains. Some 16 men and 10,000 sheep were killed by the cattle owners before the sheep ranchers finally won: six million Wyoming sheep outnumbered cattle by 7 to 1, and Wyoming led the nation in wool production.

Tower Falls in Yellowstone National Park

WYOMING WOMEN CLAIM THEIR RIGHTS Wyoming has certainly lived up to its motto of "Equal Rights" where women are concerned. In 1869 before it was even a state, it became the first U.S. location where women could vote. The first U.S. woman to hold public office was Wyoming Justice of the Peace Esther Hobart Morris, appointed in 1870. In that year U.S. women were first allowed to serve on juries, in Laramie. The world's first female forewoman of a jury was Louise Spinner Graf, chosen in 1950. The first U.S. woman elected to state office was State Superintendent of Public Instruction Estelle Reel. The first U.S. woman governor was Nellie Tayloe Ross, elected in 1924.

Wyoming women were often active in politics. In 1920 an all-woman ticket ran for Jackson city government, and won by 2 to 1 against an all-male ticket. In 1921 the women ran for re-election—and won by 3 to 1.

COAL, OIL, AND COWS Almost half Wyoming's land is owned by the U.S. government, which then leases it out for grazing, mining, and logging. More than 80 percent of state land is used for cattle. Wyoming also remains a national leader in producing sheep and wool.

Mining is the state's main business. Years ago, the Cheyenne dipped twigs in puddles of oil and lit them as torches. Now Wyoming produces a great deal of oil, natural gas, iron ore, and uranium. It has the nation's largest coal reserves and is second in coal production.

State Capitol at Cheyenne

American Samoa

The Basics

POPULATION: 67,084
AREA: 77 square miles
AREA OF TUTUILA AND AUNU'U:
53 square miles
AREA OF TA'U: 17 square miles
AREA OF OFU AND OLOSEGA: 5 square miles
AREA OF SWAINS ISLAND: Nearly 2 square miles
CAPITAL: Pago Pago, island of Tutuila
FLOWER: Paogo (Ula-fala)
PLANT: Ava
MOTTO: *Samoa Muamua le Atua* (Polynesian for "In Samoa, God is first")
SONG: "Amerika Samoa"
HIGHEST POINT: 3,160 feet—Lata Mountain
LOWEST POINT: Sea level

Samoan boys use Japanese fishing floats to store water.

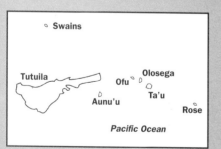

Samoan village

Picture a group of seven islands scattered across the Pacific, 2,300 miles southwest of Hawaii. This is American Samoa, the jewel of the South Pacific.

SEVEN ISLANDS   Six of American Samoa's islands are part of the Samoan chain. They are divided among three groups: Tutuila and Aunu'u; Ofu, Olosega, and Ta'u (the Manu'a group); and Rose. The seventh island, Swains Island, is 200 miles north of the rest.

Swains Island is unusual in that it has been the property of the Jennings family ever since 1856, when the American Eli Jennings and his Samoan wife settled there.

The largest and most important of the American Samoan islands, however, is Tutuila. This is the island that includes Pago Pago, the territory's capital, with its beautiful harbor and port facilities. The novel *Rain* by Somerset Maugham was set in Pago Pago. There are no other cities in the territory.

This typical Polynesian hut is woven with leaves of palm.

Only about one-third of the total territory can be used for farmland. That's because the islands aren't made of earth and stone, like the United States continental mainland. Instead, Rose and Swains Islands are made of coral—the accumulation of centuries of reefs built up from the bottom of the sea. The other islands are the remains of extinct volcanoes, mountainous, with some fertile soil in the valleys or along the coast.

These tropical islands have a warm, wet climate. Temperatures are neither too hot nor too cold, ranging from 70 degrees to 90 degrees Fahrenheit. However, rainfall averages over 200 inches a year.

A POLYNESIAN PEOPLE Most of the people living in American Samoa are Polynesians, a South Pacific native people. Their primary language is Samoan, although most also speak English.

Because, years ago, Christian missionaries went to Samoa to convert people from their native religions to Christianity, most American Samoans are now Christian. But traditional culture is still very strong in Samoa. Most people still wear their traditional garment, the lavalava. They still hollow out tree trunks to make fautasi, longboats, sometimes as much as forty feet long, propelled by many oars. They still share their traditional dance, the siva, with the many

Swains

Tutuila   Ofu   Olosega
              Ta'u
       Aunu'u
                     Rose

Pacific Ocean

tourists that come to the islands.

And most American Samoans still live in villages, with daily life focused around the family. Each family group—which might include aunts, uncles, and cousins—is headed by a family chief. The chief controls the entire family's property, is responsible for the sick and aged, and represents the family in the village council.

Gradually, however, traditional ways are being affected by modern life. In the 1960s the United States began an economic development program in the region, bringing factories and industrial development to Pago Pago. Many people left their villages to live in the city. Their thatch-roofed fale (houses) were torn down and hurricane-proof concrete buildings were put up instead.

Many American Samoan villages are built around lagoons.

Children from ages 6 to 18 were required to attend school, where they might be taught by television. No one knows how these changes will finally affect traditional life.

AMERICANS AND GERMANS The first Polynesians probably came to Samoa some 2,000 years ago, migrating from eastern Melanesia. They were joined in 1722 by the Dutch explorer Jacob Roggeveen. Over the years the United States, Britain, and France all wanted to trade with the island, and to make use of its land and waters. Finally, in 1878, the United States put forth the strongest claim by establishing a naval station at Pago Pago. In 1899 the United States, Great Britain, and Germany agreed that the United States had the right to govern the islands that are now called American Samoa. From 1900 to 1951 American Samoa was governed by the U.S. Navy. From 1951 to the present it has been governed by the U.S. Department of the Interior, which until 1978 even appointed the island's governor. Now, however, Samoans elect their own governor. They also elect one member to the U.S. House of Representatives who is allowed to vote in committees but not on the House floor.

This Tiki god is carved of mahogany.

The face of this Polynesian War God is carved to resemble a wild, tusked boar.

COCOA AND CRAFTS The leading industry in Samoa is tuna canning. In fact, over 96 percent of exports are fish products. But Samoa is also known for its cocoa—considered the world's best. And Samoan crafts are world-famous. Samoans make tapa cloth by pounding the bark of paper mulberry trees. They weave baskets and laufala floor mats from palm leaves. Other exports include tropical products such as copra, breadfruit, yams, coconuts, bananas, oranges, and pineapples. And, of course, tourism is an important part of the islands' economy.

Guam

Sunset at Agana Bay

Ceded to the United States in 1898

The Basics

POPULATION: 157,557
AREA: 209 square miles
CAPITAL: Agana
BIRD: Toto (fruit dove)
FLOWER: Puti Tai nobio (Bougainvillea)
TREE: Ifit (Intsiabijuga)
NICKNAME: Where America's Day Begins
SONG: "Stand Ye Guamians"
WIDTH, NORTH TO SOUTH: About 4 to 8.5 miles
LENGTH, EAST TO WEST: About 30 miles
HIGHEST POINT: 1,332 feet—Mt. Lamlam
LOWEST POINT: Sea level

Old Spanish Gate at Agana

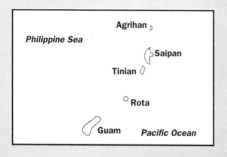

Guam's key feature is a U. S. Naval Air Base. Although Guam is far from the continental United States, it is actually U. S. territory. So the U.S. soldiers stationed on Guam can actually consider themselves right at home on the small island in the middle of the Pacific Ocean.

WHERE AMERICA'S DAY BEGINS Guam is a self-governing organized unincorporated U.S. territory. That means that the people in Guam elect their own leaders but don't have the power to affect the national U.S. government. Guam's people are U.S. citizens, but they cannot vote for president.

Guam is the southern-most of a string of Pacific islands called the Marianas, about 1,500 miles east of the Philippines and 3,700 miles west of Hawaii. It's also the largest of the Marianas. Like them, it has a warm, pleasant tropical climate and a landscape dotted with palm trees and brightly colored tropical blooms.

Water buffalo at Fort Santa Soledad

If you walked along a beach in Guam, you'd see stony coral reefs rising from the ocean. If you traveled inland you'd find mountains, and on the southern half of the island you'd find hills that were formed by volcanoes millions of years ago. Guam's northern half used to be heavily forested, but much of this land has been cleared for farms and airfields. Throughout the island, coconut groves thrive, cultivated for their sweet fruit.

Guamanians are a multiracial, multicultural people. Many are Chamorros, descended from the Indonesian and Spanish settlers who came to Guam a few hundred years ago. Others are descended from American, Italian, French, British, Japanese, Chinese, Filipino, and Mexican settlers. Because the U.S. military base is such a big part of the island's economy, about one-third of the people on the island are military personnel and their dependents. Before the United States became an important presence on the island, Chamorro was the main language. Now most people speak English. Some 95 percent of Guamanians are Roman Catholic, reflecting their Spanish heritage.

FROM MAGELLAN'S EXPEDITION TO WORLD WAR II The first Europeans to land on Guam were explorer Ferdinand Magellan and his followers, who arrived there in 1521. Forty years later Spain claimed the island for itself. Guam remained under Spanish rule for over three hundred years, until Spain lost the Spanish-American War in 1898. Then Spain gave up many of its Pacific and Caribbean possessions to the United States. One of these was Guam, which was then administered by the U.S. Navy.

Because Guam was U.S. territory, it was a logical target for Japan during World War II. The Japanese attacked Guam on December 7, 1941 (U.S. date) and captured it on Decem-

Beached Japanese barge near Inarajan

ber 10th. It took the United States three years to regain the island: U.S. forces landed on Guam on July 21, 1944, and recaptured it completely on August 15, 1944.

On August 1, 1950, Guam was declared a territory. The U.S. Department of the Interior became responsible for the land, rather than the Navy, and Guamanians became U.S. citizens and were allowed to elect their own legislature. However, until 1970 the U.S. President appointed the island's governor. Now the governor is elected.

Guam continued to have military importance for the United States. In 1954 the U.S. Air Force Strategic Air Command made Guam its Pacific headquarters.

TROPICAL FRUITS Farmers on Guam raise corn, cattle, and hogs. They also grow many tropical fruits and vegetables: cabbages, eggplants, cucumbers, long beans, tomatoes, bananas, coconuts, watermelons, yams, canteloupes, papayas, maize, and sweet potatoes. The island has traditionally relied on agriculture, but over the years some industry has developed including construction, light manufacturing, banking, and tourism. Factories on Guam make textiles and process foods.

The U.S. military base is also a major part of the economy. Some 7,200 people on Guam are employed by the U.S. government. And close to a quarter of Guam's workers are employed in service industries, many of which are set up to serve residents of the base.

Tropical fruits and vegetables are grown on farms like this one.

Puerto Rico
Estado Libre Asociado de Puerto Rico

Became a commonwealth on July 25, 1952

The Basics

OFFICIAL NAME: Commmonwealth of Puerto Rico; *Estado Libre Asociado de Puerto Rico*

POPULATION: 3,808,610

AREA: 3,435 square miles

CAPITAL: San Juan

BIRD: Reinita

FLOWER: Maga

TREE: Ceiba

MOTTO: *Joannes Est Nomen Eujus* (Latin for "John is his name")

FLAG: Five horizontal stripes, alternating red and white, with a blue triangle at the left, bearing a five-pointed white star.

SEAL: A central medallion with a lamb, symbol of St. John (San Juan) holding a white banner and resting on the New Testament's Book of Revelation, just above the commonwealth's motto. Above the lamb are the crowned letters *F* and *I*, for Spain's King Ferdinand and Queen Isabella. Around the border of the seal are symbols of the Kingdom of Spain.

SONG: La Borinqueña

LANDMARKS: El Morro Fortress, San Juan

NATIONAL PARKS: El Yunque Rain Forest

WILDLIFE REFUGE: Caribbean Islands Refuge

FESTIVALS: Kings' Day, January 6; Birthday of educator and writer Eugenio Maria de Hostos (January 11); San Juan Carnival (February); Emancipation Day— the abolition of slavery in 1873 (March 22); Birthday of Puerto Rican patriot Jose de Diego (April 16); Tropical Flower Show, San Juan (April); Eve of San Juan Bautista Day (June 23); Birthday of patriot Luis Munoz Rivera (July 17)

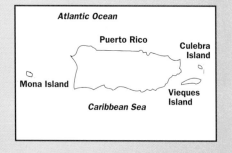
Atlantic Ocean
Puerto Rico
Culebra Island
Mona Island
Vieques Island
Caribbean Sea

Puerto Rico is so small that you can drive virtually anywhere in less than a day. Yet, the island hosts a wide variety of beautiful landscapes—mountains, beaches, rain forests. No wonder Puertoriqueños love their homeland so much!

TROPICAL BEACHES AND SPANISH FORTS The spine of Puerto Rico is the Cordillera Central, a 3,000-foot-high mountain range running through the center of the island. The range slopes steeply to the dry southeastern part of the island, and more gently to the humid, rainy northern half. The island is bordered with sandy white beaches along the warm Caribbean.

Puerto Rico's tropical climate is generally pleasant. The temperature ranges from 60 to 98 degrees Fahrenheit, with a mean temperature of 77. The warm, rainy weather makes for a long growing season, but only one-third of the island is suitable for farming. The rest is too mountainous or marshy.

Two-thirds of Puerto Rico's residents live in cities, primarily San Juan, Bayamon, Ponce, Carolina, Caguas, and Mayaguez. San Juan is by far the largest. The city is a striking mix of Spanish colonial architecture and modern luxury hotels. One of its most famous buildings is the El Morro Fortress, built by the Spaniards between 1539 and 1787 to guard the Bay of San Juan. The University of Puerto Rico, founded in

Rain forest near Santurcé

1903, has a beautifully ornamented administration building. It's also the site of lively demonstrations by students and by its unionized clerical workers.

Puerto Rico is famous for its sandy beaches, especially Luquillo Beach on the northeast corner of the island. Phosphorescent Bay, at La Parguera on the southwest coast, literally glows in the dark. That's because tiny living organisms in the water called plankton actually give off light. At El Yunque's rain forest, you can see wild parrots and wild orchids.

SUGARCANE AND OPERATION BOOTSTRAP Puerto Rico's first inhabitants were the Taino, who spoke Arawak. They were "discovered" by Christopher Columbus on November 19, 1493, during his second visit to the western hemisphere. Columbus claimed the land for Spain, and in 1508 the Spanish began to settle there. In 1515 the first sugarcane was brought from the Dominican Republic. And in 1518 the first African slaves were brought to work on the sugarcane plantations.

Like slaves in North America, slaves in Puerto Rico were cruelly treated. And, as in North America, the colonizers drove native peoples out of their lands. By 1550 Taino who had not been killed or enslaved by the Spanish had fled into the mountains. Although the French, English, and Dutch each challenged Spain's claim, Puerto Rico remained in Spanish hands until 1898.

In that year, U.S. troops landed in Puerto Rico as part of the Spanish-American War, which was fought mainly on the land of Spain's colonies. When Spain was defeated, the United States acquired Puerto Rico, along with the Philippines, Cuba, and other Spanish colonies.

Even though slavery had been abolished in 1873, workers continued to be poorly treated on the sugar plantations. By 1920 almost three-fourths of Puerto Rico's population depended on sugarcane for its livelihood. Later tobacco, mining of iron ore, and tourism became important island industries as well. And in the 1940s the United States started Operation Bootstrap, designed to lure U.S companies to build factories on the island, by offering them attractive tax breaks.

Statue of Christopher Columbus in San Juan

INDEPENDENCE, STATEHOOD, OR STATUS QUO? Puerto Ricans have been debating the best political system for their country since the first Spanish colonists arrived 400 years ago. Now there are three main opinions in Puerto Rico. Some people believe that Puerto Rico should become the 51st state, losing its identity as a nation but gaining in political influence in America. Others think that Puerto Rico's commonwealth status—with U.S. financial support but without political participation—is best. Still others want Puerto Rico to be fully independent, and they have fought for independence for many years.

Morro Castle, San Juan

FROM SUGARCANE TO TOURISM Like most Caribbean nations, Puerto Rico has had trouble achieving economic independence. That's because it produces raw materials—sugarcane, coffee, and bananas—while the more profitable work of processing materials and selling industrial goods is done by companies whose headquarters are on the U.S. mainland. As a result, the profits are taken out of Puerto Rico, even when the work is done there. There is some native Puerto Rican industry—pharmaceuticals, petrochemicals, machinery, clothing, and textiles. Tourism is also important to the economy.

One of the saddest things for many Puerto Ricans is the lack of jobs on their island. This means that they must go to the United States for work. As a result, some 2.7 million Puerto Ricans live in the continental United States. Of these, a million live in New York City. There, Nuyorican culture has developed, which in turn shapes the Puerto Rican culture on the island itself.

Fascinating Facts

PUERTO RICO'S MANY NAMES:
• The original Taino Indian name for the island was *Borinquen*.
• In 1493 Christopher Columbus called the island *San Juan* (St. John).
• Ponce de Leon renamed the capital city of Caparra *Puerto Rico,* "rich port," in 1511.
• Later, the island became known as Puerto Rico, and the capital city, San Juan.

PUERTO RICO AND THE U.S.:
• self-governing commonwealth
• residents are American citizens
• residents can vote in primaries, but not in general elections for president
• residents elect a nonvoting Resident Commissioner to Congress
• residents do not pay income tax on income earned in Puerto Rico

PUERTO RICO'S POLITICS:
• a Commonwealth Legislature with 27 senators and 51 representatives
• 78 municipalities elect their own mayors and city governments

SAN JUAN FACTS:
• estimated 1993 population—433,372
• founded in 1508 by Juan Ponce de Leon, who called it Caparra
• oldest city in any U.S. territory or state

DID YOU KNOW THAT... Although the tiny island of Puerto Rico has nearly 1,300 streams and 50 rivers, none of them is navigable.

EL YUNQUE FACTS:
• name means "the anvil"
• a mountain with a rain forest on its slopes
• the only national park that is a rain forest, home to 240 native species of trees, some of which grow nowhere else
• home to many species of birds
• unlike other rain forests, has no alligators or monkeys

U.S. Virgin Islands

The Basics

TOTAL POPULATION: 122,211

MAIN ISLANDS: St. John, St. Thomas, St. Croix

POPULATION OF ST. CROIX: 61,000

POPULATION OF ST. THOMAS: 50,000

POPULATION OF ST. JOHN: 3,000

AREA: 128 square miles

AREA OF ST. CROIX: 82 square miles

AREA OF ST. THOMAS: 27 square miles

AREA OF ST. JOHN: 19 square miles

CAPITAL: Charlotte Amalie, St. Thomas

BIRD: Yellow breast

FLOWER: Yellow elder or yellow trumpet (Ginger Thomas)

FLAG: A golden American eagle with a U.S. shield on its breast, against a white field. The eagle holds blue arrows in its left talon, symbolizing war, and a sprig of green laurel in its right talon, symbolizing peace. The blue letters *V* and *I* are to the left and right of the eagle.

SEAL: The U.S. coat of arms, with the American eagle and the U.S. shield in the center of the seal. The words "Government of the Virgin Islands of the United States" surrounds the coat of arms.

SONG: "Virgin Islands March"

HIGHEST POINT: Crown Mountain, St. Thomas—1,556 feet

LOWEST POINT: Sea level

NATIONAL PARK: Virgin Islands National Park

FESTIVAL: Carnival, St. Thomas (April)

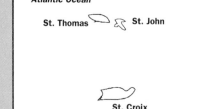

Atlantic Ocean

St. Thomas   St. John

St. Croix

Caribbean Sea

The name Virgin Islands refers to two groups of small islands between the Caribbean Sea and the Atlantic Ocean, east of Puerto Rico. One group—St. Croix, St. John, and St. Thomas—belongs to the United States and is known as the United States Virgin Islands. The other group—Anegada, Jost van Dyke, Tortola, and Virgin Gorda Islands, along with surrounding small islets—is the British Virgin Islands.

ISLAND PARADISE The United States Virgin Islands are rugged and hilly, except for the largest island, St. Croix, which is sandy and flat. When you picture the islands, think small. Their total size, only 133 square miles, would fit nine times into Rhode Island, the mainland's tiniest state. Yet they offer 117 miles of coastline—beautiful beaches along the sapphire-blue Caribbean.

The Virgin Islands were once entirely covered by the sea. Fossils of ancient animals can still be found on island shores. Once, volcanoes pushed the islands up from the ocean floor. If you walk along an island beach, you can see tiny islets jutting up from the water, like little rocks. Imagine them millions of years ago, being thrust up from the ocean by a huge, boiling volcano. Then look at them again, cool and peaceful in the island surf, some covered with green plant life.

Palm Passage on St. Thomas

Tropical flowers and trees grow all over these lovely islands. All year round you can see the scarlet, pink, and white blooms of the bougainvillea, canaria, flame tree, and hibiscus. The delightful tropical climate ranges from 70 to 90 degrees Fahrenheit, averaging a balmy 78 degrees Fahrenheit. You're likely to find good weather all year long, although there are sometimes heavy rains in the spring and fall.

The largest island of the group is St. Croix (pronounced saynh kroy), French for "holy cross." In Spanish it's called Santa Cruz, as Christopher Columbus named it. St. Croix has about two-thirds of the islands' area and is home to the cities Christiansted and Frederiksted.

St. John has villages at Cruz Bay and Coral Bay, but about three-fourths of its land is occupied by Virgin Islands National Park. St. Thomas is known for its central range of hills, from which you can see the ocean. It's also home to the islands' capital, Charlotte Amalie.

A NEW CARIBBEAN LAND The United States Virgin Islands were once home to native peoples such as the Siboney Indians, the Carib, and the Arawak from South America. The Arawak created an important invention—the hammock. These were the peoples whom Christopher Columbus found when he reached the Virgin Islands in 1493.

Mending a fishing trap

The Carib did not take kindly to the European invaders, and they fought fiercely with Columbus' crew at Sugar Bay on St. Croix. Throughout the 1500s the Caribs tried hard to defend their land from the Europeans. But in the mid-1500s King Charles I of Spain sent soldiers to kill all the Indians so that Spain could take their lands. By the 1600s when the British and Danes began to approach the islands, the native people had all been killed or chased off.

In 1607 a group of English settlers stopped at the islands, but they continued on their way to the colony at Jamestown, Virginia. For years, pirates used the island to bury their treasure. Throughout the 1600s, 1700s, and 1800s, the islands were claimed by Holland, Spain, France, England, and Denmark. (You can see the Danish influence in the "sted" endings of the names of St. Croix's towns.)

Children's parade on St. Thomas

Finally, in 1917, the United States bought its portion of the Virgin Islands from Denmark, to keep them from being taken by the Germans during World War I. In 1927 Virgin Islanders became American nationals. They were allowed a limited form of self-government in 1936 and somewhat expanded rights in 1954. Today the Virgin Islands elects a governor, lieutenant governor, and parliament to run the islands, as well as a nonvoting member to the U.S. House of Representatives.

TOURISM, RUM, AND OIL When native people lived on the islands, they fished the sea and ate the fruits and vegetables they could grow or pick wild. But the islands don't have the resources to support a modern economy.

Thus, the major industry is tourism, with a large number of visitors coming from the United States. There are some other industries too. Residents of St. John make charcoal and pick bay leaves, which are made into bay rum. Oil refineries on St. Croix produce petroleum. Other manufacturing includes watchmaking, aluminum production, textiles, electronics, and perfumes. Most goods are exported to the United States.

Fascinating Facts

VIRGIN ISLANDS POLITICS:
- administered by the U.S. Department of the Interior
- constitution—the Revised Organic Act of the Virgin Islands, passed by the U.S. Congress in 1954
- elects a governor for a four-year term with a limit of two consecutive terms
- territorial legislature—one house with 15 senators elected to two-year terms
- St. Croix elects 7 senators; St. Thomas and St. John together elect 7 senators; one senator is elected at large
- judicial system—U.S. District Court of the Virgin Islands, with the judge appointed by the U.S. president with the advice and consent of the U.S. Senate
- municipal court judges—appointed by the governor, with the advice and consent of the territorial legislature

VIRGIN ISLANDS WEATHER:
- average rainfall: 40 to 60 inches of rain each year
- average rainfall at higher elevations: 50 to 60 inches each year

VIRGIN ISLANDS TOURISM:
- more than one million tourists each year
- $10 million worth of business

VIRGIN ISLANDS AGRICULTURE:
- eggs
- beef and dairy cattle
- hogs
- pigs
- sheep
- cucumbers, peppers, tomatoes
- fruits and nuts
- grain sorghum for livestock feed

DID YOU KNOW THAT... During the 1700s landowners began developing huge sugarcane plantations on the islands. These are no longer profitable, although sugarcane is an important crop elsewhere in the Caribbean. However, you can still visit the ruins of large farms like the Princess Plantation on St. Croix.

The United States of America

Washington

Oregon

Montana

North Dakota

South Dakota

Idaho

Wyoming

Nebraska

Nevada

Utah

Colorado

Kansas

California

Arizona

New Mexico

Texas

Alaska

Hawaii

Alaska and Hawaii are not in position
and not drawn to scale.

Minnesota

Michigan

New Hampshire

Maine

Vermont

Wisconsin

Massachusetts

New York

Rhode Island

Connecticut

Pennsylvania

New Jersey

Iowa

Ohio

Delaware

Indiana

Maryland

Illinois

West Virginia

Virginia

Missouri

Washington, D.C.

Kentucky

North Carolina

Tennessee

South Carolina

Oklahoma

Arkansas

Georgia

Mississippi

Alabama

Louisiana

Florida

ALABAMA

If you would like to learn more about **Helen Keller,** who lived a full and remarkable life in spite of being deaf, mute, and blind, then visit her birthplace, "Ivy Green," at 300 West North Common Street, Tuscumbia.

The poet, educator and reformer who changed many children's lives, **Julia Tutwiler,** is honored with a memorial in her name at the Department of Archives and History at Washington Avenue in Montgomery.

ALASKA

If you're interested in outdoor sports and dogs, then visit the **Anchorage Sled Dog Racing Association,** which hosts races on winter weekends. Or see the world-famous **Iditarod,** the 1,049-mile-long dog-sled race held in March. **The Fur Rendezvous** is the site of dogsled races held in Anchorage in mid-February. For helpful information on all three, contact the

Alaskan native boy in traditional clothes

Anchorage Convention and Visitors Bureau at 524 West 4th Avenue in Anchorage, AK 99501.

The Anchorage Museum of History and Art is a treasure trove of native arts and crafts at West 7th Avenue and A Street in Anchorage.

Kodiak, the largest island in the United States is home to the Kodiak brown bear, the largest land mammal in North America.

Contact Southwest Alaska Municipal Conference at 3300 Arctic Boulevard (Suite 203) Anchorage, AK 99503.

ARIZONA

The **Grand Canyon,** the largest land gorge in the world, is 277 miles long, 17 miles wide at its broadest point, and 1 mile deep. It is in **Grand Canyon National Park,** the site of many panoramic views such as **The Watchtower** at the South Rim or **Point Imperial**—at 8,803 feet, the highest viewpoint in the canyon. Because of its remote location and heavy snowfalls, the North Rim of the Grand Canyon is closed from October to April. If you want to get "up close," the National Park Service sponsors several hikes along the many trails in and around this geological phenomenon. Contact the National Park Service at Box 129 Grand Canyon.

If you're curious about Native American life, visit **Quechan Indian Reservation.** For more information, contact the Quechan Tribal Council at P.O. Box 1352, Yuma, AZ 85364.

ARKANSAS

How are diamonds "made"? Find out at the only working diamond mine in North America at the **Crater of Diamonds State Park** in Murfreesboro.

History comes to life at **Ozark Folk Center State Park,** where the Ozark Mountain way of life is preserved and carried on through presentations of traditional dancing and singing, along with demonstrations of folk arts and crafts. This unique park is in Mountain View.

You can also explore the past at **Quapaw Quarter,** a completely restored nineteenth-century neighborhood that includes homes, churches, and some of the state's oldest buildings. It's at 1321 Scott Street, Little Rock.

CALIFORNIA

California has some of the most beautiful—and varied—scenery in the world. **U.S. 1,** an interstate highway, runs along the 400-mile-long coastline. The highway is bordered by forests: the world's tallest tree—a 365-foot-high redwood—is in Humboldt County. And **Point Reyes National Seashore** attracts many seals, birds, and migrating whales.

You can also travel the two-mile-long **"Path of History"** in **Monterey State Historic Park.** The starting point of this self-guided coastal tour is **The Custom House,** built by Mexico in 1817, and believed to be the oldest government building west of the Rockies. Contact

A beautiful Japanese garden in Golden Gate Park, San Francisco

the California Division of Tourism in Sacramento for information about these sights.

Hancock Park is the home of one of the world's greatest museums, the **Los Angeles County Museum of Art** at 5905 Wilshire Boulevard. **Hancock Park** is built on top of the **La Brea Tar Pits**, from which more than 100 tons of fossils have been removed.

The Tech Museum of Innovation in San Carlo is devoted entirely to the computer; you can visit in person at 145 West San Carlos Street, or on the **Internet** at http://www.thetech.org

Yosemite Falls, in **Yosemite National Park** rise 2,425 feet, making them the highest falls in North America. The park also offers hiking, backpacking, and camping surrounded by glacial granite peaks and clear, blue lakes.

California is home to many celebrities, but some of its "forgotten" natives claim distinction born of real-life achievement. If you would like to find out about one of them, visit the home of **Harriet Chalmers Adams,** an anthropologist (someone who studies the origins and relationships between humans and their social and cultural environments) who travelled more than 100,000 miles to explore dangerous, remote jungles and native tribes during the 1890s. It's at 605 North Eldorado Avenue, Stockton.

COLORADO

In the town of Golden, you can find out more about a famous, real-life cowboy at **The Buffalo Bill Grave and Museum** at the top of Lookout Mountain. The trip up gives you a spectacular panoramic view of Denver. To get there, take Route 5 off I-70.

St. James United Methodist Church has a **Monument to Clara Brown,** the Virginia-born slave whose hard work and faith were responsible for the founding of this pioneer church in 1872. It is at Eureka Street in Central City.

Rocky Mountain National Park in Estes Park has some of the most spectacular mountains, lakes, and wildlife in the United States. It covers 250,000 acres and offers hiking, camping, fishing and scenic drives through its wilderness.

The **Garden of the Gods** offers picnic sites and opportunities for hiking among 1,350 acres of windswept rock formations and exotic plant life. Visit them at Off Ridge Road, north of U.S. 24, Colorado Springs.

CONNECTICUT

The Peabody Museum of Natural History in New Haven is the largest of its kind in New England, and includes dinosaur fossils, birds, and meteorites. It also has exhibits of early Native American life in the area.

The **Mystic Marine Life Aquarium** in Mystic has more than 6,000 specimens and 50 live exhibits of sea life. It also presents live dolphin and sea lion shows every hour.

Did you ever wonder where your dictionary got its start? Well, it was with Noah Webster in 1806, and you can learn more about him by visiting the **Noah Webster House and Museum** in Hartford.

Hartford is also the home of the country's first public art museum, **The Wadsworth Athenaeum** (founded in 1842), which includes more than 40,000 works that span 5,000 years of art.

Emma Hart Willard began the first endowed school for girls in 1821. If you are curious about this rebel with a cause, visit her birthplace at Norton Rd. and Lower Lane in Berlin.

Mark Twain's house in Hartford, Connecticut

DELAWARE

With 175 rooms and acres of gardens, **Winterthur Museum, Garden and Library** features American art and antiques from 1640-1860. Take Route 52 in Winterthur.

New Castle, where William Penn first lived in 1682, is a completely restored colonial town of 200-year-old homes and a **Courthouse** that was the state capital during the Revolution.

Rehobeth Beach is a beautiful place to explore Delaware's largest shoreline area. With a busy boardwalk and acres of white beach, it's one of the Atlantic coast's most picturesque scenes.

DISTRICT OF COLUMBIA

Black history comes alive when you visit the **Frederick Douglass National Historic Site,** Cedar Hill. With its restored house and nine acres of land, this was the last home of the great abolitionist, who lived there from 1878 until his death in 1895. (1411 W Street, S.E.)

The **Lincoln Memorial** honoring our 16th president is one of the great public monuments in the United States. With its marble columns, long reflecting pool, and imposing statue of Abraham Lincoln by sculptor Daniel Chester French, the memorial is equally beautiful by night or day. It has been the site of numerous public demonstrations since its completion in 1914. The memorial is at the west end of the Mall.

Jazz pianist and composer "Duke" Ellington (1899-1974)

The **Smithsonian Institution,** which includes seven museums, features a variety of items ranging from Dorothy's red slippers from *The Wizard of Oz* to Charles Lindbergh's plane, *The Spirit of St. Louis,* which he flew solo across the Atlantic in 1927.

Designed by young architect, Maya Lin, the **Vietnam Veterans Memorial** in polished black granite is a somber reminder of the high price of war. Its companion, the **Vietnam Women's Memorial,** designed by Glenna Goodacre, stands nearby at 23rd St. and Constitution Ave., N.W.

Home to presidents since John Adams lived there from 1797 through 1801, **The White House** has survived fire and war, destruction and restoration. There are daily tours of its public rooms and gardens.

FLORIDA

If you're interested in ecology, **The Florida Everglades** includes the country's largest sub-tropical wilderness (with more than 1.4 million acres). Half-land, half-water, you can visit this national park in Homestead, just south of Miami.

Thomas Edison's Winter Home is the place to go to learn more about the legendary inventor—the record player and microphone are only two of hundreds of his inventions. The home includes Edison's laboratory and a museum with his inventions. 2350 McGregor Blvd. Ft. Myers, FL

Zora Neale Hurston Memorial Park is dedicated to the distinguished African-American writer whose novels have been widely praised by critics. The park is at 11 People Street in the Eatonville Municipal Complex.

In the Cocoa Beach area, **Spaceport U.S.A.** at the Kennedy Space Center presents the wonders of space travel through filmed presentations and bus tours of spacecraft hangars and rocket launch sites. Call 1-800-432-2153 for more information.

GEORGIA

The **Juliette Gordon Low Birthplace/Girl Scout National Center** is the home of the founder of the Girl Scouts of America. This beautiful old house at 142 Bull Street was the first registered National Historic Landmark in Savannah.

The **Martin Luther King, Jr. National Historic District** begins at King Center, 449 Auburn Avenue in Atlanta. The spirit of the 1960s Civil Rights movement is commemorated in a museum and library. And an eternal flame burns at the tomb of Dr. King, illuminating the words "Free at Last Free At Last Thank God Almighty I'm Free at Last."

Because 32nd President Franklin Delano Roosevelt was physically challenged by polio, he often came to Warm Springs for his health. In addition to a simple home he called "The

British actress Fanny Kemble (1809-1893) published a controversial journal after living on her slaveholder husband's Georgia plantation.

Little White House," he established a health center for others with the disease. For more information call 1-800-847-4842 (the Georgia Department of Industry, Trade and Tourism).

HAWAII

If you are interested in volcanoes, the Hawaiian islands are a great place to see them up close. **Hawaii Volcanoes National Park** covers 344 acres on the the big island of Hawaii, and features many attractions related to Mount Kilauea, the world's most active volcano.

On the island of Maui, **Haleakala National Park** begins at 7,000 feet, and continues to 9,800 where rangers can tell you fascinating information about volcanoes. You'll also get a 360-degree view of other islands in the Hawaiian chain.

The *USS Arizona* Memorial honors the memory of all those killed during the Japanese attack on Pearl Harbor on December 7, 1941. 1,102 crewmen on the *Arizona* drowned when their ship sank. The memorial is twenty minutes west of downtown Honolulu off the island of Oahu.

Craters of the Moon National Monument

IDAHO

Lunar astronauts trained at **Craters of the Moon National Monument,** which covers 83 square miles and is home to lava flows, caves, and volcanic cones. Write Box 29 in Arco, 83213.

Only seven miles south of Boise you'll find the **World Center for Birds of Prey,** home to live falcons and other birds of prey.

ILLINOIS

Jane Addams's Hull House Museum at 800 South Halstead Street in Chicago commemorates the life and work of the dedicated crusader for children and immigrants.

The **Art Institute of Chicago** is one of the world's finest museums. It features five-thousand-year-old Asian art, plus paintings and sculpture from the Middle Ages to the present. The Thorne miniature rooms illustrate every historic style of the interiors of homes. 111 South Michigan Avenue, Chicago.

The Field Museum of Natural History is packed with fascinating exhibits such as "Life Over Time," which traces the evolution of life on earth from DNA to dinosaurs. You can find more about ancient Egypt, view a

multimedia presentation of Africa, and learn about all kinds of animals from a microscopic head louse to a 40-foot killer squid.

The **Ulysses S. Grant Home** looks just as it did back in 1865 when residents of the town of Galena presented it to Grant in honor of his service to the Union. (500 Bouthillier Street.)

The capital of Springfield has many historic sites dedicated to Abraham Lincoln: the **Lincoln Home Historic Site** at 426 S. 7th Street;

A "WANTED" poster offering a $100,000 reward for Lincoln's assassin.

Lincoln Tomb State Historic Site located in Oak Ridge Cemetery; the **Lincoln-Herndon Law Offices** at 6th and Adams Streets provide a look at Lincoln's life and career before he was elected president.

INDIANA

The **George Rogers Clark National Historical Park** commemorates Clark's battle to take Fort Sackville from the British during the Revolutionary War. It is located in 300-year-old Vincennes, Indiana's oldest community.

For anyone who likes racecars and wants to know more about the world famous Indy 500, a visit to the **Indianapolis Motor Speedway Hall of Fame Museum at** 4790 West 16th Street in Indianapolis is a must.

IOWA

The Amana Colonies include 500 restored buildings that have been designated a National Historic Landmark. **The Museum of Amana History** presents documents and artifacts relating to the nineteenth-century settlement of the area by German/Swiss immigrants. Call 1-800-245-5465.

The Davenport Municipal Museum has a large collection of Grant Wood paintings and memorabilia for those who would like to find out more about the man who painted the famous *American Gothic.*

Take a trip back in time to an eighteenth-century Iowa Indian village, nineteenth-century working farms, and an 1875 town. It's all at **Living History Farms,** a 600-acre open-air museum in Urbandale.

KANSAS

The **Amelia Earhart Birthplace** is the first home of the great aviator, and contains memorabilia of her life. (223 North Terrace in Atchison.)

Although born in Denison, Texas, Dwight D. Eisenhower moved to Kansas with his family when he was two years old. **The Eisenhower Center** complex includes his boyhood home, a museum and library dedicated to the 34th president of the U.S. You can learn more about his life from his youth through his success as a World War II general to his popular presidency. The center is at S. Buckeye St. at 4th Street in Abilene.

The **Kansas Cosmosphere and Space Center** in Hutchinson houses more than $100 million worth of exhibits that explain the history of space exploration. It also has a planetarium. Call 1-800-397-0330.

KENTUCKY

Early American history comes alive at **Fort Boonesborough State Park** in Bluegrass. This reconstruction of one of Daniel Boone's early forts also includes a museum and demonstrations of pioneer crafts. 1-800-255-7275.

White Hall State Historic Site in Richmond is the home of nineteenth-century abolitionist Cassius Marcellus Clay, for whom boxer Muhammed Ali was named at birth.

LOUISIANA

The site of the **Battle of New Orleans** honors the memory of General Andrew Jackson and his soldiers who won a decisive battle against the British on January 8, 1815. Call 1-800-334-8626.

Horses dot the landscape all over Bluegrass country in Kentucky.

The **Louisana Children's Museum** features hands-on exhibits and activities. It's at 428 Julia Street in New Orleans.

Melrose Plantation on Route 119 in Natchitoches is the site of African House, a museum that shows the art of internationally acclaimed African-American painter Clementine Hunter.

MAINE

Acadia National Park has beautiful stretches of shoreline and the highest mountains along the East Coast. It offers hiking, biking, camping, and boating.

The **Acadian Whale Watcher** takes you out to see the great whales that swim off the coast of Maine.

You can find out what it is like to be a lobster catcher, shopkeeper or computer expert when you visit the **Children's Museum of Maine** in Portland.

MARYLAND

The **Banneker-Douglass Museum** honors the lives and work of scientist Benjamin Banneker and abolitionist Frederick Douglass. (84 Franklin Street in Annapolis.)

The **Clara Barton National Historic Site** was the home of the Civil War nurse and founder of the American Red Cross. (5801 Oxford Road in Glen Echo.)

Fort McHenry National Monument and Historic Shrine in Baltimore harbor is the site of a naval victory over the British during the War of 1812. The battle inspired Francis Scott Key to write "The Star-Spangled Banner."

MASSACHUSETTS

The **African Meeting House** was built in 1806, making it the oldest standing African-American church building in the United States. (8 Smith Street in Boston.)

The **Emily Dickinson Homestead** at 280 Main Street in Amherst looks exactly the way it did when the popular poet lived there in the nineteenth century.

A good way to get acquainted with the historic city of Boston is to take a walk on the three-mile-long **Freedom Trail** that winds past sixteen of the city's most important sites. Call 1-800-888-5515.

MICHIGAN

The **Henry Ford Museum and Greenfield Village** in Dearborn is America's largest indoor-outdoor museum. Its exhibits show how the United States changed from a rural to an industrial society in areas such as communication, transportation, domestic life, agriculture and industry. The complex also has 80 historic buildings including one of Thomas Edison's laboratories. At 20900 Oakwood Boulevard.

The **Sojourner Truth Grave** in Oak Hill Cemetery is the burial place of the great nineteenth-century

Michigan's Upper Peninsula is home to wildlife such as this elk.

African-American speaker and abolitionist. It is located at South Avenue and Oak Hill Drive in Battle Creek.

More than 100 years old, the **Grand Hotel** on Mackinac Island is a Victorian masterpiece that features the world's longest porch.

MINNESOTA

The birthplace of the present-day Twin Cities is commemorated at **Fort Snelling State Park,** where you can see the historic fort built in 1819 at the junction of the Mississippi and Minnesota rivers. The park is just south of downtown St. Paul, at Route 5 and Post Road.

Henry Wadsworth Longfellow's famous *Song of Hiawatha* was inspired by Minnehaha Falls. "This is the forest primeval," wrote the poet. Now it's **Minnehaha Park,** on the Mississippi River, just outside of Minneapolis. Above the waterfall is a statue of Hiawatha and Minnehaha. You can walk, jog, bike, or roller-skate for 15 miles along Minnehaha Parkway, on the banks of Minnehaha Creek.

For visitors who like the wilderness, a trip to the **Boundary Waters Canoe Area** in northeastern Minnesota offers over 1,000 rural lakes surrounded by dense forests. To rent a canoe, or just to find out more about the area, contact the Ely Chamber of Commerce, 1600 Sheridan Street, Ely, MN, 55731, or 1-800-777-7281.

Nearby, the **Vermilion Interpretive Center,** 1900 E. Camp Street, has exhibits on Minnesota's famous iron range, the fur trade, and Native Americans.

MISSISSIPPI

The lovely old town of Natchez survived the Civil War almost untouched, so today it's one of the best places to visit the plantation homes and townhouses built by rich cotton merchants in the early nineteenth century. In 1932, the women of Natchez started offering tours of these homes—many of which are privately owned and still in use, and can be seen only twice a year, for three weeks in October and four weeks in March and April. For a historic tour, contact the **Pilgrimage Tour Headquarters,** 220 State St., Natchez, MS, 39121, or call 1-800-647-6742. You can also get a **carriage tour** of downtown Natchez.

In June, visitors to Biloxi can see the **Blessing of the Shrimp Fleet.** For information about this historic ritual, contact the Biloxi Chamber of Commerce, 39501.

MISSOURI

Branson is the new country-music capital of the United States, growing so fast that some believe it may rival Nashville. Branson is home to such halls as the Roy Clark Celebrity Theatre and the Cristy Lane Theatre. If you drive along Route 76, you'll encounter miniature-golf courses, bumper cars, souvenir shops, and other amusements.

Just east of Kansas City is the **Harry S Truman Library and Museum** (U.S. 24 and Delaware Street) and the **Truman Home** (219 N. Delaware Street), both located in Independence, the former home of the U.S. President. The President and First Lady Bess Truman spent their summers here while Truman was president.

George Washington Carver, the famous African-American botanist who discovered many new uses of the peanut, was born about 70 miles west of Springfield. Today, the **George Washington Carver National Monument,** off Route V, marks his birthplace.

Fans of Laura Ingalls Wilder's "Little House" books will want to visit the **Laura Ingalls Wilder Home** (Route A) in Mansfield, about 40 miles east of Springfield on Route 60. This is where the author lived while writing her famous series. Here you can see some of her handwritten manuscripts—written in pencil on school notebooks—as well as the original version of Pa's fiddle.

Another famous author lived in Missouri—Samuel Clemens, better known as Mark Twain. You can visit the author's boyhood home, now the **Mark Twain Home and Museum,** 208 Hill Street, Hannibal. Not too far away, at Route 79, is the **Mark Twain Cave,** the model for the one where Becky Thatcher and Tom Sawyer get lost in *The Adventures of Tom Sawyer*. For more information about the cave, contact the Hannibal Visitors and Convention Bureau, 320 Broadway, Box 624, Hannibal, MO 63401.

MONTANA

One of the most awesome sights to be found anywhere in the United States is the real glacier to be found at **Glacier National Park**. Contact National Park Service, West Glacier, MT 59936. This park preserves more than one million acres of mountains, waterfalls, and lakes, populated with elk, deer, wolves, and other Rocky Mountain wildlife. The 50-mile **Going-to-the-Sun Road** runs through the park; you can travel it by car, on horseback, or in a guided bus tour.

NEBRASKA

The Pulitzer-Prize-winning author Willa Cather lived in Red Cloud, where you can find the **Willa Cather Historical Center**. At 326 N. Webster Street. Five miles to the south is the **Cather Memorial Prairie**, a 610-acre area dedicated to preserving the plains that the author loved so much.

If you drive along the Great Platte River Road (take I-80 west from Omaha and Lincoln), you'll encounter the **Stuhr Museum of the Prairie Pioneer** in Grand Island (at the junction of U.S. 34 and U.S. 281). Here you'll find artifacts of American Indians and of the Old West, including a 60-building "Railroad Town" that features a restored farmhouse and people wearing old-fashioned costumes. The Railroad Town is closed from mid-October through April, so call to make sure it's open when you go.

NEVADA

Valley of Fire State Park offers dramatic landscapes on Route 169, in Overton, just 55 miles northeast of Lake Mead. There you can see many colorful sandstone formations as well as the petroglyphs (picture writing on rocks) of the ancient Anasazi Indians.

About 25 miles east of Las Vegas is the impressive **Hoover Dam** (Route 93, just east of Boulder City), built in the 1930s on the wild waters of the Colorado River. You can visit the 727-foot-high structure every day except Christmas.

NEW HAMPSHIRE

The poet **Robert Frost** lived in Franconia, where you can visit his home on Ridge Road. See the landscape that inspired such great works as "The Road Less Traveled."

Visit **Canterbury Shaker Village**, south of Lake Winnipesaukee, for a look at the history of this nineteenth-century community whose crafts and simple way of life are famous to this day.

The highest mountain in New England is **Mount Washington**, in the **White Mountains** of northern New Hampshire. The 750,000-acre White Mountain National Forest is a wilderness area that stretches all the way up to the Canadian border.

NEW JERSEY

The famous Revolutionary War heroine, "Molly Pitcher," got her nickname at **Molly Pitcher's Spring**, now on Wemrock Street off Route 522 in Freehold. Here Mary Hays carried water to the thirsty fighting troops, who created her nickname by calling out "Molly, pitcher!" whenever they wanted water.

Science lovers won't want to miss the **Liberty Science Center** at **Liberty State Park** in Jersey City (at Exit 14B off the New Jersey Turnpike). The center features three floors of hands-on exhibits plus a huge Omnimax theater with an 88-foot-wide domed screen.

People who think of New Jersey as an urban state will be glad to visit the **Pinelands National Reserve** for a taste of the wild side of the Garden State. You can find hundreds of creeks and streams suitable for canoeing in this 1.1-million-acre park near Chatsworth, the nation's first national reserve.

NEW MEXICO

Carlsbad Caverns National Park has one of the world's largest cave systems, with 77 caves, some as deep as 750 feet, others big enough to hold 14 Houston Astrodomes. The park can be entered at 3225 National Parks Highway.

A yucca plant in White Sands National Monument, New Mexico

In Santa Fe, the **Wheelwright Museum of the American Indian** (704 Camino Lejo) is housed in a building in the form of a traditional Navajo hogan. Inside, you can see the arts and crafts of many different native cultures.

NEW YORK

Do you like dinosaurs? Are you interested in wolves and bison? Do you want to find out more about Native Americans, Inuit, and many other cultures? Then you shouldn't miss a visit to the **American Museum of Natural History**, home to over 30 million artifacts and located at Central Park West and 77th Street in New York City.

Overlooking the Hudson River, Sunnyside was the home of writer Washington Irving (1783-1859).

For a look at the history of women's rights, stop by the **Susan B. Anthony House** at 17 Madison Street, Rochester, home of America's most famous crusader for women's right to vote.

The largest urban zoo in the United States is the **International Wildlife Conservation Park,** or the "Bronx Zoo" for short. Located at Fordham Road and the Bronx River Parkway in the Bronx, New York City, the conservation park features tram rides through simulated wilderness areas where you can see lions, tigers, bears, and more exotic animals roaming outside of cages.

Baseball fans will surely want to see the **National Baseball Hall of Fame** on Main Street in Cooperstown. There you'll find displays, paintings, and audiovisual presentations that tell about baseball's heroes and recount the history of the game.

Harriet Tubman, herself an escaped slave, made many trips to free other Southern slaves. During the Civil War, she served as scout and spy for the Union. When the war finally put an end to slavery, she settled in Auburn, where you can now visit the **Harriet Tubman Home** (180 South Street, Route 34).

NORTH CAROLINA

Discovery Place is a fascinating hands-on science museum at 301 N. Tryon Street in Charlotte. There you'll find aquariums, an indoor rain forest, a planetarium, a touch tank, and a huge Omnimax theater.

On December 17, 1903, Wilbur and Orville Wright made the first airplane flight, in their plane, the *Flyer.* You can see a replica of this famous aircraft at the **Wright Brothers National Memorial** in Kill Devil Hills (U.S. 158 Bypass).

NORTH DAKOTA

In the state capital of Bismarck, the **North Dakota Heritage Center** exhibits Native American and pioneer artifacts as well as natural history displays. Visit the center at 612 East Boulevard.

President Theodore Roosevelt always credited North Dakota's rough country with helping him to regain his health. Now you can visit the **Theodore Roosevelt National Park** (Box 7, Medora, ND 58645), which is divided into two halves, with 50 miles of Badlands running in between. Scenic drives through the park ask drivers to slow down in order to protect the bison, wild horses, mule deer, pronghorn antelope, and bighorn sheep that still live in this area. You might start your tour seven miles east of Medora on I-94, at the **Painted Canyon Overlook and Visitors Center**, where picnic tables offer tourists both a great view and a chance to eat. One segment of the park includes Roosevelt's **Elkhorn Ranch.**

OHIO

One of the first nationally recognized African-American poets, Paul Laurence Dunbar, was born in Dayton, where today you can visit the **Paul Laurence Dunbar House** at 219 North Summit Avenue. Dunbar's most famous line (later picked up by Maya Angelou for her autobiography) was "I know why the caged bird sings."

Paul Laurence Dunbar (1872-1906)

At the **Mound City Group National Monuments,** some 24 prehistoric Indian burial mounds have been preserved.

Neil Armstrong, the first man on the moon, is honored at the **Neil Armstrong Air and Space Museum** off 1-75 between Cincinnati and Toledo, in Armstrong's home town of Wapakoneta. If you want to feel what a space trip might be like, take exit 111. (The museum is closed from December through February.)

OKLAHOMA

Along Route 123 in northeastern Oklahoma is **Woolaroc,** a drive-through wildlife preserve where bison and 40 other animal species roam—so obey the rules and stay inside your car! At the center of the preserve is a museum packed with Native American art as well as artifacts from pioneer days. (For information, write Woolaroc, Box 1647, Bartlesville, OK 74005.)

Just north of the state capital, Oklahoma City, is the **National Cowboy Hall of Fame and Western Heritage Center,** home to paintings, sculpture, and other artifacts of cowboy life, as well as a re-created frontier town that features a sod house, saloon, and mine. Kachina dolls, used to teach Hopi children about sacred spirits of the dead, can be seen at this museum, at 1700 N.E. 63rd Street.

OREGON

Have you ever seen a 6,800-year-old lake? You'll get your chance at **Crater Lake National Park** (Box 7, Crater Lake, OR 97604), where you can see the result of the volcano that destroyed Mount Mazama. The empty

Crater Lake is one of the most beautiful bodies of water in the United States.

cauldron of the former mountain soon filled up with rain and snow, creating a sapphire-blue lake so clear that sunlight reaches down into the water for 400 feet.

At Washington State Park in Portland, see the **Statue of Sacagawea,** a monument to the young Native American woman who served as a translator on the historic Lewis and Clark expedition through the Northwest Territory.

PENNSYLVANIA

Today, most people have heard about the dangers to the environment. But 30 years ago, the concepts of pollution and ecology were still unfamiliar ideas. Rachel Carson's book *Silent Spring* began the modern movement to save the environment. You can see the natural landscape that inspired this important author at the **Rachel Carson Homestead,** 613 Marion Avenue, Springdale.

The turning point of the Civil War was the Battle of Gettysburg, commemorated today at **Gettysburg National Military Park** (97 Taneytown Road). Stand on the ground where so many soldiers fought and died, and learn more about this historic battle from the markers and plaques that honor this site.

The **Frances Ellen Watkins Harper House** (1006 Bainbridge Street, Philadelphia) was once home to the nineteenth-century lecturer and crusader for African-American rights. Harper's most famous book, the novel *Iola Leroy,* painted an optimistic picture of what African-Americans might achieve once the Civil War had ended slavery.

RHODE ISLAND

Through the eighteenth and nineteenth centuries, America's aristocrats went to the seaside community of Newport to build lovely mansions and enjoy the summer weather. **Hunter House** (54 Washington Street), built in 1748, remains a stunning example of colonial architecture.

Also in Newport, **Touro Synagogue** still stands. Dedicated in 1763, this is the oldest surviving synagoge in the United States.

SOUTH CAROLINA

The first shot of the Civil War was fired at Fort Sumter. This famous moment is commemorated at the **Fort Sumter National Monument** in Charleston Harbor, Charleston.

In Columbia, the **South Carolina State Museum** (301 Gervais Street) is housed in a renovated textile mill, honoring

The Corn Palace in Mitchell, South Dakota was built in 1892.

the industry that created the state's wealth. The museum includes exhibits of archaeology, fine arts, science and technology. Check out the gift shop for some unusual souvenirs.

SOUTH DAKOTA

Over 1.3 million acres of western South Dakota is preserved in the **Black Hills National Forest,** an area that the Sioux considered sacred ground. To reach this fascinating part of the country, take Rural Route 2. For more information, write Box 200, Custer, SD 57730.

For more on the Indian point of view, visit the **Sioux Indian Museum** (515 West Boulevard), which exhibits artifacts from Sioux and other American Indian peoples.

You might also visit the **National Hall of Fame for Famous American Indians,** on U.S. 62 East near Anadarko.

Back in the Black Hills National Forest, 21 miles southwest of Rapid City on U.S. 16, is **Mt. Rushmore National Memorial** (Box 268, Keystone, SD 57701), the granite cliff where the giant faces of Presidents George Washington, Thomas Jefferson, Abraham Lincoln, and Theodore Roosevelt are carved. Sculptor Gutzon Borglum worked on the monument for more than 14 years, and even then the work had to be completed by his son, Lincoln. From June to mid-September, a dramatic lighting ceremony at dusk shows off the carving to its best advantage.

TENNESSEE

What do Elvis Presley and Dolly Parton have in common? They both recorded famous hits at the legendary **RCA Studio B** in Nashville. You can visit this historic studio when you buy a ticket to the **Country Music Hall of Fame and Museum** (4 Music Square E.).

Check out a different type of music in Memphis at the **W.C. Handy Memphis Home and Museum** (352 Beale Street). Handy is considered the creator of modern jazz.

If Handy was king of the blues, another Memphis resident, Elvis Presley, was king of rock and roll. You can visit Presley's famous estate, **Graceland,** 12 miles southeast of downtown Memphis. If you want to visit, make a reservation (1-800-238-2000); tours include a trip through the mansion, automobile museum, and burial site, along with a view of Elvis's two private jets and a piano covered in gold.

If you prefer presidents to rock stars, don't miss the home of U.S. President Andrew Jackson, **The Hermitage,** 4580 Rachel's Lane, Hermitage. (Rachel was the name of the President's wife.)

TEXAS

The unofficial state motto is "Remember the Alamo," commemorating the famous battle between Texans and Mexicans at the fort in San Antonio. You can visit **The Alamo** at Alamo Plaza, where you can learn more about the 189 volunteers who died in the historic battle in 1836, including famed U.S. pioneers Davy Crockett and James Bowie.

Davy Crockett is also honored at **David Crockett National Forest,** Ratcliff Lake, 1240 East Loop 304, Crockett. In the piney woods of east Texas, you can find places to hike, canoe, camp, and picnic.

In Big Bend, over 800,000 acres of canyons, desert, woodlands, mountains, and lakes are preserved in **Big Bend National Park** on U.S. 385. This wildlife area is the state's major national attraction, as it reveals millions of years of erosion that have created a junglelike floodplain, the Chihuahuan Desert, and the Chisos Mountains, home to black bears, mountain lions, coyotes, deer, jackrabbits, and over 430 species of birds, including the roadrunner.

UTAH

Picture a stone cathedral spire, a deep canyon, or a colorful stretch of desert. These are only some of the unique geographical features you might find in **Canyonlands National Park,** south of Moab (Route 313, Moab, UT 84532). This park is divided into three distinct areas, each with its own visitor center.

Dinosaur National Monument features the prehistoric remains of the earth's ancient beasts. For more information, write Box 128, Jensen, UT 84035.

If choir music appeals to you, you shouldn't miss a concert at the world-famous **Mormon Tabernacle** at Temple Square in Salt Lake City. Besides dramatic concerts on Thursdays and Saturdays, the Tabernacle buildings and grounds introduce visitors to the Mormon religion, including exhibits and art with religious themes.

VERMONT

Anyone who likes eating ice cream should make a point of touring **Ben and Jerry's Ice Cream Factory,** Route 100, one mile north of I-89 in Stowe. Tours take you through the entire ice-cream-making process, from receiving the milk to adding the mix-ins, with free samples at the end. The factory also includes a gift shop, playground, and, of course, concession stands serving ice cream.

One of the Revolutionary War's earliest heroes was Ethan Allen, leader of Vermont's Green Mountain Boys. The **Bennington Battle Monument** at 15 Monument Avenue honors these fighting men.

Have you ever wondered what an early American farm was like? You might find out at **Shelburne Museum,** a complex of 35 buildings that houses one of the largest Americana collections in the United States. The drive to the museum—located on U.S. 7 just outside of Burlington—offers some lovely views.

VIRGINIA

Monticello is the magnificent mansion that President Thomas Jefferson designed to overlook the majestic

Carter's Grove Plantation, Virginia

countryside. Like all southern plantations, Monticello was built and maintained by slave labor. Today, you can visit Monticello by taking Route 53 out of Charlottesville.

The man who wrote *Up from Slavery* is honored at the **Booker T. Washington National Monument,** marking the birth of the great African-American educator and statesman. Take Route 3 out of Hardy, or, for more information, write Box 310, Highway 122, Hardy, VA 24011.

In Jamestown, near the Old Church Tower, you can find the **Pocohantas Statue,** dedicated to the memory of the young Native American woman who, in 1607, helped save the first British colonists from starvation. Jamestown includes many other references to the proud history of this early colony.

A later period in U.S. history is commemorated in Staunton at the **Museum of American Frontier Culture** (230 Frontier Drive). The building has been restored to re-create early American farm life, showing the animals and crops that would have been raised on eighteenth-century farms.

WASHINGTON

About 85 miles southeast of Seattle is **Mt. Rainier National Park,** a 400-square-mile wilderness area whose visitor center offers a 360-degree view of the famous mountain. For more information, write the Superintendent's Office, Tahoma Woods, Star Route, Ashford, WA 98304.

Throughout the Pacific Northwest are tributes to Lewis, Clark, and Sacagawea, explorers of the Northwest Territory in the early 1800s. Near Iwalco, a small fishing community of about 600 people, you can find the **Lewis and Clark Interpretive Center,** which documents the 8,000-mile round-trip journey, starting in Wood River, Illinois, and turning around at the mouth of the Columbia River.

WEST VIRGINIA

One of America's many unsung female heroes was Agnes Jane Reeves Greer (1880-1972)—inventor, business-woman, and architect. You can visit **Greer Mansion** at Cheat Lake in Morgantown to learn more about this remarkable woman.

Years before the beginning of the Civil War, abolitionist John Brown and a small band of antislavery activists staged his famous raid on Harpers Ferry. This

The majestic Grand Teton mountains in Wyoming

action is commemorated at **Harpers Ferry National Historical Park** (Box 65, Harpers Ferry, WV 25425), where the Potomac and Shenandoah rivers join.

WISCONSIN

Years before Golda Meir became the prime minister of Israel, she was a public school teacher. Visit the **Golda Meir School**, named in her honor, located in Milwaukee at 1555 North Martin Luther King, Jr., Drive.

Ella Wheeler Wilcox was once one of the country's most famous poets. You can learn more about this writer at the **Ella Wheeler Wilcox Birthplace** at County Trunk A at Scharine Road in Johnstown.

One of the U.S.'s best-loved family resort areas is **Wisconsin Dells**, located between Tomah and Madison. For nearly 15 miles along U.S. 12 (south of I-90/94), you can see huge eroded rock formations that were created over thousands of years, as the Wisconsin River bit into the earth's soft limestone. Almost three million visitors come to the Dells each year to enjoy the area's water parks, miniature golf courses, theme parks, and other amusements.

WYOMING

Wyoming is the land of national parks, most notably **Yellowstone,** which in this state you can reach through Mammoth. The first reports of this amazing national park—reported in St. Louis newspapers in 1810—were considered tall tales. Now, of course, we know that there are indeed giant elk, steaming mud pots, spurting geysers, and dramatic waterfalls in this beautiful national park, which in 1872 became the country's first.

Grand Teton National Park is also an exciting place to visit, offering lakes, mountains, and views of moose and bison along the Snake River. Contact The National Park Service, Drawer 170, Moose, WY 83012.

In Cody, the **Buffalo Bill Historical Center** (720 Sheridan Avenue) includes a number of museums with a western theme: **Plains Indian Museum, Cody Firearms Museum,** the **Buffalo Bill Museum,** and the **Whitney Gallery of Western Art.**

PUERTO RICO

The **Walled City of San Juan** includes Puerto Rican family treausres from the sixteenth and seventeenth centuries.

The **El Yunque** is a dramatic national park, where visitors can see many tropical plants, flowers, and animals.

U.S. VIRGIN ISLANDS

The **Christiansted Historic District** is probably the most interesting place to visit in this American possession, located at Harbor and West Streets, Christiansted, St. Croix.

These fiction and nonfiction books can tell you more about life in each state or territory.

ALABAMA

Alabama Bandits, Bushwhackers, Outlaws, Crooks, Devils, and Characters. Carole Marsh. The title says it all.

A Christmas Memory, Truman Capote. The author remembers a beloved aunt from his childhood.

Helen Keller's Teacher, Margaret Davidson. The true story of Anne Sullivan Macy who became Helen Keller's teacher and lifelong friend.

To Kill a Mockingbird, Harper Lee. In this classic story, a child tries to come to terms with racism and the fight for justice in a small town in the 1900s.

ALASKA

Call of the Wild, Jack London. In this story, a dog starts his life as a civilized pet but ends up a wild wolf in northern Alaska.

Julie of the Wolves, Jean Craighead George. Thirteen-year-old Julie is lost in the Alaskan wilderness—but gradually she is accepted by a pack of Arctic wolves that teach her to survive.

Racing the Iditarod Trail, Ruth Crisman. All about Alaska's most famous dog race.

Thunderfeet, Alaska's Dinosaurs and Other Prehistoric Critters, Shelley R. Gill. They're long gone but interesting to imagine.

ARIZONA

Anpao: An American Indian Odyssey, Jamake Highwater. A brave young man undertakes a quest that takes him across the face of the ancient world.

The Call of the Canyon, Zane Grey. This classic Western includes many beautiful descriptions of the Arizona landscape.

The Enemy Gods, Oliver LaFarge. The author paints an authentic portrait of Navajo life.

ARKANSAS

The Enduring Hills, Janice Holt Giles. This novel takes place in Arkansas's Ozark Mountains and tells about life and customs there.

True Grit, Charles Portis. A Yell County farm girl goes to Fort Smith and persuades a U.S. Marshal to help her track down her father's killer.

CALIFORNIA

California Blue, David Klass. John and his father get into an environmental tug-of-war after John discovers a new sub-species of butterfly.

Child of the Owl, Laurence Yep. When Case goes to live with her grandmother in San Francisco's Chinatown, she learns about her Chinese heritage.

The Great American Gold Rush, Rhoda Blumberg. How the discovery of gold at Sutter's Mill changed California forever.

Island of the Blue Dolphins, Scott O'Dell. An Indian girl left by her tribe survives alone for 18 years on a bleak island off the coast of California. Based on a true story.

Local News, Gary Soto. Thirteen wonderful stories about Mexican-American teens living in California.

Manzanar, John Armor and Peter Wright. A nonfiction account of the California internment of Japanese-Americans during World War II. Photos by Ansel Adams.

COLORADO

The Mountain Lion, Jean Stafford. A brother and sister have an unhappy youth until they escape to a Colorado ranch.

Tales, Trails, and Tommyknockers. Myriam Friggins. Stories from Colorado's past.

CONNECTICUT

Country Place, Ann Petry. This African-American author grew up in Old Saybrook and set this novel in the town of Lenox.

A Connecticut Yankee in King Arthur's Court, Mark Twain. A classic humorous tale of time travel.

DELAWARE

Delaware Timeline: A Chronology of Delaware History, Mystery, Trivia, Legend, Lore and More.

Voices of the River: Adventures on the Delaware River. Illustrated by Jan Cheripko.

DISTRICT OF COLUMBIA

First Children, Growing up in the White House, Katherine Leiner. Fascinating accounts of the lives of young people who have called the White House "home."

How the White House Really Works, George Sullivan. Home, office, museum and tourist attraction—how the White House operates. A fascinating behind-the-scenes look at America's "home."

FLORIDA

Jonah's Gourd Vine, Zora Neale Hurston. An Alabama cotton picker becomes a preacher in a small Florida town.

Strawberry Girl, Lois Lenski. Adventures of a girls in the Florida lake country.

The Yearling. Marjorie Kinnan Rawlings. Jody and his pet fawn are inseperable as they grow up in the Florida Everglades.

GEORGIA

Cold Sassy Tree, Olive Ann Burns. It's 1906, and things turn topsy-turvy when 14-year-old Will Tweedy's grandmother dies and his grandfather remarries.

Kidding Around Atlanta: A Young Person's Guide to the City. Anne Pedersen. What you might want to see and do in one of the South's most popular cities.

When Birds Could Talk and Bats Could Sing, Virginia Hamilton. A retelling of African-American folktales collected in the 1880s by journalist Martha Young. Illustrated by Barry Moser.

HAWAII

The Day Pearl Harbor Was Bombed: A Photohistory of World War II, George Sullivan. This arresting account is done is magazine format.

At the Gateways of the Day, Padraic Colum. The author adapted these stories from Hawaiian folklore.

Mark Twain's Letters from Hawaii, edited by A. Grove Day. These 25 travel letters from the famous American author detail a four-month visit to Hawaii in 1866.

'Olelo No'eau: Hawaiian Proverbs and Political Sayings, Mary Kawena Pukui. Reading these proverbs is a great way to get a feeling for the way Hawaiians look at things.

IDAHO

Stomp Ranch Pioneer, Nelle P. Davis (Idaho Yesterdays Series). A deeply moving novel about a pioneer woman farmer.

In Tragic Life, Vardis Fisher. This is the first of four autobiographical novels set in Idaho about a boy from a Morman pioneer background.

ILLINOIS

Across Five Aprils, Irene Hunt. On a southern Illinois farm during the Civil War, Jethro is loyal to the Union and his beloved brother is a Rebel.

Dandelion Wine, Ray Bradbury. This classic fantasy novel is set in a small Illinois town.

The Great Fire, Jim Murphy. Vivid, first-hand accounts of the 1871 Chicago fire make this nonfiction gripping.

INDIANA

Except for Me and Thee, Jessamyn West. The details of life in rural Indiana come alive in this novel about a Quaker family during Reconstruction.

Girl of the Limberlost, Gene Stratton Porter. The writer's detailed account of Indiana wildlife in this novel make the place come alive.

Jokelore: Humorous Folktales from Indiana, Ronald Baker. This collection of funny stories gives the flavor of Indiana life and sensibilities.

IOWA

Charlie Young Bear, Catherine Von Ahnen. Iowa's Mesqkuakie Indians receive payment for their lands in the 1950s.

True Tales from Iowa's Past, O. J. Fargo. Short nonfiction chapters about Iowa history.

Iowa Past to Present, People and the Prairie, Dorothy Schweider. A young people's history.

High on the Hog, Kimberly Olson Fakih. Trapp spends a rewarding summer on her great-grandparents' Iowa farm before moving to New York City.

An Occasional Cow, Polly Horvath. A New York City kid finds summer in Iowa a lot more exciting than she imagined.

KANSAS

Folklore from Kansas: Customs, Beliefs, and Superstitions, William E. Koch. A collection of ghost stories and folktales from Kansas.

The Learning Tree, Gordon Parks. A novel based on the author's own life tells of a black child growing up in a small town in the 1920s.

Lost Star: The Story of Amelia Earhart, Patricia Lauber. An award-winning biography of a Kansas native and America's most famous female aviator.

KENTUCKY

Cloud-Walking, Marie Campbell. A collection of the tales of mountain people.

The Court Martial of Daniel Boone, Allan W. Eckert. An historical novel based on the events of 1778.

Mountain Path, Harriette Simpson Arnow. A rural school teacher reaches out to the children in her community in this semi-autobiographical novel about the Cumberland region.

Singing Family of the Cumberlands, Jean Ritchie. This memoir of a folk musician born in the Cumberlands in 1922 includes traditional songs and is illustrated by Maurice Sendak.

LOUISIANA

The Autobiography of Miss Jane Pittman, Ernest Gaines. The fictional memoirs of a 100-year-old ex-slave about her life on a Louisiana plantation.

Creole Folk Tales, Hewitt L. Ballowe. These tales give the flavor of life in Louisiana's Mississippi Delta.

Other Voices, Other Rooms, Truman Capote. An old plantation is the setting for this novel about an adolescent's self-discovery.

Sounder, Bill and Vera Cleaver. Heartwarming novel about an African-American boy, his imprisoned father, and their dog.

MAINE

Especially Maine: The Natural World of Henry Beston, Henry Beston. A naturalist tells about the state that he loves and has observed for many years.

The Edge of the Sea, Rachel Carson. A beautiful and perceptive book by a Pulitzer prize-winning writer.

Folklore and the Sea, Horace Beck. This book of maritime legends includes many set in Maine.

Rebecca of Sunnybrook Farm, Kate Douglas Wiggin. High-spirited Rebecca grows up in Maine at the turn of the century.

The Maine Woods, Henry David Thoreau. The nineteenth-century author recalls trips to Mount Katahdin, Moosehead Lake, and the West Branch of the the Penobscot.

MARYLAND

Awesome Chesapeake, David O. Bell. The bay around which much of Maryland's history and economy are grounded is brought to life.

Maryland: Its Past and its Present. The interesting history of the nation's seventh state.

Jacob Have I Loved, Katherine Paterson. The sibling rivalry of twins, Louise and Caroline, who live on an island in the Chesapeake where their father harvests oysters and crabs, is the theme of this novel.

MASSACHUSETTS

April Morning, Howard Fast. Fifteen-year-old Adam Cooper becomes a man on the day of the Revolutionary Battle of Lexington.

Johnny Tremain, Esther Forbes. Johnny goes from being an arrogant young apprentice to a dedicated helper of the colonists in this Revolutionary War tale.

Little Women, Louisa May Alcott. The four March girls must learn to find their own identities in this story about a Massachusetts family during the Civil War.

Nightbirds on Nantucket, Joan Aiken. An English girl lost at sea is rescued by a New England whaling vessel and taken back to Nantucket where a hilarious mystery unfolds.

Samuel Eaton's Day, Kate Waters. A vivid photo recreation of a Pilgrim boy's daily life on Plimouth Plantation.

MICHIGAN

The Dollmaker, Harriette S. Arnow. During World War II, a gentle mountain woman brings her family to Detroit where she tries to hold on to her mountain customs and values.

Michigan's Past and the Nation's Future, Bruce Catton. The author explores Michigan's history in this contemporary book about the Wolverine State.

We'll Race You Henry: A Story About Henry Ford, Barbara Mitchell. This partly fictionalized biography focuses on race cars.

MINNESOTA

Lake Wobegon Days, Garrison Keillor. These playful stories are a fictionalized version of the popular radio talk show host's own childhood in Minnesota.

We Made It Through the Winter: A Memoir of a Northern Minnesota Boyhood, Walter O'Meara. Surviving the frigid Minnesota winter was an even greater challenge one hundred years ago when O'Meara was a boy.

MISSISSIPPI

Collected Stories, Eudora Welty. One of Mississippi's finest writers, born in Jackson, tells classic tales of small town and rural life.

A Treasury of Mississippi Folklore, B.A. Botkin. A rich collection of myths, legends and stories.

MISSOURI

The Adventures of Tom Sawyer, Mark Twain. Tom Sawyer enjoys the free and easy life of a boy in Hannibal, Missouri, in the middle of the nineteenth century.

Flood: Wrestling with the Mississippi, Patricia Lauber. What happens when a rain-swollen river overrides its banks? And how can people who live along it protect themselves?

Hilly Billy, Rose Wilder Lane. Laura Ingalls Wilder's daughter wrote this description of the customs and speech of the Ozark Mountains.

MONTANA

The Big Sky, Alfred B. Gutherie. A boy runs away from home to join the Blackfoot in the Teton Mountains in the 1820s.

A River Runs Through It and Other Stories, Norman Maclean. This autobiographical narrative of growing up in rural Montana centers on trout fishing in the Blackfoot River.

Sweetgrass, Jan Hudson. This award-winning novel shows how a 15-year-old Blackfoot girl proves herself in a terrible year for her tribe.

NEBRASKA

The Buffalo Wallow, Charles Tenney Jackson. The author recalls his boyhood in a prairie sodhouse in the 1890s.

Prairie Songs, Pam Conrad. A beautiful, illustrated novel of how one family thrives on the harsh prairie life.

Signs, Omens and Portents in Nebraska Folklore, Margaret Cannell and Emma L. Snap. Ghost stories and legends from the state are collected in this volume.

NEVADA

Between Two Worlds, Candice Ransom. The true story of a nineteenth-century Paiute woman's struggle to resist removal of her people to a Washington state reservation.

Roughing It, Mark Twain. The 25-year-old author remembers life in Virginia City as a journalist.

NEW HAMPSHIRE

The Isles of Shoals in Lore and Legend, Lyman Rutledge. This volume collects folklore about one of New Hampshire's most beautiful spots.

An Old Town by the Sea, Thomas Bailey Aldrich. This nonfiction account of Portsmouth draws on the author's childhood memories of that city, where he lived in the middle of the nineteenth century.

NEW JERSEY

The Chinaberry Tree, Jessie Redmon Fauset. This novel by one of the few women writers of the Harlem Renaissance explores life in a small black community.

The Folklore and Folklife of New Jersey, David S. Cohen. This is a contemporary collection of New Jersey folklore, compiled in 1983.

A New Jersey Reader, Henry Charlton Beck. This anthology of stories includes both fiction and historical material in its portrait of New Jersey's history and folklore.

NEW MEXICO

Book of the Hopi, Frank Waters. This nonfiction work tells of Hopi folklore, history, and customs.

Cuentos: Tales from the Hispanic Southwest, José Griego y Maestas and Rudolfa A. Anaya. This is a bilingual collection of tales collected from Spanish-speaking families in northern New Mexico and southern Colorado.

The House at Otowi Bridge: The Story of Edith Warner and Los Alamos, Peggy P. Church. This story of a woman who lived at Los Alamos at the time of the creation of the atomic bomb also conveys the way the nuclear project affected the region.

House Made of Dawn, N. Scott Momaday. A contemporary Indian attempts to recover the mystical tradition of his ancestors in this groundbreaking novel.

Indeh: An Apache Odyssey, Eve Ball. The oral history of the Apaches tells of their life in the land that became New Mexico.

Journey to the People, Ann N. Clark. A teacher and writer who won the 1953 Newbery Award remembers her life in New Mexico.

NEW YORK

Behind the Lines, Isabelle Holland. A young Irish maid gets caught up in the New York City race riots during the Civil War.

The Contender, Robert Lipsyte. Alfred, a black dropout, enters the Harlem Training Center for Boxers, hoping to become a contender for the championship.

Nilda, Nicholasa Mohr. Nilda, who lives with her large, affectionate family in Spanish Harlem, begins the painful process of growing up.

The Rifleman, John Brick. The life of Timothy Murphy, upstate hero of the Revolution, is the basis for this historical novel.

Remember the Ladies: The First Women's Rights Convention, Norma Johnson. A clearly written account of the event with many photos and interesting facts.

The Sketch Book, Washington Irving. This volume of essays and German folktales includes "Rip Van Winkle" and "The Legend of Sleepy Hollow."

Trimmed Lamp, and Other Stories of the Four Million, O. Henry (William Sydney Porter). These New York short stories feature O. Henry's classic "surprise ending" as they portray the lives of working men and women in early 20th-century New York.

We Shall Not Be Moved, Joan Dash. A compelling, nonfiction account of the 1909 strike by teenage girls working in the shirtwaist factories of New York.

NORTH CAROLINA

The Land Breakers, John Ehle. This novel tells of pioneer life beyond the Blue Ridge in the eighteenth and nineteenth centuries.

My Folks Don't Want Me to Talk about Slavery: Twenty-one Oral Histories of Former North Carolina Slaves, Belinda Hurmence (editor). This collection of oral histories presents new insight into slavery and the Civil War.

The Ragged Ones, Burke Davis. This historical novel of the Revolution is noted for its realism and accuracy.

Rough Weather Makes Good Timber: Carolinians Recall, Patsy M. Ginns. In 1977, the author collected these stories and proverbs from North Carolina residents.

The Swamp Fox, Noel Gerson. General Francis Marion, the "Swamp Fox," is the subject of this historical novel.

Where the Lilies Bloom, Vera Cleaver and Bill Cleaver. In this lyrical novel, 14-year-old Mary Call promises her dying father that she will keep the family together.

NORTH DAKOTA

American Daughter, Eta Bell Thompson. This is the autobiography of an African-American woman who moved with her farming family to the small town of Driscoll in 1914.

Badlands and Bronco Trails, Lewis F. Crawford. The story of Ben Conner, a pioneer in the days after the Civil War.

Dakota Diaspora: Memoirs of a Jewish Homesteader, Sophie Trupin. The author remembers life in one of the few Jewish immigrant communities of North Dakota.

Dust Bowl Diary, Ann Amie Low. The author remembers

life on a stock farm in southeastern North Dakota in the late 1920s.

Hunting Adventures in the West, Theodore Roosevelt. The author, who became a U.S. President, worked on a ranch in North Dakota in the 1880s, and wrote this memoir of his favorite hunting trips.

OHIO
Arilla Sun Down, Virginia Hamilton. A seventh grader from a small Ohio town, Arilla Mooning Running Adams, comes from an interracial background, part black, part Indian.

Ballads and Songs from Ohio, Mary O. Eddy (compiler). The author compiled versions of 25 English and Scottish popular ballads and almost 300 European and Native American folksongs.

The Bent Twig, Dorothy Canfield Fisher. This novel about the family of a college professor is based on the author's experience of Columbus in the late nineteenth century.

The Second Bend in the River, Ann Rinaldi. The daughter of settlers in 1798 befriends Native American chief, Tecumseh.

Leafy Rivers, Jessamyn West. This historical novel is set in Ohio Territory around 1800.

OKLAHOMA
Bound for Glory, Woody Guthrie. The songwriter and singer tells the story of his life from his upbringing in Okemah through his involvement with social protest in the 1930s and 1940s.

A Girl from Yamhill: A Memoir, Beverly Cleary. The popular author tells the story of her life.

Sequoyah, Grant Foreman. The biography of the Cherokee leader recounts how he invented a way of writing down his language.

The Way to Rainy Mountain, N. Scott Momaday. The author, a Native American novelist, created this account of the folklore, history, and present life of the Kiowa Indians of the Wichita Mountains.

The Will Rogers Book, ed. Paul M. Love. Rogers was a popular, homespun philosopher in the 1920s and 1930s. Some of his work is collected in this volume.

OREGON
Across the Wide and Lonesome Prairie, Kristiana Gregory. The Oregon Trail Diary of Hattie Campbell. A fictional account inspired by historic events.

Big Sam, Sam Churchill. A lumberjack recalls his life at the beginning of the 20th century.

Oregon Folklore, Suzi Jones (editor). These folktales include ghost stories, love stories, and legends.

PENNSYLVANIA
Fabulous Valley, Cornelia Parker. This novel tells of the 1859 discovery of oil in Pennsylvania.

Gettysburg, Stephen Longstreet. This historical novel describes there actions of ordinary townspeople to the great battle.

The Killer Angels, Michael Shaara. This Pulitzer Prize-winning novel tells of the Battle of Gettysburg from the point of view of officers on both sides.

The Patch Boys, Jay Parini. This novel tells of coming of age in an Italian-Polish mining community in 1925.

Spellbound: Growing Up in God's Country, David McKain. The author recalls growing up in a small town in the Alleghenies in the 1940s and 1950s.

RHODE ISLAND
I Seek a City, Gilbert Rees. This fictional autobiography of Roger Williams tells of his quest for religious freedom.

Our Own Kind, Edward McSorley. An Irish immigrant family struggles to survive in South Providence in the early twentieth century in this historical novel.

Saltbound: A Block Island Winter, Chilton Williamson, Jr. The beauties of Block Island are chronicled by this Rhode Island resident.

SOUTH CAROLINA
The Day Fort Sumter Was Fired On: A Photo History of the Civil War, Jim Haskins. Tells the effects of this military event on women, slaves, and children as well as the men who fought there.

Folk Song in South Carolina, Charles W. Joyner. One of the best ways to learn about a people is through their songs, as this volume demonstrates.

Jesse Jackson, A Biography, Patricia McKissack. A lively and even-handed story of the life of this South Carolina presidential candidate.

Scarlet Sister Mary, Julia Peterkin. The author was an owner and manager of a plantation near Fort Motte. She wrote several novels, like this Pulitzer Prize-winner, about the lives and folklore of the Gullah people.

A Short Walk, Alice Childress. This historical novel tells of an African-American woman who gets involved in Marcus Garvey's campaign for returning to Africa.

SOUTH DAKOTA

Bury My Heart at Wounded Knee: An Indian History of the American West, Dee Brown. The Sioux Massacre of the nineteenth century is the point of departure for this historical narrative about American Indians.

Dakota Dream, James Bennett. After dreaming of a life away from orphanages and foster homes, a boy escapes to a Sioux reservation.

Land of the Spotted Eagle, Luther Standing Bear. In this 1933 memoir, a Dakota chief writes about his people and the land they inhabit.

Little House Series: By the Shores of Silver Lake, The Long Winter, Little Town on the Prairie, These Happy Golden Years, Laura Ingalls Wilder. Novels from the famous Little House series set in Smet, South Dakota, where the author grew up.

TENNESSEE

Chariot in the Sky: A Story of the Fisk Jubilee Singers, Arna Bontemps. This 19th-century historical narrative tells the story of the internationally renowned Fisk Jubilee Singers.

The Hawk's Done Gone and Other Stories, ed., by Mildred Haun. This collection draws on the lives of the East Tennessee mountain people.

TEXAS

Make Way for Sam Houston, Jean Fritz. This biography captures the spirit of this larger-than-life hero.

Old Yeller, Fred Gipson. In this classic story, a boy and his dog have many adventures in the Texas hill country.

UTAH

Saints of Sage and Saddle: Folklore Among the Mormons, Austin E. Fife and Alta Fife. The Mormons were the first European Americans to settle in Utah. These are their stories.

Wind in the Rock, Ann Zinger. This essay describes the natural beauty of five southern Utah canyons.

Why the North Star Stands Still and Other Indian Legends, William R. Palmer. The author collected these tales of the native peoples of Utah.

VERMONT

Understood Betsy, Dorothy Canfield Fisher. A popular classic about Elizabeth Ann and the fearful new life she meets in the wilds of Vermont.

Hill Song: A Country Journal, Lee P. Huntington. The author shares the beauties and challenges of each of the Vermont seasons.

VIRGINIA

Grandfather Tales: American English Folktales, ed., Richard Chase. These stories were collected from North Carolina, Virginia, and Kentucky, reflecting the English heritage of all three states.

The Double Life of Pocahontas, Jean Fritz. A biography of the Indian girl who befriended white settlers in seventeenth-century Virginia.

When Will This Cruel War Be Over? Barry Denenberg. The fictional Civil War diary of Emma Simpson.

A Picture of Freedom, Patricia McKissack. The fictional diary of Clotee, a slave girl on Belmont Plantation in 1859.

Thomas Jefferson: The Man With a Vision, Ruth Crisman. This biography recounts the many achievements of our fourth president: statesman, writer, musician and architect.

WASHINGTON

Great Son, Edna Ferber. This novel chronicles four generations of a Seattle family from 1851 to 1940.

Haboo: Native American Stories from Puget Sound, Vi Hilbert. This collection of Indian folklore was compiled in 1985.

WEST VIRGINIA

The Telltale Lilac Bush and Other West Virginia Ghost Stories, Ruth Ann Music. West Virginia mountain people told the author these scary tales.

Up from Slavery: An Autobiography, Booker T. Washington. One of America's most influential African-American leaders tells of his early life in Malden, where he worked in a saltworks, in a coal mine, and as a domestic servant.

WISCONSIN

Caddie Woodlawn, Carol Ryrie Brink. This delightful novel about a red-haired tomboy and her brothers in early Wisconsin won the Newbery Award in 1936.

Little House in the Big Wood, Laura Ingalls Wilder. This timeless classic tells the story of a log-cabin family in Wisconsin in the 1800s. Illustrated by Garth Williams.

Rascal, Sterling North. The author relates his boyhood adventures with a pet raccoon in rural Wisconsin.

WYOMING

Bendigo Shafter, Louis L'Amour. Set in Wyoming, this Western novel was written by one of America's most popular authors.

My Friend Flicka, Mary O'Hara. In this beloved classic novel, Ken is delighted when he gets his own horse, Flicka, on his Wyoming ranch.

One Day at Teton Marsh, Sally Carrigher. The author describes the ecology and wild life of a pond near Jackson Hole.

Shane, Jack Shaefer. This classic Western recounts the struggle between farmers and ranchers in the 1890s.

PUERTO RICO

Puerto Rico in Pictures. The life and history, culture and geography of this rich land.

The Three Wishes: A Collection of Puerto Rican Folk Tales, Ricardo Alegría. Puerto Rican stories and legends give readers the flavor of life on the island.

Index

PHOTO CREDITS

All photos courtesy of Archive Photos with the exception of the following: p. 47 Ralph Bunche, p. 50 Ida B. Wells-Barnett, p. 72 Toni Morrison, p. 79 Marion Anderson, p. 89 Barbara Jordan, p. 121 Paul Laurence Dunbar, all courtesy of The Schomburg Center for the Study of Black Culture, a division of the New York Public Library, Astor, Lenox and Tilden Foundations; p. 2 Folk Dancers courtesy of the Alabama Bureau of Tourism; p. 8 President William Jefferson Clinton, p. 16 Henry Hudson, p. 30 Raggedy Ann doll, p. 42 Cal Ripken Jr., p. 48 snow scene, p. 49 Laura Ingalls Wilder, p. 58 desert scene, p. 63 Bill Bradley, p. 98 coal miners, p. 100 Green Bay Packers, all courtesy of Scholastic Inc.